Colour in the
Winter Garden

Colour in the Winter Garden

Revised and Enlarged Edition

Written and illustrated by

GRAHAM STUART THOMAS

OBE VMH DHM VMM

Gardens Consultant to The National Trust

Sagapress/Timber Press
Portland, Oregon

First published 1957
Second edition 1967
Reprinted 1971
Third edition 1984
Paperback edition 1994

Paperback first published in North America in 1994
by Sagapress, Inc./Timber Press, Inc.
The Haseltine Building
133 S.W. Second Ave., Suite 450
Portland, Oregon 97204–3527, U.S.A.

ISBN 0–88192–285–4

Contents

Illustrations

BY GRAHAM STUART THOMAS

List of watercolours

Between pages 66 and 67

List of colour photographs

Between pages 162 and 163

5. The Heather Trial at Wisley, photographed in January. Those in flower are cultivars of *Erica carnea* (*E. herbacea*) and *E.* × *darleyensis* both of which tolerate some lime in the soil. Those in the distance show the remarkable colours given by the foliage of cultivars of *Calluna vulgaris*

6. The contrasting tints of *Cornus alba* 'Sibirica' (red) and *C. stolonifera* 'Flaviramea' (yellowish), photographed at Wisley in winter

7. *Mahonia* × *moseri* showing its winter colour

8. The rare *Rhododendron ponticum* 'Foliis Purpureis' whose leaves are bronze-green in summer and the colour of a copper beech in winter, if grown in full sun. It is compact growing with the normal lilac-coloured flowers

9. *Cotoneaster* 'Cornubia' (red) and 'Rothschildianus' (yellow). Two strong-growing hybrids photographed in early February at the Savill Garden

10. *Rhododendron* Praecox in early February with *Erica carnea* 'Springwood White' in the background

11. *Rhododendron* Nobleanum 'Venustum' flowering in January. Successive crops of buds open from late autumn onwards during mild spells

12. *Primula vulgaris sibthorpii*, in flower in January. It is the pink representative of our common primrose in the Caucasus

13. *Narcissus* 'Jana', a cultivar which regularly flowers in February

List of line drawings

Scale: The drawings are reproduced three-quarters of natural size except those marked † *(half size) or* ★ *(actual size).*

Author's Note
and Acknowledgments

The appearance of my first book, *The Old Shrub Roses*, which has brought me much warm encouragement and friendship from all over the world, had one rather unfortunate effect. Being so specialized a subject it has tended rather to give me the title of a 'rose specialist', to the exclusion of other horticultural subjects. I feel, therefore, that I must now explain that this Winter Flower book was started many years ago, before I became so enamoured of roses, and was laid aside temporarily in order to provide the public with the fruits of my work among the roses. The present book, I hope, will perhaps dispel the erroneous conclusion, and I would hasten to assure my future readers that I am equally interested in summer flowering plants of all kinds!

In writing a book it seems inevitable that one's friends should be brought into the scheme, and, being friends, that they contribute their ideas and advice generously. To all those who have helped me with this book, therefore, I tender my best thanks. In particular am I grateful to Mrs Gwendoline Anley and Mr William T. Stearn for much helpful criticism; to Mr James P.C. Russell for his assistance with the rhododendron chapter, to my brother, Mr Geoffrey W. Thomas, and Mr Richard G. Schardt for their help in reading the proofs; and to Mr H.E. Beale, Mr G.R. Barr, and Mr Norman G. Hadden for information about certain plants.

The RHS *Dictionary of Gardening* has been the main work of reference, but at times I have almost despaired of understanding the confused and constantly changing nomenclature of the wide variety of plants dealt with in the following pages. I hope, however, that the synonyms given may be a help to seekers like myself. Recourse to the Lindley Library of the Royal Horticultural Society has resulted as usual in the complete co-operation of the Librarian and staff.

Permission to quote poems on pages 1 and 140; 57; 84; 112 and 159 respectively is gratefully acknowledged to Messrs Michael Joseph Ltd and the Hon. V. Sackville-West; the Society of Authors and Mrs Cicely Binyon; *The Observer*; the Clarendon Press; Messrs Faber & Faber and Mr A.T. de la Mare.

I am grieved that time has taken its toll of an old friend during the preparation of the book; A.T.J., so well known by his initials throughout horticulture, has left a great gap in his passing. He was to have written a foreword. The preparation of the book and its illustrations was greatly fostered by his constant encouragement.

1984 Edition

Various adjustments were made in the previous edition and reprint, but so much has happened since the book was first written, and so many new plants have appeared, that this edition has been entirely revised and in many parts re-written. My thanks are due to Mr John Bond for help with the Rhododendron notes.

Graham Thomas

To the memory of my Father and Mother
who encouraged me in all things

Winter

The golden leaves of autumn days
Are tossed and driven along the lanes
And let the rays of winter's sun
Alight on shining holly blades.
No longer pools of darkness lie
Under the trees now barely branched,
But beams of amber from the sky
Weave through the mesh of twigs above,
And cast long shadows on the clear
And verdant field, stealing across
The hedge and dyke, and bringing light
To homesteads set with lichened tiles,
A blended veil of green and gold,
Sienna brown and grey.
    Now the dark greens of lively shrubs
Stand forth again in glittering array;
New vistas open wide, whose line and form
Have been obscured by summer's leaves.
    The stage is set for winter flowers
That brave the winter's cold; the nodding blooms
With fragrance sweet and gentle tints
That suit our altered scene;
The lustrous leaf with silver striped, or gold,
The shining berry the birds avoid
And vivid flames of osier stems: all these
Do prime our plots in darkest days
And fill our jars indoors.
    For winter brings us many joys;
The fleeting light of lowly sun,
Bespangled rime and softly mounded snow,
The migrant fieldfare and the robin's song;
Christmas – and catkins on the hazel bough
That speak to us of spring.

Argument

Gardener, if you listen, listen well:
Plant for your winter pleasure, when the months
Dishearten; plant to find a fragile note
Touched from the brittle violin of frost.

V. SACKVILLE-WEST
from *The Garden*

In wooded country my own choice of the year's pageantry of beauty is that of winter, on those mild days when the wind comes from the blessed south-west. The warm Gulf Stream, which plays so great a part in our climate, is then more evident in its beneficence than in the summer, when the sun's greater power warms us independently. We frequently have many weeks in midwinter, here in Surrey, when the damp air enriches all the colours of the landscape. The tints of the lichens on tree and hedgerow, tile and wall, stand out in contrast to the pale sky or darkling bank of violet cloud. The beeches and the poplars, birches and willows in particular have a special appeal when their wet twigs are lit by the sun against a rain cloud. Looking into the haze of twigs, glistening in tones of brown, green and purple, the wonderful contrast against the velvety cloud is a sight which lives with me throughout the year.

The landscape is infinitely varied. Here may be acres of tilled land with lively rows of vivid green young corn blades running to the horizon; there are sere, creamy-yellow of the wiry tussocks of grasses on our commons, seen among thickets of green gorse and broom, and the grey-green Scots pines, their branches supported by their warm reddish stems. There may also be white-stemmed birches, and brown bracken fronds, enriched almost to a chestnut colour after the rain, in rivalry with the brown of a beech hedge. White sands and chalk, grey clays, and loams of every tint of brown, support a vegetation either wild or cultivated, giving us a wealth of tones and form. It is not until the leaves fall that the enchantment of the open heads of the trees is apparent. In this the common ash stands out in striking value; it is always a graceful tree and its open head and thick, knobbly twigs are perfect from a scenic point of view. Many a lovely summer view is obscured by a massed dome of leaves, and winter shadows slanting over the undulating meadows are far more interesting than their summer counterparts.

It is only when spring brings its tender green in dappled contrast, or when autumn fires the rides, that winter's softer tones are eclipsed. But how rare are those spring and autumn days. Our climate is so fickle that a combination of the season's fleeting beauties with one of those occasional days of sunshine is rare indeed. When the leaves have fallen, we have three months at least before that brief miraculous passage of time that we call spring, which again and again and with never-failing, breath-taking loveliness, is spread before us.

Perhaps it is because I long for spring from August onwards that it seems to me so short. Each year a day or two out of the little store transcends all others. So soon do the trees take on their rich greenery, the fields lose their green lines and become waving masses of blades, and the streams and ditches, so full of early interest, become smothered with coarse weeds. And yet how the fullness of summer soaks into our beings! It is indeed the changefulness of our changing seasons that weaves the pattern of our lives, giving us no static period of monotony.

But this book is about winter, and to winter with its icy winds, its frosts and snows, I will return. In counties other than those which are wooded even the milder weather may be a trial. Where mountains prevent the low winter sun from reaching the cold earth, or where the land is so flat that its only winter beauty, apart from the thin, low pattern of field and hedgerow, is the great arc of ever-changing sky, winter may well be wished away.

It may be felt that autumn would join hands with spring were it not for the almost inevitable spells of icy weather, and that to ourselves winter is only true winter when such conditions obtain. In other words, that late autumn is sometimes separated from early spring only by a short week or two of weather which is so inimical to growth of all kinds that this book would thereby be considered a mere joke. But I think it will be allowed that our winter may be given a period of four months, from the time when the poplars and limes shed their leaves in Early November until the bursting of the hawthorn into tiny green leaves in March. Let this then be our winter, the period which I will discuss in these pages. I am never far away from flowers or leaves. My year is wrapped up with them, and I want my winter to have as much of their company as is possible. This is my reason for writing these chapters, for so few gardeners give much thought to this aspect of gardening, although it is true that the cult of the flowering shrub has done much to change this, and perhaps no shrub so much as the Fragrant Guelder.

Never has gardening been more to the fore than it is at the present day. We have only to look on the newsagents' counters where about a dozen magazines devoted entirely to horticulture are displayed weekly, to say nothing of the further dozen which have special gardening pages. Then we have our great national newspapers with their weekly columns, and at the other end of the scale the many books published every year on special aspects of horticulture, and the rising membership of the gardening societies.

To London gardeners a special winter attraction must be the seasonal shows in the Royal Horticultural Society's halls, where exotic flowers from warm greenhouses, bulbs and other flowers in and out of season, and a host of greenery, flowers and berries from shrubs may be seen and enjoyed in comfort. But we cannot all visit the shows and not all of us have the space, the means, or the time necessary, to run a greenhouse to provide blooms for the home. And so I want to do my best to call attention to the numerous hardy trees, shrubs and plants that any of us with a small or large garden may choose from, to provide colour and interest from our windows in winter, to furnish the garden, and provide material for decorating the house.

A flower, whether small or large, lasting or fleeting, rare or common, has a beauty not possessed by anything else in this world, and as such is worthy of our closest attention. To exquisite form is given, perhaps, a royal cloak of jewelled colours, a miraculous texture, or a delicious fragrance. In some flowers we find all four qualities combined. Let me not convey, however, that the flowers which appear during our colder months can compare in brilliance with the more obvious beauty that the summer's sun draws forth; rather let me say that they have charm, and that their beauty is the more appreciated on account of their scarcity.

Up to the present the flowers of winter have not been 'improved' by our busy hybridists. It is just as well, for a great size of bloom would be an easy prey to the buffeting wind and driving rain of the dark months. Besides, it is not a blaze of colour I think that we should expect from our gardens in winter, but rather an embellishment and interest which can satisfy through many weeks.

It is a common idea in gardening to have beds near the house planted annually with two sets of plants which provide colour during April and May, and then again from July to the end of September. This means that for just that time of the year when a little colour and interest are needed – often for four months of less enjoyable weather – we look upon raked soil, with a few sprigs of greenery from serried lines of wallflowers, or leafless twigs of roses. This method of providing colour is perhaps an outmoded form of gardening, but far be it for me to push forward a rule for garden owners. The inexhaustible joy of gardening is that no two plots need be the same, nor, in my experience, are they ever alike. Even if the same plants are grown, the owners' tastes will dictate a different arrangement. But it does often occur to me how much more enjoyable the views from the windows might be if we concentrated our attention on *plants* rather than on *flowers*. In other words, garden-furnishing comes from leaves and their contrasting shapes and disposal, which are with us for six or twelve months, rather than from flowers which often have a duration of only two or three weeks.

Especially is this true of our winter flowers. As I have said, none has been fancied by the hybridist, except for the winter-flowering pansies and a few selected hellebores and little bulbs, and we are thus using nature's wildings in an unalloyed state. And the use of this kind of plant for display at any time of the year awakens us to a far more refined and interesting beauty than the production of prize blooms of selected man-made strains.

It is a strange fact, by the way, that the majority of the florists' flowers have poor leaves. It is not that the beauty of the leaf has decreased as the size and colours of the flower have developed, but that the plants have as a general rule quite simple, ordinary foliage.

One of the great things in growing 'species' – the technical term for nature's wildings – as opposed to 'varieties' or 'forms', is that we at once become more conscious of the beauty of the entire outline of the plant, the poise of its blooms, the grace of its stems, and above all the value and individual beauty of its leaves. There are of course exceptions, but it will be acknowledged that where the flowers and leaves remain in nature's original proportions, a greater value is attached to the latter.

Unlike many of our popular summer flowers upturned to the sun, the flowers of winter are frequently nodding, thus sheltering their vital parts from damage by the weather. This gives them a special appeal to me. But it is not only the flowers themselves that I write about; with them are all the multitudinous shapes and shades of green or burnished leaves, some decorated with white or yellow, and the green, brown, red and orange twigs of shrubs and trees, and the brilliant berries. These, their form and texture, their uses for groupings or isolation, their love of sun or shade, and preference in the way of soils and conditions provide us with an inexhaustible study. And it is a study which, except with the bulbs, can help to provide permanent features in the garden, to give it a furnished appearance throughout the year, and to cover the ground with luxuriant foliage, thus greatly reducing labour.

It will be realized from the above paragraph that gardening for winter effect lends itself par excellence to the 'new gardening' – the growing of trees and shrubs and permanent herbaceous plants in more or less natural arrangement and conditions – the gardening which seeks to cope with the largest area with the least labour and for the longest enjoyment. If it can be said that there is a revolution in gardening today it is this new feeling for furnishing the ground and garden with stalwart plants and shrubs. For if the ground be covered with a colonizing, healthy, low herbaceous plant as *Tiarella cordifolia*, *Bergenia*, or Lily of the valley, or with dwarf shrubs like heather or Sun Rose, little cultivation or attention is necessary, provided that the right choice has been made and that the plant is growing thickly and well. These plants form the immediate cover for the foreground and for patches running back into the bigger shrubs. Under the shrubs a litter of fallen leaves, augmented by those gathered off the lawns and paths, and other decaying matter, provides another form of ground-cover, through which bulbs will healthily push their stems. When once these two forms of ground-cover are on their way to fulfilment the days of the spade and hoe are numbered.

This kind of gardening is useless if one grows 'flowers'. The popular strains of flowers prefer what we may call the old-fashioned vegetable-garden cultivation: deep digging, manuring, hoeing and staking. Then we may expect perfection from our dahlias and sweet peas, our gladioluses and chrysanthemums, and many other favourite flowers.

We have in our collection of winter plants and shrubs just those permanent things which will blend together; the hellebores and early bulbs will thrive under the Autumn Cherry, the cyclamens under the Strawberry Trees, and the Mountain Heath will smother weeds over wide stretches of border, giving their eight or twelve weeks' display every year: provided, I must repeat again, that the right choice has been made. Gardening is the most difficult of arts, for not only must we visualize the colour, quality, and season of each plant, long before its maturity and also in a dormant planting period, but also we must make a great effort to select those plants which will do best in our respective sites. A contented plant, be it ever so common, is better than a rarity pining for more suitable conditions.

I can think of no more rewarding planting than a great collection of these evergreens and flowering shrubs for winter, mixed with bulbs and hardy plants. I would arrange my planting so that my vantage-points were towards the east, north, and west, for in winter especially we need the sunlight to strike upon the plants and light them for our eyes. In the summer, when the sun is more over our heads, often the opposite would be equally desirable. One of the best backgrounds for winter planting is a thicket of silver birches; their stems are very attractive, but the masses of small, purplish-brown twigs create the very best contrast that I know for greenery of all kinds. Behind them would be another thicket, of evergreens to keep at bay the icy winds from the north and east. There is no doubt that the winter heather is one of the finest of all ground-coverers on acid or limy soil, and sheets of the various pinks and whites in winter create a more solid effect than all the other shrubs and plants put together. These, then, would be in the foreground, running back in tongues of colour, to where the Winter Sweets and jasmines, backed by evergreens of varying tints and outlines, would be crowned with the arbutuses and cherries. And in moister, lower parts great clumps of red Dogwoods and orange willows would flame in sunlight, or smoulder dully on cloudy days.

But such is not likely to be my good fortune. I therefore put my winter-flowering plants in my front garden, where I can see them daily, going to and fro, and there is never a week without a bloom during open winter weather.

Another good use of these winter delights in smaller gardens is to dispose them among those whose display comes at a different period. Thus a border mainly devoted to spring- and summer-flowering shrubs can well have groups of winter heaths, bulbs and hellebores in front, while behind the summer herbaceous border can be placed winter- and early spring-flowering shrubs, whose beauty will be revealed when the border flowers are dormant. In this way will colour and interest be maintained throughout the year.

But let us now leave these generalizations and examine for their colour and interest the various inmates of our imaginary winter garden, taking them one by one in horticultural groups.

The trees, shrubs and plants mentioned in this book are mostly of wild types and have been grown and observed during the period stated in Surrey. A much more varied list might be obtained by a gardener in the sheltered coombs of Cornwall or the warmer parts of Ireland or Scotland, while a very much smaller number would be the result along our north-east coasts, or inland in perhaps the North Midlands. Surrey is, after all, not a bad county, although it is much colder than many gardeners in the Midlands and North realize. In Woking we are midway between Wisley and Aldershot where low readings of the thermometer are frequently given, owing partly, I believe, to the quickly chilling effect of sandy soils.

1. Trees

A garden in these days is a small thing compared with its usual interpretation one hundred, or even only fifty, years ago. There are so many more plots today which have pretensions to being called gardens that this reduction of the size of the individual is a small loss compared with the greater national area devoted to gardening. This means that there are more gardens today needing plants and shrubs than those needing trees. But there is generally room for one tree in every garden, and it is always comforting to remember that, although they create shade which is inimical to the majority of the popular florists' flowers, there are many extremely charming plants available which actually grow best in full or partial shade.

Among the few hardy trees that can be called winter-flowering is one of the most valuable of all garden trees. The Autumn Cherry, since first it came to these shores from Japan in 1911, has been gaining steadily in popularity, until today it occupies a high place among the many favourite cherries. In time this cherry, *Prunus subhirtella* 'Autumnalis', makes an open-headed tree, but is not of heavy growth, and, in spite of its size, is so valuable on account of its blossom that it should be in all but the smallest gardens. Very often, before the small leaves fall in a shower of yellow, the tiny white flowers throng the twigs, increasing through open weather in November to a cloud of white. When fading they turn pink, giving a soft glow along the branches. Unless the weather be mild, it usually ceases then and new buds open again in the early year. When the sun shines, the black, knobby twigs freely set with blossoms are a lovely sight. Its exquisite pink variety, *P.s.* 'Autumnalis Rosea', does not flower so freely in the autumn as the white kind, holding its geatest display until the spring.

Prunus subhirtella 'Autumnalis'

Nor does it appear to make so large a tree in maturity, although it is just as vigorous as the white type as a youngster.

As Collingwood Ingram pointed out in his exhaustive book *Ornamental Cherries*, the Autumn Cherry can be cut in bud and will last for weeks in water. A particularly fresh and charming effect was once shown in the class for floral arrangement at the Royal Horticultural Society's Hall. It was there used with single pink chrysanthemums, and many of us were quite enthralled with the simple beauty.

Much less known is another pretty cherry which also flowers during mild spells from November to April. This is *P. serrulata* var. *semperflorens*, or 'Fudan-Zakura' ('Shikizakura'), a large shrub or small tree, forming a fairly close, rounded head, and bearing single blush-pink flowers fading to white in reddish sepals.

In February or in an exceptionally mild January, the Chinese *P. conradinae*'s protruding stamens give promise of opening buds; it has small, single blossoms of blush-pink, set on smooth, brown twigs, and makes a fair-sized tree. The semi-double form is the one usually planted, but I must confess to a greater liking for the single-flowered species. This does not make a very strong plant as a sapling, but gradually grows into a beautiful round-headed tree up to some 20 feet in height in sheltered conditions. At Kew and at Winkworth Arboretum there are handsome specimens; the bark is richly coloured and the flowers create a shimmer of pink in February. Another Chinese *Prunus*, generally in flower in February, is *P. davidiana*; throughout the summer the leaves of David's Peach – for this is no cherry – hang like slim javelins in cool green from the wide-spraying stems. In autumn they fall early after turning to soft orange-pink. The stemless blooms stud the whippy branches with soft pink. It has much to recommend it throughout the year but, for blossom alone, the slender, erect-growing, pure white variety, *P.d. alba*, is superior, and its blooms have a rounded perfection of outline very good to behold. These both make trees of some 18 feet in height, much like that of an Almond or fruit tree. The almonds themselves are March flowers, but the form *P. dulcis* (*P. communis*) 'Praecox' may be relied upon to flower in February. It is a smaller tree and has smaller flowers than the common almond, but is valuable for its flowering season.

Few winter flowers give me more satisfaction and enjoyment than the named flowering forms of the Japanese Apricot, *P. mume*. According to the severity or otherwise of the winter, they flower between the end of December and the beginning of March; in fact I have sometimes enjoyed them at Christmas. Alone among species of *Prunus*, their flowers need to be at least half open before picking them for indoors; tight buds do not respond well to warmth. And what a scent they have; it is powerful – two sprays will scent a room – and deliciously sweet, haunting and indefinable. The flowers cast their scent freely on the air, and if one of the kinds were in the front garden of every house, what a fragrant way we should have! Each tree – or large shrub, depending on how you grow it – will last a month at least in bloom, and the buds on the strong young twigs open later than those on weak old twigs. I think perhaps my favourite is the semi-double white, *P.m.* 'Omoinomama'. Translated this means 'to have its own way' in reference to its amusing habit of producing occasional pale pink flowers, or single petals of pink. I have long grown this and a single rich dark pink one named 'Benichidori' ('Flight of red plovers'). At Kew I have seen 'Yaekankobai' ('Many-petalled red winter plum'), single pink and 'Touzibai' ('Winter plum') single white. A large

Prunus davidiana alba

semi–double blush is 'Kenkyo' ('Blush') while yet another, 'Kyokkho' ('Deep red') seems identical with 'Benichidori'. There is also a weeping form 'Pendula'. These cultivars have reached Kew from a conservation society, the Flower Foundation of Japan. Although the first two and some others have been in cultivation in this country for over thirty years, they have remained unnoticed by all but a few discerning gardeners; they are quite hardy, easily grown and must surely soon become better known. Their flowers withstand all but the most severe frosts.

The pink Manchurian Apricot, *P. mandshurica*, is free flowering and also beautiful but lacks the entrancing fragrance of *P. mume*.

Two species of *Prunus* were shown at a February meeting of The Royal Horticultural Society, the one an early form of a well-known cherry, *P. incisa* 'Praecox', and the other a peach, *P. kansuensis*. Both make compact small trees and are valuable for the abundance of their small blush-tinted white flowers.

One of the most reliable of flowering *Prunuses* is the Cherry-plum or Myrobalan, *P. cerasifera*. This is a small, quick-growing green-leafed tree, a common hedging shrub, with abundant white blossom. It is usually at least a fortnight earlier than its better known purplish-leafed form, *P. cerasifera* 'Pissardii', whose pink blooms usually appear in March. *P.c.* 'Hessei' has white flowers which are produced regularly in February, but its purplish calyces give it a warm tint.

The various *Prunus* trees are not difficult to satisfy in the way of soil, the cherries even thriving on chalk, but the two peaches are often short-lived and sometimes show profuse 'gumming'. There is no cure for this; they are trees which should be given sheltered positions and all the sunshine possible. Peaches and cherries seem loath to put up with coarse grass around their roots – in fact I know of no trees that are so intolerant of company of this kind – and they do best therefore in cultivated ground.

One hears much of the Glastonbury thorn – *Crataegus monogyna* 'Biflora' (*C. oxyacantha* var. *praecox*) – but I do not think it can be considered of great use and beauty for the average garden. The legend tells us that our present trees are direct descendants from the staff of Joseph of Arimathea, which, being thrust in the ground on that Christmas Day of long ago at Glastonbury, burst at once into flower, in Divine proof of his mission. The fact is that trees do bear flowers and leaf spasmodically through the winter as well as bearing a crop of blossom at the proper flowering time.

Among true evergreen trees there is one that must find mention here, and that is *Eucalyptus gunnii*. In October and into November its quaint, greenish flowers appear and are very beautiful when examined closely, while its slender stature and flimsy greenery create a new birch-like note in the garden. It is, in maturity, a large tree, but is only hardy in our warmest counties. Those from upland provenance in Tasmania are likely to be proof against our winters. In direct contrast may be placed the magnificent *Corylus colurna*, a hazel from Turkey. A stout trunk covered with flaking grey bark bears a great head of branches, a fine sight in February when hung with the long catkins in clusters and singly. It is being used as a street tree in London and elsewhere. With this, in moister parts, may be placed our own native alder, *Alnus glutinosa*, whose purple buds and coppery catkins appear in the same month. It is a tree of large proportions, but so cheering is the promise of a catkin foretelling spring that it may well merit inclusion in larger planting schemes, but a compact small tree is one which might be deferred for Chapter 6 because both its twigs and catkins are a bright orange throughout the winter: it is *A. incana* 'Aurea', while even more brilliant in its colouring is 'Ramulis Coccineis'.

The most interesting group of poplars in winter is that of the aspens; *Populus tremula*, the Aspen Poplar itself, is most beautiful when hung with its long and fluffy grey catkins, enriched with the crimson of hundreds of young stamens, but *P. canescens*, the Grey Poplar, sometimes considered a hybrid between *P. tremula* and *P. alba*, is even more noticeable. Here the male catkins are equally richly coloured and the tree has a grandeur of port which is unique; the huge trunk, of a strange, greenish-cream colour heavily marked with the black 'necklaces' of the lenticels and the black scars from lopped branches, presents a very striking appearance. The branches are very brittle and the tree is short-lived. In common with the aspen it produces abundant suckers which can be a terrible nuisance in a small garden.

The remainder of our trees are usually seen as large shrubs with one or more stems. For long-lasting colour and interest *Parrotia persica*, a member of the Witch Hazel clan, takes an important position, its wide-spreading, fan-like branches making a large and characteristic specimen and needing much space for its appreciation. One of the most magnificent specimens I know is growing in Westonbirt Arboretum in Gloucestershire; here the 30-foot long, nearly horizontal branches are in marked contrast to a group of dark green columns of *Calocedrus* (*Libocedrus*) *decurrens*. Two trees overshadow the winter garden at Polesden Lacey on chalk. As a lawn specimen it is superb: it will thrive in any reasonable soil. It is delightful in spring in its fresh silkiness; the leaves on the ends of the main branches begin to take on burnished tints at the end of June, increasing in colour and brilliance towards autumn, when those in the centre of the bush change colour and on dropping reveal rounded buds of brown velvet thickly studding the twigs. These, in February, open and disclose the tight bunches of crimson stamens.

Though trees in some respects of the word, I will leave the hamamelises until the next chapter, and likewise the willows, and this leaves us *Arbutus*, *Azara* and *Cornus mas*. The last, the so-called

Cornus mas

Cornelian Cherry, has nothing to do with the cherries, except that it bears round, red, fleshy fruits in summer, no mean attraction after its lovely clouds of starry, yellow blossoms in February. A large shrub of some 12–18 feet, it creates a bright picture in full flower, especially when grouped with its red-twigged relatives – varieties of *C. alba* – and is frequently brilliant in its October tints, thriving on almost any soil.

Azara gives us *A. microphylla* from Chile, whence it reached these shores some eighty years ago, a dainty tree-like evergreen up to some 15 feet, beset with tiny, rounded leaves on spraying branches giving a ferny effect. On examination it will be seen that the 'lobes' of the leaves are in truth large overlapping stipules, and not leaves at all. The orange-yellow flowers once again are insignificant but their vanilla scent is very sweet during warm spells in February and March.

We are left with the arbutuses, and of all our garden treasures these are some of the most dignified and satisfying. From their shaggy or peeling soft brown or reddish bark, to their glossy, firm, evergreen leaves, and nodding groups of dainty, urn-like, green-white flowers, they are truly aristocratic. *Arbutus unedo*, usually seen in big, bushy trees, up to 15 feet or so and as much through, is naturalized in the extreme south-west of Ireland, although its real home is the Mediterranean region, and is the only true late autumn- or winter-flowering species. It has a very beautiful variety (*A.u. rubra* or 'Croomei') which is vegetatively propagated for its large, rosy-pink bells and dark red fruits. It is possibly more useful for smaller gardens on account of its more bushy growth. The resultant fruits of the species, which take a year to ripen to their orange-red, may be seen hanging with the flowers, and give the plant its name, Strawberry Tree.

Arbutus unedo

A. unedo has mated with *A. andrachne* and produced *A.* × *andrachnoides* (*A. hybrida*). Flowers are borne in late autumn or spring, as *A. andrachne* is a spring flowerer. Two fine specimens grace the top terrace at Bodnant. Although these are members of the great Heath Family, Ericaceae, they thrive on limy soils as well as on those of an acid tendency. In fact, one of the finest specimens of *Arbutus* I know is on a sharply sloping chalk bank near Winchester. All species have great beauty of bark and are discussed again in the chapter devoted to this character (Chapter 6).

It is hardly surprising that this chapter should be so short. Anything that flowers during cold weather would normally respond most easily to varying temperatures and therefore it would derive most benefit from being near to the ground. Several other chapters go on interminably, so many are the species to be mentioned. But flowering trees are not really very important in our winter garden; the design should be snug and well backed with evergreens and the open tracery of surrounding trees that will lead the eye aloft on sunny days, and give beauty at other times of the year.

2. Deciduous Shrubs

Among the hardy deciduous shrubs we find many of the best winter flowers, and they are, moreover, mostly suitable for the average garden. It will be best to consider first the largest, and, having given *Parrotia* a place among the trees, I cannot do better than turn straight to its relatives the Witch Hazels, for they attain a tree-like dimension, but generally lack the single stem that constitutes a tree. Just as the deciduous shrubs take a high place among plants generally in the winter garden, so do these members of the genus *Hamamelis* deservedly take pride of place among the deciduous shrubs. They are the very life of the winter garden. Of all the flowers they seem best qualified to withstand sharp frosts; even after snow and icy winds their flowers seldom suffer much, and provided there are mild spells to encourage them, some kind or other may usually be had in flower from October to March.

Hamamelis virginiana is the true Witch Hazel, and an extract from its leaves and bark is used in medicine. All species bear hazel-like leaves, although they are not related to the catkin-bearing trees botanically, but earned their name from the use to which they were put by the early settlers in North America, where their resemblance prompted the use of the Virginian species for water-divining. Before the leaves have fallen the strange little flowers of this early autumn species appear; they are mere wisps of greeny-yellow, with a peculiar fragrance, and they hang on until the end of November or later.

In December or January, even before the first aconite, the best-known species, *H. mollis*, comes into flower. Usually seen in shrub form up to about 8 feet in height, with its soft, furry twigs, large, velvety foliage assuming a golden-yellow in October, and flowers which are the finest in the genus, it is justly popular. A more lovely sight could not be found during the whole gardening year than its bright, canary-yellow blooms with maroon eyes spangling the ascending twigs above a carpet of the pink winter-heath, *Erica carnea* 'King George'. Other plants may have their charm and attraction, but to me this companionship is the essence of winter gardening. The colour goes on for weeks, through storm and shine unperturbed, and the amazing warm fragrance of the hazel is carried far on the air.

The attraction of the hazel's flowers is closely characteristic of all the species. The calyx is maroon-coloured inside and the twisted strap-shaped petals, forming a cross, are of varying tints of yellow in contrast, with an eye-like glint in the centre from the yellow stamens. With the flowers are the nutty husks from the previous year's flowers, each enclosing four beautiful, polished, black seeds, precision-shaped and neatly marked with white where they were attached to the base of the husk.

The Chinese *Hamamelis mollis* has proved a great success at Wisley, and on January 12th, 1932, an Award of Merit was granted to a beautiful, pale yellow form named *H.m.* 'Pallida', which was raised there. This is the form I unhesitatingly chose for my garden. It is possibly the most telling hazel extant, but were it otherwise, such is the value of this species that any variety would be welcome. A strange, short-petalled variety which originated in France some time ago is known as *H.m.* 'Brevipetala'; the colour is the notable thing about this variety, for it is of ochre-yellow. When it has made a good sized bush it is impressive in flower, as it is the warmest tint among yellows for the dawn of the year. A form known as 'Coombe Wood' no doubt originated in Veitch's nursery, but has never become well known. It is a most appealing shrub, with more arching growth than the type, and the flowers, very large and well formed, are held in a nodding position, like those of *H. japonica* var. *arborea*. The scent and foliage are in the general run of excellence. 'Goldcrest' is another good variety, flowering later; it was raised at Bodnant.

This great species is closely followed by the lesser lights of the genus, from Japan. I use the word 'lesser' only as applied to floral display, for *H. japonica* itself is a strong grower, reaching some

10–15 feet, with open, wide-spreading growth and fan-like branches. It has a moderate fragrance, but the flowers are of a telling pale yellow, nearly as large, in a good form such as 'Sulphurea', as those of *H. mollis*. It often opens with *H. mollis* in early January, but the old leaves rather spoil the effect as they frequently cling to the stems, hiding the flowers. The next to open is usually *H. japonica* var. *flavopurpurascens* (usually known as *H.j. rubra*) whose yellow is suffused with the maroon of the calyx. In some years this variety flowers abundantly, but is not reliable. Although its colour is by no means as bright as the others, it has the sweetest, softest fragrance of them all.

More tree-like than its species, *H.j.* var. *arborea* has a most striking fan-like growth, and its dark yellow flowers are neat and very twisty, of an essentially Japanese style, while the last to flower in February and into March is *H.j.* 'Zuccariniana' whose flowers are of citron-yellow and give off a strong and penetrating odour much like that of *Cornus mas*. Apart from its later-flowering period, it has not much garden value except as a young plant, when it usually flowers freely. I suspect it would repay some hard pruning as an old shrub, for it develops into a weak-looking, goblet-shaped shrub some 12 feet high and wide.

Such is the popularity of the Witch Hazels that many hybrids have been raised, in this country, on the Continent and in the United States. One of the oldest is 'Hiltingbury', named after Messrs Hillier's Winchester nurseries. The flowers are comparatively small, of red-brown, but it is chiefly noted for its red autumn colouring, most others turning to yellow. Another seedling raised by Hilliers is 'Carmine Red', referring to the flowers. Because they are crosses between *H. mollis* and *H. japonica* these hybrids are known as *H.* × *intermedia*. The richest and most conspicuous in its reddish colouring is 'Diane' which originated in Belgium. 'Luna', on the other hand, tends towards the greenish-yellow of 'Zuccariniana'. There are several of orange tone, notably 'Jelena', also from Belgium, named after Mme Robert de Belder of the famous Kalmthout Arboretum. This has large, richly scented flowers and is often in flower by Christmas. 'Orange Beauty' is similar. There is no doubt that the lighter coloured cultivars, such as 'Pallida' and 'Sulphurea', are the most conspicuous in the garden, but in the winter scene a flower of any colour is valuable and hence we can enjoy these more subdued tones. From the Arnold Arboretum in the United States comes 'Arnold Promise': it is a strong, tall grower and one of the latest to flower with flowers of a brilliant clear yellow. I think this plant has a great future; it grows well at Wisley. Many of these may be seen at Wisley; some are in the comparatively new area devoted to winter flowering plants at the east end of the Trial Ground.

Hamamelis vernalis, like the autumn-flowering *H. virginiana* from eastern North America, is not of great importance, but flowers during the first months of the year. All the better species and varieties are doubly valuable on account of the usually glorious yellow of their autumn tints, thus being in the front rank of plants for our purpose. In spite of *H. mollis* and *H. japonica* having been in cultivation for over a century, they are not yet common, perhaps partly because they are slow to increase, and also because they will only thrive on lime-free soils; they prefer a medium loam well mixed with humus, but something short of this will suit them, so long as they are not waterlogged or given lime. They have such a beautiful mode of branching that pruning is highly undesirable, but as one must cut them occasionally for the house, it is fortunate that they speedily grow again. The flat, fan-like growths of *H.j.* vars *arborea* and *flavopurpurascens* will grow out for 10 feet or more in one direction, and the poise and line are scarcely equalled in the shrub world, except in the noble *Parrotia*.

Much of the charm of winter gardening – and of our rooms – is provided by the Winter Sweet, so aptly named in English, but which the botanists have variously christened *Calycanthus praecox*, *Meratia praecox*, or *Chimonanthus fragrans*. At the moment both Rehder and Bean (latest editions) concur in calling it *Chimonanthus praecox*. Such unanimity is a pause in horticulture worth noting; these changes of nomenclature during the two hundred years or so since it was introduced to the Western Hemisphere from China have harmed it not one jot!

It is a twiggy shrub of some 7 feet square and high, and when its leaves have fallen it has a grey appearance. The rounded buds open in midwinter and in the type species the flowers have a grey tint too, but the fragrance is sublime. How blest are we gardeners who know these flowers of winter! One small twig with half a dozen flowers will scent a room with sweet spiciness as good as summer's best, but the stiffly nodding, dirty cream flowers with their maroon-red inner petals have none of the soft charm of summer flowers. The petals are transparent and frail and they do not stand much frost. This colourless form of the species is seldom seen outside botanic gardens, forms varying to a rich

Chimonanthus praecox

yellow tint being far more common in cultivation, but all these tints have a true wintry look about them, their petals being partly trans-parent and revealing the soft maroon-shaded central petals within their cup-formation. A much more brilliant plant is *C.p.* 'Grandiflorus'. The flowers of this are widely open, of bright straw-yellow, revealing a dark maroon centre composed of shorter petals, also reflexed. It creates quite a bright effect, but to my mind is coarse and overbearing, lacking all the charm of the type, nor has it so delicious a scent. But even that is not the most brilliant. One dull afternoon in January I went to Kew: the most lovely sight greeted me on the wall of the Cambridge Cottage Garden, where a plant of the superlative *C.p.* 'Luteus' had been trained to cover many square feet. The flowers open wider than those of other varieties and all the

Chimonanthus praecox 'Luteus'

petals are broader, of a clear, light yellow, heralding the glory of the forsythia in March. Some writers persist in stating that this variety has no fragrance; this is quite wrong. I find it almost as scented as the species itself. As yet but seldom seen, when it becomes known it will surely be a popular plant, for it appears to be as good and hardy a shrub as the species, but once again it is a slow plant to propagate. Although perfectly hardy, these Winter Sweets do need all the sunshine they can get to ripen their wood; moreover, they often take some years to begin flowering regularly in rich, deep soil. Grown on or near a west wall they will get the full benefit of the sun in summer and shelter from frosty winter mornings, and in my experience they flower best in such conditions and in rather poor soil.

The honeysuckle's scent is almost proverbial, so that it is not surprising to find two fragrant, winter-flowering species in this genus. *Lonicera standishii* and *L. fragrantissima*, both found just over a hundred years ago in China by Robert Fortune, are two bushy shrubs about 6 feet high, with small cream flowers an inch or so long and wide. That of Standish is deciduous and rather gaunt in growth, while *L. fragrantissima* is somewhat lax and open, and is semi-evergreen.

Lonicera fragrantissima and *standishii*

The flowers of both are creamy white.

Except perhaps by the purists, I think the above two species will be neglected in the future by discriminating gardeners in favour of L. × *purpusii*, probably a hybrid between the two, with a better habit than either. It is midway in character between its parents, although showing something of the bristly leaf stalks and calyces by which L. *standishii* can most easily be distinguished from L. *fragrantissima*. It originated in the Darmstadt Botanic Garden in the early twenties, being a chance seedling found near the two species. All kinds will fortunately thrive in soil of almost any quality. In the garden these shrubs and the Winter Sweets are usually fairly dense to the ground, and in consequence cannot be suitably underplanted as can the open-growing Witch Hazels. Rather are they of the type of shrub for grouping, having no particular growth-style of their own. Larger growing is *L. setifera*, a species from the Assam Himalaya with bristly stems. Seldom does the first month of the year go by without the appearance of the bunches of pale pink sweetly scented flowers.

Another valuable genus is that of the viburnums. Leaving *Viburnum tinus* for consideration in the chapter on evergreens (Chapter 3), there are several excellent shrubs taking as high a place among the winter garden plants as other species do in the full tide of summer, and again in the autumn pageant.

Introduced by Purdom and Farrer, the superlative *V. farreri* flowered for the first time in this country in 1920 and ever since then has been increasing in popularity. It has for long been known as *V. fragrans*, but as this name was used earlier for a different species, it has been discontinued, largely through the researches of Professor W. T. Stearn. Finding the name inadmissable, he proposed in 1966 that it be changed to *V. farreri* in honour of him whose introduction and praise ('the best beloved and most universal of garden plants all over North China') had caused it to be so well-known over here. Not all such name-changes are so felicitous! It is one of the earliest of winter flowers to open, for frequently on a November day its branches may

Viburnum farreri (V. fragrans)

be seen wreathed with its blush-white flowers opening from rosy buds, and its amazing scent of heliotrope is carried freely on the breeze. It delights in a fairly moist soil, but needs full sunshine to set its buds well, and has the excellent habit of continually pushing up fine, straight shoots from the base, which, as the years pass, gradually branch and arch outwards. When mild weather obtains they are literally smothered with rounded heads of little trumpet blooms. The Fragrant Guelder does not last well indoors, but it is a help to put cut sprays outside or in the larder at night, where they will not suffer from the drying air of the rooms. This Fragrant Guelder, as Sir William Beach Thomas so aptly called it, has a white cultivar 'Candidissimum', showing greener wood and bud scales, and is greenish-yellow in the bud. It has a quiet beauty of its own but is by no means as ornamental as the usual type. The flowers and growth are generally smaller, too. *V.f.* 'Nanum' is also sometimes grown, but this does not flower very freely until the dense plant has reached a height of 3 feet or so, when a peppering of its pinkish blooms transforms a somewhat dull little bush into a hummock of fresh beauty.

Lovely as our remaining species are, they cannot compare with *V. farreri*. *V. grandiflorum*, heralded with acclamation from Bhutan in 1914, has not proved a good garden plant. Its winter hardiness appears now to be without question, and it does produce most lovely, silvery-pink bunches of trumpet flowers in the *farreri* style in winter, but the growth is more gaunt and open. A good white form is named 'Snow White'; it was collected in Nepal by Donald Lowndes in 1950. On the other side of the scale is the half-evergreen *V. foetens*, with stiff, yet drooping bunches of similar flowers in creamy-white, borne on smooth, fat twigs. Like the others, its flowering period is long, and I have seen it at Leith Vale, Ockley, and at Wisley in flower in November. Good reports have reached me of *V. foetens* from Edinburgh, where it has formed a large, rounded bush, flowers freely, and is not harmed in the bud by frost. Botanically, both *V. grandiflorum* and *V. foetens* are grouped together by Rehder, but from a horticultural point of view they are totally distinct; the latter seems to prefer some shade.

An interesting and beautiful hybrid was raised at Bodnant, Lord Aberconway's famous North Wales garden, between *V. grandiflorum* and *V. farreri* named *V. × bodnantense*. This has the same long-flowering period as *V. farreri* and its flowers and habit are midway

Viburnam foetens

between the two species. At Bodnant it is considered a really good hybrid and it certainly makes a strong bush, but it unfortunately inherits the gaunt growth and tender flowers of *V. grandiflorum* and cannot compare in general usefulness for the garden with *V. farreri*. When cut for indoors this hybrid has an advantage over *V. farreri*, since its flowers do not fall so quickly; scent and beauty may be assured for a week at least in rooms. It is important to get the 'Dawn' or 'Charles Lamont' form of *V.* × *bodnantense*; another hybrid was made by Messrs Notcutt of Woodbridge from *V.f.* 'Candidissimum'; it has white flowers and has been named 'Deben' after the local river. A little of the less pleasant fragrance of *V. grandiflorum* has been imparted to these hybrids, but the result is, nevertheless, delicious. These viburnums need constant moisture below ground to grow really freely; the

Fragrant Guelder is one of the first shrubs here in the South to show signs of unhappiness in hot weather.

Another fine hybrid *Viburnum* commemorating its raiser *V.* × *burkwoodii* (*V. carlesii* × *utile*), is becoming well known, and in sheltered districts might be classed as an evergreen. With us in Surrey it generally retains a few dark, glossy leaves through the winter, and flowers in mild October and November periods and also in April and May. While its flowers lack the exquisite quality of those of *V. carlesii*, it has won a high place among hardy shrubs on account of its hearty nature, graceful free growth, and early-flowering habit. A sister seedling is called 'Park Farm Hybrid' and has blooms of a better quality, richly tinted with pink in the bud. For some mysterious reason this plant was not selected to bear the raiser's name, although in the more considered opinion of many of us it is the superior plant. Both may reach to 7 or 8 feet in height and width in time, but it is not unwieldy and can be suitably reduced, enabling it to be grown in narrow borders and on walls and fences. *V.* × *b.* 'Chenaultii' is of the same parentage and values, from France.

A strange shrub, *Prinsepia utilis*, was exhibited in early February at a Royal Horticultural Show; it apparently makes a very large arching shrub with green shoots and long green spines. The small racemes of tiny flowers are greenish white. It is one of the less attractive members of the Rose Family, and the second name refers to the oil extracted from the seeds. A white-flowered form of the Flowering Currant, *Ribes sanguineum*, usually flowers well in advance of the pink kinds and has considerable charm; this was at the same Show.

While the best of the forsythias are too late for our category of winter flowers, there are two species which do flower in February or early March. One is *Forsythia giraldiana*, which Farrer introduced in 1914 from Southern Kansu, and which is tall and graceful, but only a pale ghost of its later brethren; the other is *F. ovata*, a useful compact shrub up to some 5 feet. This is one of the many good things that have reached us via the Arnold Arboretum from Wilson's collecting in Korea. The small, nodding, fragrant flowers have great charm, but a good, deep golden-yellow form should be sought, as it varies considerably. The late John Coutts, when Curator of Kew, picked out some excellent forms and was good enough to share them with his friends.

Of recent years the related genus *Abeliophyllum*, of which there is only one known species, *Abeliophyllum distichum*, has found its way into gardens. Mr Coutts was also concerned particularly with this shrub and exhibited it in February 1944 at Vincent Square, but it had been received in this country in 1937. It is a very hardy shrub from the Chincen Hills in Korea, and bids fair to be a useful addition to our winter garden. The name refers to the likeness of the leaves to those of an *Abelia*, being smaller than those of forsythias. It is a neat, twiggy plant, and very beautiful in February when closely covered with the sprays of small, deliciously scented, starry, ivory-white flowers opening from pink-tinted buds in the best forms. I think it may become a popular plant when its qualities are better known, for, like the forsythias, this member of the Olive Family appears to thrive in any ordinary soil, but needs hot sunshine in summer to encourage it to flower freely.

With all this abundance of exotics, it is good to turn to a British plant – also native of Europe and Siberia – which stands in the front rank of February- and March-flowering shrubs. This is the Mezereon, *Daphne mezereum*. As with so many daphnes, it is by no means easy to please, but usually thrives in a cool, retentive soil, and there is no greater joy in the earliest months of the year than a free-grown bush of 3 or 4 feet with its numerous spires of soft, old-rose, starry flowers, closely pressed to the twigs. It lasts well indoors and is as fragrant as any of the previous shrubs. Its poisonous red berries, ripening in July, have given fanciful writers an opportunity to discover something sinister in its colour or scent, but neither itself nor its even more delightful creamy-white variety (with yellow berries) can be passed over on that account. The white form known as 'Bowles's Variety' is the most desirable, and grew to a considerable height in the garden of that doyen of horticulturists at Myddelton House. Another kind, which I have not seen, is recorded with double white flowers, but whether a double white would be a worthy addition is a different matter altogether. *D.m.* 'Autumnalis' ('Grandiflora') is a form which starts flowering in early autumn, and I am glad to find that this plant is still in cultivation. These Mezereons make a very splendid display during mild spells and their flowers will stand a hard frost without being harmed. They have a rather stiff, upright habit and need a soft patch of greenery near by as a contrast, and, for all but the autumn-flowering form, *Nuttallia cerasiformis* can well be used. In January the leaf buds of this wide-spreading shrub begin to open, and by mid-

Daphne mezereum

February they present so massed an appearance that the shrub is a cloud of palest green. The insignificant cream flowers are sweetly scented, but in Surrey do not open until March, followed on female plants by strings of miniature purple plums at midsummer.

If I were making a winter garden I would always try to have a nut in it somewhere. There is nothing quite like the charm of a catkin in the early year, and, if neither the Cob nor Filbert, nor their copper-leafed variants be needed, and the Turkish Hazel be too large, then we can turn to that strange Gloucestershire foundling, *Corylus avellana* 'Contorta'. The spiral twists and tortuous turns of every twig are amusing to contemplate in nudity in winter, but when February comes the perpendicular line of the yellow catkins gives a subtle quietness to the huddle of branches. Careful gardeners may like to train up the main branches on canes for a few years to give their plants grace and balance.

Some of the willows, and notably early-flowering forms of *Salix caprea* (Pussy Willow or Palm), may be found in flower in February, and if cuttings are made they will keep this early-flowering propensity. *S. caprea* is too large, however, for the average garden, but there are two charming smaller species which flower very early; one, *S. gracilistyla*, liking a damp spot and producing quantities of silvery, slim 'palm' on woolly twigs, is a native of Japan and Korea. The other, *S. irrorata*, from New Mexico and Arizona, will thrive in quite dry sandy soil, and makes a twiggy bush with its annual growth heavily covered with a white waxy 'bloom'. The bursting pink-tinted catkins make a pretty picture in January and February. Both *S. gracilistyla* and *S. irrorata* will reach some 10 feet in height in time, but the former is usually seen as a low shrub, and the latter is not coarse-growing and can easily be kept within bounds. It is surprising that they are not better known, as they are not new to cultivation, but such plants do not of course rely upon popular appeal for their inclusion in gardens. A form of *S. gracilistyla*, 'Melanostachys' ('Kurome'), was brought from Japan in 1950. It is an extraordinary plant, small growing, and bearing small black catkins with red anthers in the early year. There is nothing like it and it captivates some people. *S. daphnoides* might be classed as a tree, but these others are shrubby kinds; the most showy of *daphnoides* forms is 'Aglaia', with bright, plum-red bark, and large male catkins, but its relative *S. acutifolia* is possibly the most beautiful Pussy Willow for cutting for the house; its branches are delicate and thin, with the pinkish-silver tufts, turning to yellow, sprinkled along their arching length. Another strong-growing shrubby willow for February flowering is *S. aegyptiaca* (*S. medemii*), which has long catkins of greenish yellow. The Persian form which is usually grown makes a very large, tall shrub or small tree.

Every breeze, or a child's finger, moves the catkins of the nuts, and their pollen floats away to drift on to the crimson tassels of the female

Stachyurus praecox

flowers. Not so do the *Stachyurus* flowers dangle. Surprise is always noted in a beholder's eyes when we shake a branch hung well with the ropes of cream bells, like white currants, in February. The stalks are stiff and do not move. *Stachyurus praecox* is the species usually seen and its reddish bark gives this rather quiet shrub a wider appeal. Its distribution in Japan is repeated across the narrow seas by *S. chinensis*, a similar species in China.

Our last paragraph shall be devoted to the 'Japonicas'. They are, it is true, really spring-flowering shrubs, but never a winter goes by without that useful variety 'Aurora' showing colour from October onwards, its great goblets of coppery-salmon lasting and opening so well in water. Other kinds, especially the common red one, follow suit. Their nomenclature is confusing, and should therefore be placed on record at every opportunity. The red Chinese Quince, long known as *Pyrus* or *Cydonia japonica*, should now be known as *Chaenomeles speciosa*, while our other old friend, the dwarf, orange-red Japanese *Cydonia maulei*, becomes *Chaenomeles japonica*. How difficult our worthy confrères the botanists make things for us gardeners may be judged by the close of this chapter and the beginning of the next.

3. Winter Flowering Evergreen Shrubs

Fair pledges of a fruitful tree,
Why do ye fall so fast?
Your date is not so past,
But you may stay yet here awhile
To blush and gently smile
And go at last.

ROBERT HERRICK (1591–1674)
from *To Blossoms*

The great genus *Berberis* has several sections of distinct types and the various species are native of temperate zones in both hemispheres, but we are concerned at present only with certain members characterized by their leaves which are of many divisions, or pinnate. On this account they are classed in a separate genus, *Mahonia*.

I approach with some trepidation the group headed by *Mahonia japonica*. For many years a gaunt shrub with long leaves composed of holly-like lobes, and producing erect, 6-inch spikes of primrose yellow bells scented like Lily of the valley in winter and earliest spring, was grown under this name. It is a native of China and its proper name is *M. bealei*. Its more richly endowed relative is the magnificent shrub long known by this latter name and is a native of Japan, and should be called *M. japonica*. The difficulty is not minimized by the fact that books and catalogues are slow in getting up to date in this respect, and one can never be sure which plant is being discussed.

The true *M. japonica* is one of the most impressive of foliage plants, and its long stems, reaching to some 8 feet in places sheltered from hot sun and wind, are always well clothed in the handsome pinnate leaves, long and graceful and less prickly than those of the usurper already described. Deliciously scented, the flowers are borne from the tops of the stems on long curving racemes up to a foot in length, and each bloom is a primrose-bell of many petals opening wide in clement weather. As with all barberries, the stamens respond to a touch and alertly move to enclasp the stigma. This is a shrub of rare and constant beauty, the leaves being gracefully curved in spite of their stiffness, and the contrast of the very pale undersides against the dark upper surfaces is as noticeable as in some rhododendrons.

Although it is looked upon as a genuine species, the true *M. japonica* does not in my experience set good seed, while the unwanted *M. bealei* sets ample quantities; this is a strange fact, in view of the new names.

Mahonia bealei

Mahonia japonica

There is still room for a possible improvement on both, namely, a
plant with the superlative growth and large flowers of *M. japonica*
with its long racemes held more erect, as in *M. bealei*. Since everyone
is not yet up to date in the nomenclature of these two kinds, it is as well
when ordering a plant or writing about it to speak of '*M. japonica* –
formerly *bealei* – the best lax-flowered kind'. This should avoid confusion in what is a most tiresome teaser. These mahonias do not object
to lime but are lovers of humus and cool soil and conditions –

semi-woodlanders, in fact, and thriving best when sheltered from strong winds; they will grow in almost any cold, north-facing corner, even under trees. On the other hand, when grown in full sun, the leaves frequently develop bright reddish tints – ideal for the flower arranger.

One of the most valuable of autumn-flowering shrubs, and one of the most striking of all hardy foliage plants, is a more recent introduction from China, whence Major Johnston brought seeds in 1931 – *M. lomariifolia*. It occurs in north-east Upper Burma, China, Yunnan, South Sichuan, and Formosa, and plants from the colder localities should be useful here. Although not hardy enough for general open situations in Surrey, the strain in cultivation is nevertheless worthy of a sheltered westerly corner where its upright, bamboo-like stems can have space to throw out horizontally the fine long leaves, hard and leathery, like those of a *Cycas*, and divided into many lobes. In October, and lasting well into November, the bunched spikes of rich, brilliant yellow flowers appear at the top of the stems, supported by the toby-frill of leaves. Seen thus, it is a very noble sight and carries the palm-like tradition of these greater mahonias to the fullest extent. We frequently lose its leaves and stems in the winter, but so far it has always grown again from ground-level, and after several favourable seasons, if it attains a height of some 9 feet, it may be expected to flower. It is one of those striking plants that, once seen, one never forgets. At Hidcote there is a fine specimen of this splendid shrub, growing in a fully exposed position 550 feet above sea-level. Very cold winters have harmed it, but it is still thriving. The first and succeeding generations raised from this plant are proving to be of increased hardiness. To come upon it in November bearing a dozen or more heads of rich, canary-yellow flowers, each composed of many spikes bearing in all hundreds of blooms, is a very great experience.

At the Savill Gardens, Windsor, there are natural hybrids of this species and *M. japonica*. One was named 'Charity'. It has reached some 7 feet high and wide, and bears handsome foliage, intermediate between the parents. The light yellow flowers, slightly scented, are borne for many weeks in erect spikes, larger and better displayed than in *M. lomariifolia*.

The name 'Charity' has an interesting background. Messrs L.R. Russell bought some seedlings of *M. lomariifolia* from The Slieve Donard Nursery in Northern Ireland, the source of so many good plants. Sir Eric Savill purchased some of these from Mr Russell and specially asked for the inclusion of one which bore broader leaves. When this grew it was considered without a doubt that it had *M. japonica* for one of its parents. When exhibited in November 1957 this was given a Preliminary Commendation by the Royal Horticultural Society (later First Class Certificate – FCC) and was named 'Charity' by Sir Eric because Mr. Russell had been good enough to let him have the special seedling. Subsequently named *M. × media*, this same cross has occurred elsewhere. I think the finest is *M. × media* 'Lionel Fortescue'; it has brilliant yellow more or less erect racemes of flowers and is usually the first to open. After it and 'Charity' are past their best, Norman Hadden's 'Underway' comes into flower, with large creamy yellow flowers densely disposed on erect spikes. The foliage of all is splendid, dark green above and much paler beneath, achieving 18 inches in lengh or more. Although they get large and wide in time, they respond well to reduction by pruning or very severe frosts, and one single head of flower spikes surrounded by a great collar of leaves is enough to grace any room. Until these fine plants had been raised there was no evergreen of such splendid quality to lighten dark November. Several other seedlings have been raised, some being hybrids with the next species.

Another fine plant at Windsor is *M. acanthifolia*; this was given an FCC by the RHS in November 1958. A crown of leaves cut from a healthy young plant measured over 5 feet across. It is sturdy and luxuriant with handsome pinnate leaves, but is not reliably hardy. The flowers are of bright yellow and somewhat fragrant. *M. napaulensis* is a pleasant enough plant but neither the flowers nor the leaves are in so exalted a class as those mentioned above.

We have already (page 15) looked at the noble arbutuses, since they rapidly take on the dimension of trees, but with them flower two large shrubs, *Osmanthus heterophyllus* (*O. aquifolium*, *O. ilicifolius*) and *Elaeagnus macrophylla*. Truly autumn-flowering, they continue well into November and delight us with their far-reaching scent. The *Osmanthus* might at first sight be taken for a neat-leafed holly, but on closer inspection it will be seen that the leaves are borne in opposite pairs, not alternately as with the 'tree that bears a crown', in the words of the old carol. The flowers are creamy-white, and small, huddled amongst the leaves, and would not always be noticed except for their scent. As a shrub, it is a compact grower and always looks glossy and neat, but reaches large proportions, 8 feet or so high and through, in time. It thrives in sun or shade in acid or limy soil.

Of a similar size, but by no means as hardy, *Elaeagnus macrophylla* is at once a lax grower, and yet always well furnished with twigs and its lovely leaves. In shape broadly oval, they are covered with silvery scales. When young they are brilliantly silvery to the point of whiteness, but the upper surfaces become greener and polished with age, while beneath the silver remains in contrast. The creamy–silvery bells are beautiful too, in a quiet way, and add their scent to what is undoubtedly a much–neglected shrub. A related species, less striking in every way but a good evergreen, is *E. pungens*; this also produces creamy-scented bells in an unobtrusive way in late autumn; for the hybrid between the two, *E.* × *ebbingei*, see page 82.

Before we return to the plants flowering in the early year, I must mention a few half-hardy shrubs for late autumn-flowering and suitable for warm walls and sheltered corners. In November I have had *Grevillea rosmarinifolia*, a native of New South Wales, in flower; it produced quantities of its lovely pink bloom, typically Proteaceous with their long styles. Then again a leguminous shrub – *Coronilla glauca* from South Europe – flowers in mid-November regularly against a south wall. The gold of the gorse is there and the scent too – by day, not by night – but it is a meek little bushy plant with neat, lead-green foliage, and will not stand up to our worst winters. The clusters of small pea-flowers rise to open and deflect again to ripen their seeds. Probably less hardy is *C. valentina*, an equally reliable winter-flowering sub-shrub.

Those shrubby veronicas from the Southern Hemisphere, now called *Hebe*, present us with many kinds which flower well into the autumn – and in winter in mild districts, particularly maritime. It is really the end of their flowering period, for they start to flower in the summer. As a general rule the larger the flower spike the more tender they are, being mostly hybrids of *H. speciosa*. They are all good evergreens, with opposite pointed leaves, of lustrous green sometimes touched with purple, and bear the flower spikes in every upper leaf-axil. Some famous varieties near to *H. speciosa* are 'Simon Deleaux' (coppery crimson), 'Veitchii' or 'Alicia Amherst' (violet-purple) and 'Gauntlettii' named after the Chiddingfold firm so famous in the early part of this century. 'Midsummer Beauty' and 'Hidcote' (lavender-blue), 'Great Orme' and 'Carnea' (pink) are less in flower-spike size but still highly ornamental. There are many smaller cultivars such as 'Hielan' Lassie', 'Mrs Tennant', 'Bowles' Hybrid', 'Autumn Glory' and 'Mrs Winder'; the last is noted for its purplish foliage and violet-blue flowers. But they all, to me, smack more of the summer and early autumn than of the winter for Surrey, in which county few are really hardy. To this little group of tender, small shrubs can be added another which in Cornwall achieves considerable size. The aromatic leaves nearly obscure the small white flowers in the early year; it is *Atherosperma moschatum*, another Southern Hemisphere shrub. All of these shrubs will be seen at their best in Cornish gardens.

That diverse race the buddleias give us another shrub for sheltered places. On the wall of the Long Garden at Cliveden, Buckingham-shire, one may see in November a small-leafed plant, *Buddleia auriculata*, from South Africa, set freely with small, creamy spikes like some miniature *B. davidii (variabilis)*. The scent is as unforgettable in its warm richness as that greenhouse inmate the East Indian *B. asiatica*, whose flowers in long, drooping spikes will scent a whole house in February. The hybrid Broom, *Cytisus* 'Porlock' (*Cytisus monspes-sulanus* × *C*. × *spachianus* (*C. racemosus*)), will stand several degrees of frost. This is an admirable large shrub for sunny spots in warm localities, very much like the fragrant broom of the florists, but more hardy on account of its parentage. These two paragraphs certainly cover some tender subjects which would be killed or severely maimed in very severe winters, but they are thrifty plants needing nothing but a reasonable garden soil and ample sunshine, and the reward of a plant a few years old smothered with flower is well worth the risk of a loss in an occasional winter.

If I were asked what evergreen shrub I would grow, given space, for winter flowers, I should have difficulty in choosing between *Mahonia japonica* and *Garrya elliptica*. The scent of the former weighs the scales heavily. But of all winter-flowering shrubs, to me the *Garrya* is typical of the season, and the promise of warm days to come. It is, I suppose, its relationship to the nut with its catkin-flowers – that true winter emblem of spring – which appeals so strongly.

It is a shrub of greens in varying tints. Not altogether defiant of frost, and deserving a sheltered spot, it has great quality in its bushy, well-filled growth, and in the rounded, sculptured leaves of sombre dark tint which are a wonderful foil to the decorative beauty of the flowers. Very few female plants are seen, and the male is the plant to

Garrya elliptica

grow, for the beauty of the staminate flowers closely worked into green strings. As January passes to February they elongate until one day on the sunny side of the shrub one sees the transformation. The dull green strings have become unravelled, as it were, and every flower is a cream and green tassel, the whole a miracle of loveliness – a quiet harmony of colour and contrasting form. It should be grown on a sheltered wall in cold districts. This is a good, thrifty evergreen for chalky and other soils, but like so many other things, it seems to do even better on a good medium loam. Though strictly belonging to the chapter devoted to berries, the female *Garrya* has a unique and quiet beauty in those seasons when it is heavily hung with its fruits. These are ripe in winter, and when contrasted with the creamy green of the male flowers and the soft, dark green leaves, the strings of small 'berries' show their strange green and purple colouring and silky sheen to advantage. 'James Roof' is the name of a male form with particularly long strings of flowers and good catkins raised in California.

Some excitement has occurred recently, both in Seattle, USA, and in Ireland because of a natural hybrid which occurred in a garden at Seattle between *G. elliptica* and *G. fremontii*. Subsequently seeds of the hybrid were sent to Lord Talbot at Malahide Castle, near Dublin, and further abnormalities have been observed. The original has been named 'Pat Ballard' and its long male catkins are of a richer tint than typical *G. elliptica*. Dr Charles Nelson of the National Botanic Gardens at Glasnevin, Dublin, wrote a full account of the whole matter in the University of Washington Arboretum Bulletin Vol. 43, No. 3; Dr Nelson has recently written me with news of yet another seedling bearing purplish racemes. These hybrids have been given the name of *G. × issaquahensis*; it commemorates the place, near Washington, USA, where Mrs Ballard lives. It is a tongue-twister but the better for being understandable!

No chapter on winter-flowering evergreens would be complete without reference to camellias. Now that their tenderness has been exploded, and their claim to hardiness is fully established, we can look forward to their increased popularity in all gardens on acid soils. We will consider them again as evergreens in the chapter devoted to foliage, but some varieties at least do produce flowers in mild spells in winter before the main collection opens in spring. Sheltered on the east by a wall, these lovely shrubs would get some little protection for their early blooms. Those fortunate enough regarding climate will wish to wrestle with the incomparable but rather tender *Camellia reticulata*. The best-known form is the semi-double, now rechristened 'Captain Rawes'; this is tolerably hardy, while the fully double 'Robert Fortune' is reported to be less hardy. It has been reintroduced to our gardens from Europe, having been almost extinct for many years since being brought from China in the last century. The single-flowered form more recently introduced by George Forest appears to be as hardy as, or even hardier than, 'Robert Fortune' and seedlings raised in this country will probably be successively more hardy. They all have flowers of great magnificence, and the collection of old Chinese varieties from Yunnan which are now creeping into cultivation will do much to increase interest in this fine genus, satiated as we have been with the formal floral styles of *C. japonica* for a hundred years.

C. sasanqua, a native of China and Japan, forming in the wild dense thickets up to 20 feet, has been much used in the past by the Japanese, and many forms have been evolved. Forms of this species coming my way have mostly been single, of a lovely pale rose-pink. Seen on a wall at Kew, no hardy November flower can compare with its wild-rose beauty, and this species has the added attraction of a delicate fragrance. In the Savill Garden in Windsor Great Park a most beautiful rich rose-pink form is growing, and flowers abundantly lighting a 10-foot wall with warm colour, perhaps the most telling of all shrubs in flower at that time of the year. Numerous Japanese varieties are now coming into cultivation in this country and the United States, and a great range of single and semi-double forms in a variety of floral styles and colours will be available in the future. One of the richest in colour that I have seen is called 'Crimson King'; the fine single blooms with their circle of golden-yellow stamens bring all the warmth of spring into a dull November day. When these really exquisite shrubs are distributed it will indeed be a boon to have such blossom at such a time. A considerable collection grows at Dunster Castle, Somerset.

Both *C. saluenensis* and *C. sasanqua* are more graceful in growth and have smaller leaves than the usual garden hybrids of *C. japonica*, and lack their highly polished surfaces. They make admirable wall-shrubs, and, as mentioned for *C. reticulata*, they would thrive best with a westerly aspect, thus giving them the benefit of some sun and at the same time keeping them cool at the root. For, like rhododendrons, they need a medium rich in humus, and cannot tolerate dryness any more than stagnation.

C. saluenensis was found in Yunnan by Forrest during the 1914 war. Only really hardy in sheltered gardens, it produces from February to April dainty single blossoms varying from white to crimson in the wild, with a tuft of cream stamens. So far it has only been my good fortune to see a soft shell-pink form, with wide-open blossoms.

Of late years possibly the most free-flowering and magnificent of all camellias has come to the fore. Indeed, the late Lord Aberconway, writing of it in the Royal Horticultural Society's *Journal* for August 1949, went so far as to say 'one of the best shrubs that has ever been introduced to our gardens has been the late Mr J.C. Williams's hybrid of *Camellia saluenensis* and *C. japonica*'. This has been named *C.* × *williamsii*, and the form most commonly grown so far is known as 'J.C. Williams', but other crosses between the two species are becoming available also. Combining the refinement of *C. saluenensis* with the vigour of *C. japonica*, this race should become widely grown, and the single and half-double forms so far seen are as beautiful as a flower can be, in a variety of pink shades, many showing the circlet of golden-tipped stamens. 'J.C. Williams' is proving to be a fine, hardy shrub in all but the most exposed positions, and is exceptionally free-flowering. Together with *C. saluenensis*, these camellias flower mainly in March and April but in sheltered gardens the flowers may confidently be expected in a mild February, in particular 'Bow Bells'. Occasionally some *C. japonica* varieties appear at the same time; *C. japonica* 'Nobilissima' followed by 'Gloire de Nantes'. 'Yoibigin' and 'High Hat' and a few others may be expected in mild Februarys, or even earlier, but in general I feel that these brilliant and rather over-bearing shrubs belong to spring rather than winter.

Writing in the Royal Horticultural Society's *Journal* for November 1951, Charles Williams of Caerhays Castle, Cornwall, mentioned how several of his crosses between *C. saluenensis* and *japonica* 'are open from January to May inclusive and a few from November to December', and cut sprays of a very early seedling received an Award of Merit on December 5th, 1950, which had first opened on November 3rd. This was called 'November Pink'. He went on to say that he could have picked open flowers at any time between the above dates – partly, of course, a tribute to the mild climate of Cornwall. I well remember these blooms coming before the committee, and, with them, though not successful in obtaining awards, were a cross between *C. saluenense* and *taliense*, also from Caerhays, and *C. sasanqua* from Colonel S.R. Clarke, of Borde Hill, Sussex. I think this paragraph may well encourage us to hope that the camellia will, in due course, provide some very good winter flowers, which in colder districts would be admirable in slightly heated greenhouses, where their culture out of doors was considered too risky.

C. cuspidata crossed with *C. saluenensis* has resulted in *C.* × 'Cornish Snow'. The small flowers are cupped, semi-double, of pure white and slightly fragrant. A pale pink form is called 'Winton'. It has not suffered from cold winters in my garden and flowers in February.

It is, I think, unfortunate that such a grand evergreen as *Fatsia japonica* is so seldom seen nowadays. This was at one time a popular room-plant in common with that other celebrated Japanese, the *Aspidistra*. Sometimes it is seen gracing a tiny front lawn, but is deserving of a wall or sheltered corner and it is encouraging to see it being used in municipal plantings in London and elsewhere. While it is quite hardy its long stems and huge leaves require some shelter from gales. The ascending stems, rising sometimes to 12 feet, give off side branches, and each bears a crown of deeply divided, palm-shaped, smooth leaves of rich green, and the flower heads – clustered drum-sticks of tiny cream blooms – appear at the apex of each crown. There are few more handsome evergreens, and, as a November-flowering shrub which is not particular as to soil, provided it has reasonably good fare, it might well be more commonly grown. In the return to favour of its near relative the ivy, in its many beautiful forms, perhaps we may see a portent.

Sycopsis sinensis, a compact, upright Witch Hazel relative, hides its orange-coloured tassels among the thick array of its drooping spear-shaped leaves. This is a very attractive evergreen of particularly dusky hue.

And the Laurustinus? Shall this maligned shrub, *Viburnum tinus*, that 'harbours dirt and smells of cats', shall this Cinderella of our shrubberies find a place in this book? Assuredly; here we have a shrub which is hardy and produces quantities of ruddy buds in autumn, opening to white blooms in mild weather and continuing in attractive appearance until early spring releases the sap. The big, rounded masses of greenery some 10 or 12 feet across are the very thing for the backbone of the garden and for softening the corners of buildings. It is usually hardy enough in the south, although it may suffer in a hard winter; its larger-leafed varieties seem less hardy but are not impor-tant, *V.t.* 'Lucidum' having more attractive foliage and finer, pure white flowers, while the form *hirtum* has bristly stems and foliage. 'Eve Price' has deep rosy-red buds. My choice of the lot would be

Sycopsis sinensis

'Gwenllian', which is of more compact growth than the others, flowering freely when small. The comparatively large pink-tinged white flowers are usually accompanied by metallic blue berries, giving a delightful effect. It was raised by Sidney Pearce of Kew and named after his wife. All forms in favourable seasons produce fruits later of this metallic blue, but they are seldom observed, tucked away under new growths. I would place this species right in the front rank of evergreen shrubs and would include it in the first six shrubs I would choose for almost any garden, but I should keep it away from the house, for in common with most other species its objectionable smell is noticeable in damp mild weather.

Only in very warm and sheltered gardens do the various species of *Pieris* flower early enough to be included in this book, but a form from Japan of *P. japonica* called 'Christmas Cheer' starts flowering at or soon after that date. All pierises are handsome evergreens. *P. japonica* when hung with its compound racemes of little creamy bell flowers is most appealing; 'Christmas Cheer' is pink in the bud, and 'Daisen' a rich pink.

While no shrub garden is complete without its important pieces, it is equally true that to link these together and create a harmonious whole we must have our drifts and groups of smaller things, and in this category I would put the sarcococcas and daphnes. *Daphne × hybrida* (*dauphinii*), a cross between *D. odora* and *D. collina*, is a small, glossy-leafed shrub whose clusters of rosy-purple, sweet, starry flowers are borne from autumn until spring in mild spells. *D. odora*, its parent, is perhaps the most penetratingly delicious of all scented shrubs – a

Daphne × hybrida (D. dauphinii)

Daphne odora

fruity, exhilarating scent to inhale deeply again and again – and it is tolerably hardy with me. The long, leathery leaves are edged with yellow in the variegated form, which appears to flower more freely than the type. Although a native of China and Japan, this is also known as *D. indica*, and has been grown in this country since 1771. It is best in our warmest counties. Its white flowers are purple in the bud, but there is also a pure white form 'Alba', with non–variegated leaves which also seems tough and hardy in the same corner. *D. blagayana* is not truly winter-flowering, but in early seasons its prostrate stems may be expected to yield some clusters of its scented, cream stars in February where they poke forward out of their cairn of stones. For that is the approved way of growing this vigorous though perhaps short-lived species, which likes rooting in limy loam under the cool-ness of small rocks. I think the usual cause of failure with it is that its needs are not fully understood. It likes a large area which it can colonize by degrees, ever questing for fresh ground and rooting as it goes under its stones. A very rare and strange species which loses its leaves in summer but bears them in winter is *D. jezoensis*. It is quite low growing, sometimes nearly prostrate but a cheering sight when bearing its brilliant yellow starry flowers in the depth of winter. It is a native of Honshu, Japan.

We occasionally see *Daphne bholua* at shows or in gardens. It is partially or sometimes evergreen and some forms are tender. Dr Geoffrey Herklots introduced a form from near Khatmandu, and one of the progeny has thriven at the Savill Gardens, with wall protection, and has been named 'Sheopuri' after the mountain on which it grew.

Daphne laureola

Sarcococca ruscifolia, S. hookeriana digyna, S. humilis

Another, 'Gurkha', introduced by Major Spring-Smythe from Eastern Nepal is thriving in Hampshire. They have white flowers, purplish in bud and are sweetly scented. There is no doubt we shall hear more about these in future years; meanwhile I would refer you to *Daphne*, by C.D. Brickell and B. Mathew.

That cousin of the daphnes, *Edgworthia papyrifera* (*E. chrysantha*), is deciduous, but I include it here for convenience. It is only hardy in Surrey in sheltered positions, but is of rare beauty in a mild February, when its flowers appear at the tips of the twigs like yellow daphnes in tight bunches enwrapped in silky down.

For underplanting in groups beneath large shrubs and trees – for they delight in shade and shelter – are our native Spurge Laurel, *Daphne laureola*, with its pale green, tubular, fragrant flowers and the sarcococcas, those little-known bushes of the Box Family. The Spurge Laurel has a dwarf, very compact variety *philippi* which makes a good hummock of green. The sarcococcas are very much underlings; just pleasant small shrubs of neat and bushy habit, until on some soft January day a puff of air brings to you the warm sweetness of their flowers, which are little more than tufts of stamens and stigmas. *Sarcococca ruscifolia* and *S. humilis* have broadish leaves and creamy flowers, while *S. hookeriana digyna* has narrow leaves, an erect growth, and flowers tinted pink. It is certainly the most ornamental and one of the nicest small shrubs of its type that I know, though *S. hookeriana hookeriana*, with soft green leaves and white flowers, is also conspicuous in flower and berry.

4. Heathers

The most important thing in designing a garden is to get the right shapes and balance between path and lawn and the planting space. The next most important thing is to introduce a style of planting which will embellish and furnish the whole during whatever period or periods the garden is called upon to serve; and the finishing touch to this is that the planting shall be knitted together with a permanent, if possible evergreen, underplanting.

This is a chapter on heathers, and the above remarks will serve to show what importance should be attached to them. For they and their kind are the very plants that can make or mar a garden, by their arrangement. One hears so much about 'grouping' these days; every-thing must be planted in groups for effect, regardless of its character. To my mind this is utterly wrong. How can one group Japanese cherries, every tree and every variety of which has a singular individu-ality and mode of branching of its own? How group *Cotoneaster salicifolius* with its strong, yet graceful lines? Why should we mass together striking shrubs like *Viburnum plicatum* and *Rhododendron* 'Amoenum'? How can we enjoy a mass of *Verbascum vernale*, whose great leaves and tower of yellow demand space around them? And even among the lowlier plants there are similar examples.

Let us see what alternative we can find for the above examples, chosen without any more thought and time than it takes to write them down. If in a big park a mass of colour is needed from a tree, *Malus* of the *floribunda* persuasion will be admirable: they have little stance and quality; again, we might select *Berberis* × *stenophylla*, with its thicket-forming branches of roses like *Rosa* 'Andersonii' for big groups of shrubs. In the flower border heleniums and gaillardias will knit

themselves into groups and all will be well, but for the lowly foreground stretches choose heathers and Sun Roses, *Potentilla fruticosa*,
dwarf rhododendrons, bergenias, and others.

Grouping is right and vitally *necessary* in any garden if carried out
with the right plants – those plants of a colonizing tendency and of
little individuality in regard to 'line'. In the winter garden especially,
heathers stand out, to my mind, as the first essential to successful
design, when planted in drifts and stretches in front and around their
larger neighbours. Without them any winter garden will be a collection of plants, and of all gardens this is the most tedious to those who
seek refreshment from it. There are splendid examples of drift planting at Wisley, the Savill Garden and also at the Botanic Garden at
Ness on the Wirral.

There are fortunately no 'ifs and buts' about these drifts of pink
winter-flowering heathers. Their roots are not dependent upon those
bacteria – peculiar to most Ericaceous plants – which die on exposure
to lime, and therefore cannot transmit the goodness from the ground
to the roots. *Erica carnea* and *E. erigena* (*E. mediterranea*) and their
hybrids – all we need for our purpose – will grow in somewhat limy
soils as well as in acid ones. A good light loam suits them well, but
in impoverished or limy gardens the addition of leaf-mould or peat
will be beneficial. Considering how much they benefit from wind
and sunshine, it is surprising how they thrive in sheltered and often
shady gardens.

For general purposes there is nothing, I think, so good as the
ordinary *E. carnea*. This, the Mountain Heath, also called *E. herbacea*,
is a sturdy, bushy plant up to 9 inches or so in height, making a close
thicket of tiny twigs set with tiny, bronze-green leaves, and by August
the new season's buds, arranged in closely packed spikes some
5 inches long, may be seen. These usually begin to open in December
and the drift gradually takes on a rosy-pink glow. Anything more
fitting as a ground-cover for hamamelises or other open-growing
shrubs, or for planting in drifts along the path, I cannot imagine. This
valuable plant has been segregated into a number of forms, and that
known as 'King George' usually opens its flowers in late December. It
is a compact type with deep rosy blooms. 'Queen Mary', 'Mrs Samuel
Doncaster', 'Winter Beauty', and other old varieties crowd the lists,
and all give just that different tint that is needed for a succession of
groupings.

Some few years ago a fine white was discovered in Italy and named 'Springwood', after the discoverer's Scottish home. This has the longest spikes of any and the long individual flowers are capped by their protruding light brown stamens with finer effect than in the pink forms. It is extremely vigorous and a first-class carpeter – it is nothing to find single plants covering 12 or 20 square feet – but unfortunately it has an almost horizontal habit, with the result that on flat ground its blooms are not seen to best advantage; but when planted on slopes this habit becomes an asset. Generally known as 'Springwood White', it has a lovely pale pink counterpart, 'Springwood Pink'; this is slightly less vigorous, but both are most admirable weed-smothering plants. *E.c.* 'Rubra' is a richly coloured form, and a considerably darker one, 'Vivellii', has coppery dark foliage and rich carmine-crimson flowers which do not open until March: it is of very compact, dwarf growth. A number of newer varieties should be watched; several have given an excellent account of themselves at Wisley. 'December Red' flowers both early and late, while 'Alan Coates' is a good plant for earliest spring. Both are vigorous yet compact. Another splendid variety in these darker shades is 'Ruby Glow'. As so often happens in almost any genus, the darker flowered forms are less vigorous than the paler forms, and I often wonder why this should be so.

Two rather newer cultivars are 'Startler', coral pink, and 'Rosy Gem', bright pink, neat and bushy. The most pronounced advance in rich colouring is found in the splendid 'Myretoun Ruby', raised by Allan Porteous in Wigtonshire, Scotland, in 1965. This is a strong grower, flowering in February and March, of rich purplish carmine; it is brighter, larger and a better grower than the darkest hitherto, 'Vivellii'. There is no more delightful a companion for these pink heaths than *Hebe pinguifolia* 'Pagei'; it is of the same height and habit and has pale glaucous leaves throughout the year.

E. erigena, long known as *E. mediterranea*, is not so hardy as *E. herbacea*, which is imperturbable, and it does not flower until April or May, but some compact types are earlier (February–April) and shorter. Among them may be numbered 'Brightness' (pink) and 'W.T. Rackliff', which is an improvement on the old 'Alba'. But they really are at their best after February. A most useful addition to the colour range is 'Irish Dusk' found by David McClintock in Co. Mayo in 1966. In addition to bronzed foliage it has flowers of coral pink and seems to be quite hardy and early flowering.

With *E. erigena*, *E. carnea* has produced a very hardy hybrid, *E. × darleyensis* (which used to be known as *E. mediterranea hybrida*), a strong grower up to 18 inches in height and producing its lilac-pink spikes of bloom from November till March. A richer coloured and more compact type is known as 'George Rendall', and I feel this is bound to become popular. A seedling occurred in A.T. Johnson's delightful garden in the Conway Valley, North Wales, against a plant of 'Ruby Glow' and near to *E.m.* 'Hibernica', and these are therefore the supposed parents of a magnificent plant, named *E. × darleyensis* 'Arthur Johnson'. Being the grateful recipient of a plant years ago, I can vouch that this is indeed a magnificent version of our old friend, with flower spikes up to 9 inches long. It makes a rich green, spreading bushlet, up to 2 feet high, and produces its deep lilac-pink flowers without stint from January to March. This appears to me to be the most valuable of all our winter heathers. To the same group belongs a useful white variety, 'Silberschmelze', but it is not a clean white.

Equally suitable for grouping in lime-free and more sheltered gardens is one of the tree heaths *E. lusitanica* (*E. codonodes*); this makes a bushy plant up to 4 or 5 feet on this side of the country and yearly gives abundant bloom in the best style of the tree heaths. The tiny, pinkish buds produced in thousands on big, branching spikes open to scarcely bigger white tubes in December and remain in beauty till the spring. In large gardens a few plants of this notable heath will give a smoky effect in flower, unlike any other shrub, which has a background to hamamelises and, later, the bursting forsythias, provide a remarkable suggestion of distance with their soft tints.

Apart from the above true winter-flowering types there is a late-flowering form of the common ling; this, A.T. Johnson's special foundling at Hyères, *Calluna vulgaris* 'Hiemalis', contributes to the flora of November, and is thus an exceedingly valuable plant. It is hardy but unfortunately does not seem to have the long life for which the other forms are noted. The slender spires of starry blooms are of soft lilac-pink, just as one might find on our commons in August, and it is therefore a useful plant for grouping with the latest colchicums and crocuses. This useful plant has become very rare, possibly extinct; I should like to acquire it again.

Apart from the winter-flowering heaths many gardeners admire the winter tints of the summer-flowering kinds – *Erica vagans*, *E. cinerea* and *Calluna vulgaris*. The brown bells of *Erica vagans*, the Cornish heath and the grey-brown of some of the callunas are particularly pleasing in the heath garden, and do truly give colour to the winter garden. Among taller kinds I would specially call attention to *E. stricta* (*E. terminalis*), whose rich, dark green bushes up to 5 or 6 feet in height make so splendid a windbreak or background and bear rich brown flower heads all winter. But along with the dead heads of herbaceous plants these tints speak to me of autumn and a past season, not a new season and a true awakening in the dead of the year manifested by all the other plants in this book. And so I leave their inclusion to individual taste, but it must be remembered that they will tolerate little or no lime, apart from *E. stricta*, which will even grow on chalk.

The planting of heaths of all kinds is best done in spring, but care must be taken to see that their hair-fine roots do not get dry. The winter-flowering and Cornish types can safely be increased by division and layering, with every hope of their success, but, as a general rule, I prefer small plants from cuttings. A handful of peat-moss or leaf-mould mixed with the soil around the root of a newly planted heather is a great help in assisting it to settle down quickly, and a mulch of similar materials in the first few seasons before the plants have spread will also be found a good help. When the plants have spread together their own growth carpets the ground and keeps it cool, without which good flower spikes will not be freely produced.

Little cultivation is necessary beyond an annual clipping over of all kinds in the spring. The summer-flowering groups may be done as soon as their dead tops can be dispensed with and the winter and spring sorts as soon as their flowers are over. Clipping can be done best with small shears, and the contours of the plants or groups should be followed to give a natural effect.

Heathers are what may be termed children of the open air. On their native hillsides the wind keeps them bushy and well filled, animals browse on them and fires sere them periodically to the ground. In the garden clipping is necessary to ensure that much twiggy growth is made, so that they remain compact. Neglected plants become a prey to heavy snow and collect dead leaves, with the worst possible results in time. This open-air feeling about heathers is frequently the cause of their exclusion from the confines of a garden. They do indeed need planting in big sweeps with suitable trees and other plants to create a 'heath' effect. However, practically all the shrubs we grow are found in great colonies in the wild, and yet we are content to have an odd specimen or two in our gardens. Shall not the winter-flowering heathers therefore be allowed even in the most formal parts of our gardens, to give colour at a time when it is most needed?

Some heathers are even useful in a third degree, that of the foliage. All have a rich, velvety, dense appearance, and stand in contrast to bigger and more distinct foliage as a cushion does towards sound. We can get really brilliant colour from heather foliage; the well-known *Calluna vulgaris* 'Serlei Aurea' has rather pale greenish-yellow leaves all the year round, and is vivid in winter. This is one of the best white-flowering lings, and an old-established, vigorous favourite. A more recent and splendid white is 'Gold Haze'. I mention these two first because I find that in the late summer, when they are in flower, white tones better with the brilliant foliage than the typical heather colour. In this way some of the newer, most brilliant heathers in foliage – such as the dazzling ones from J.W. Sparkes of Worcestershire, 'Golden Feather', 'Blazeaway', 'Multicolor', 'Robert Chapman' and 'Orange Queen' – are even unpleasant in flower, as is the still newer and even more brilliant 'Sir John Champion'. But anyone looking for winter colour and remembering the display in the Wisley Trials will overlook, probably, the floral colour. At the other end of the colour range the vigorous *C.v. hirsuta* has subdued greyish foliage.

In the heaths *Erica cinerea* 'Golden Hue' and 'Golden Drop', the bright, yellowish leaves turn to brilliant coral-pink and terracotta-crimson respectively, and provide one of the most vivid sights in the winter garden, likewise 'Valerie Proudley', a yellow-leafed form of *E. vagans*. The little collection is of immense value in lime-free soil; for those of us who garden on limy soil, we have recourse only to *Erica herbacea* 'Aurea', whose foliage turns yellow in winter, and 'Anne Sparkes', whose foliage is coppery; both make surprising contrasts to the deep-pink flowers. Seen in a mass, there is no doubt that the foliage of the various heathers can compete in brilliance with *anything* – flower, berry, or foliage – *throughout the gardening year*. And for a rich green velvety effect I know of no shrub more precious than *E. arborea alpina*, a great bush up to 6 or 8 feet in height and quite hardy, but demanding a lime-free soil.

5. Climbing Plants

Most shrubs can be successfully grown by training them on walls. It is generally a question of forethought and suitable training and pruning. A wall in a keen gardener's garden is generally a choice spot for his most treasured possessions, because of the very human desire to grow something that cannot be expected to thrive in the open. No matter how cold or how mild our climate may be, we gardeners always enjoy the triumph of making a plant from a still warmer country feel at home by trickery! And so we grow our half-hardies on warm south and west walls, and carefully arrange shelter for our other walls, or use them for the provision of shade for plants which otherwise would not find a congenial home in an open garden.

Although quite hardy in themselves, there are plants among those in this book which deserve a place on a wall where their frail blossoms will give some protection from a sudden snap of frost. There is no need to give up such positions to the stalwarts like *Hamamelis* and *Daphne mezereum*, which stand a deal of cold, but give space to your Winter Sweet, *Buddleia auriculata*, *Camellia sasanqua*, *reticulata*, and *saluenense*, *Grevillea rosmarinifolia*, *Viburnum grandiflorum*, and *Lonicera* × *purpusii*. The *Buddleia* and *Grevillea* are ardent sun-lovers, of course, but the others will thrive on a wall or fence facing north-west, which may well be given to them, but a place should be kept for the yellow Winter Jasmine, *Jasminum nudiflorum*.

This plant is among the first half-dozen I would put in any garden, if for no other reason than that it provides flowers for the house from October to April regularly and abundantly. Picked in bud they

Jasminum nudiflorum

invariably open well and a succession can thereby be maintained. Yellow jasmine is the very centre around which gather all the delights of the temperate world mentioned in these pages. Brought by that great seeker Robert Fortune from China in 1844, it has increased in popularity until it is the most commonly planted of all our winter shrubs. It seems to thrive anywhere, but the longest and best shoots come from a cool north wall. As many as possible of these should be left on the plant; they will provide the best future-flowering shoots and do not look so well in the house as the twiggy, branching pieces. The removal of the latter will prove ideal pruning. That beautiful species *J. mesnyi* (*J. primulinum*) is only hardy in the mildest localities, but where it can be induced to thrive the effect of its blooms will be unsurpassed by any other member of the genus from the Temperate Zones. Frequently of a 'double' nature, the blooms are of a similar yellow to *J. nudiflorum*, but are much larger. The plants are obviously related and hybrids may yet give us something good, although *J. mesnyi* has not so far, I believe, set seed in this country.

For soils suiting camellias and the like, and for cool northern walls, it would be worth trying the lovely *Lapageria rosea* in favoured districts. One of the very few woody members of the Lily Family, it is an evergreen climber whose glistening, tubular, crimson flowers always excite interest from August until late into the autumn. This and a paler form are superbly illustrated in the volume on *Climbing Plants* in that remarkable 'Present Day Gardening' series published by *The Gardeners' Chronicle* many years ago. These lovely things prefer a cool soil rich in humus such as one would give a rhododendron. If in a cold winter they should be killed to the ground, they will usually shoot again, and their flowers are worth a long wait. It is worth noting that the name *Lapageria* is derived from 'de la Pagerie', the maiden name of the Empress Joséphine, and thus commemorates one whose influence on horticulture was very considerable, through her garden at Malmaison.

Besides these two distinct plants there are two *Clematis* species from Southern Europe to consider. They are not showy, but have a dainty charm. Of the two I prefer *Clematis cirrhosa balearica* (*C. calyina*) from the Balearic Isles to *C. cirrhosa* itself, whose natural distribution is wider; its foliage is extremely neat, beautifully divided, and of a dark glossy texture which shows up the soft, creamy-green, bell-like flowers splashed inside with tiny mahogany marks. It thrives on a wall

Clematis cirrhosa balearica

at Wisley. In the Ranunculaceae, which often have no distinction
between petals and sepals – both being confined botanically into the
'perianth' – it is remarkable to find that these two species do have a
little cup-like bud-protector, called an involucre, which distinguishes
them from all other species. Another species in this same group is
C. napaulensis, sometimes called *C. forrestii*. This native of Northern
India and neighbouring parts of China is only a success in our very
mildest counties or in a cold house; the beauty of the creamy flowers is
enhanced by their purple stamens. It flowers from December
onwards.

Fortunately the two European clematises and the Winter Jasmine
thrive almost anywhere; the clematis certainly likes the sun to remind
it of its Mediterranean home, and a reasonably well-drained soil, but
the jasmine will do well in cold, dark spots and also on hot, dry slopes,
on chalk, loam or sand. What more could be said of a beautiful plant?

The chapter on Berries will call to mind many excellent shrubs like pyracanthas and cotoneasters which can be trained on walls. These large-growing shrubs and the smaller cydonias are very happy as a rule on north or even west walls, leaving our warmer walls for the tempting 'half-hardies' mentioned at the beginning of this chapter.

Some of us are fortunate in having walls into which it is simple to fasten supports for wires; otherwise the gables and iron pegs in the ground will provide initial places of fixture. Most gardeners have large nails or 'vine-eyes' fixed during building into new walls, which avoids the later damage of nails and plugs. One of the most satisfactory and long-lasting means of training plants on to walls is by fixing pig wire – a large, 6-inch mesh, strong galvanized netting – between windows up to the required height. This is most excellent, as it will encourage twiners, and also it is a simple matter to push leading shoots of shrubs behind the mesh, where they will remain firmly and permanently.

One other point should be remembered in planting such things as camellias and lapagerias which will not tolerate lime. Though the natural soil may be lime-free, it is not uncommon to find builders' debris containing lime in the ground near the house; this must of course be removed and replaced with suitable material for these particular beauties. A final warning is to keep climbers away from down-pipes; strong growers will be apt to force the pipes from the wall.

6. Trees and Shrubs with Coloured Bark

. . . *While sallow Autumn fills thy lap with leaves;*
Or Winter, yelling through the troublous air,
Affrights thy shrinking train
And rudely rends thy robes.

WILLIAM COLLINS (1721–1759)
from *To Evening*

The silver birch stands pre-eminent among trees in winter. When all else is green and grey and brown, its sinuous trunks, in silver-white, enhanced by the corky, black fissures, strike a note of light contrast, and their reflection in lake or stream accentuates their cold nakedness. But be sure when planting birches to get the kind with the whitest bark, *Betula pendula* (*B. verrucosa*), whose rough, warted twigs show its divergence from the other native, *B. pubescens*, which has velvety twigs. Both of these species were at one time called *Betula alba*. They are rather greedy-rooted trees, but I would put in a plea for their more usual inclusion in even smaller gardens, for a tree or a group does give a wonderful sense of space and freedom, only otherwise attained by the use of the Scots pine *Pinus sylvestris*. It is fitting that these two natives should head this chapter, for the white of the birch is not more lovely than the warm red-brown of the pine's trunk in maturity. The latter is, however, a large tree with greedy surface roots and is best planted on the outskirts of the garden or even right outside it, were that possible.

Returning to the birch, it is natural that a tree so noticeable and so lovely should have several varieties in cultivation, and amongst these I would draw special attention to the Swedish cultivar *Betula pendula* 'Dalecarlica' (*laciniata*), whose smooth, white trunks, drooping twigs and daintily cut leaves bring it to the front rank of birches. Then there is Young's lovely weeping form *B. pendula* 'Youngii'; the main shoot of this should be trained up as high as possible while still small, so that the beauty of its weeping branches and branchlets does not altogether shroud the creamy stem. One occasionally happens upon wild trees of similar habit, and at Edinburgh Botanic Garden there is a wonderul specimen of *B. pendula* 'Tristis', whose erect white trunks and branches reach up widely before letting fall their tresses of weeping twigs, purple-brown and shining as are those of all these kinds. It is not until one sees a magnificent specimen like this that one realizes that 'Young's Weeping Birch' is not grand enough for some important positions where one would like a full-scale weeping willow, but where perhaps the ground may be too dry. For such positions the Edinburgh birch would be admirable.

For a more dainty screen than the Lombardy poplar some gardeners plant the erect-growing *B.p.* 'Fastigiata'. Eventually making a rather wider plant than the poplar, it is very lovely with its sinuous white branches. Around the lake at Kew and in dry positions have been planted a number of specimens of *B. platyphylla szechuanica*; this birch has an extra white bark and also rather larger leaves than our natives, and is, like all these trees, of rapid growth. I always remember very vividly an autumn day at A.T. Johnson's garden in North Wales where a lovely young specimen of *B. ermanii* grew in a grassy glade. The creamy stem of the birch soared aloft, the track, as it were, of the rocket-shower of drooping twigs and golden leaves, many of which dappled the lawn.

There are some very remarkable birches at Grayswood Hill, Haslemere, and here again *B. ermanii* is present in a great specimen with a huge branching bole in soft buff colour. In addition, I would mention in this garden a fine specimen of *B. utilis*. This species, though it has not quite such a graceful habit as some other birches, is remarkable for the height to which the milk-white bark peels. Even branches near to the top of the tree and of a thickness no greater than one's finger are white, and its erect growth makes it very suitable for smaller gardens. This Himalayan birch is reputedly not too hardy, but even so, it has been in cultivation for nearly a hundred years and deserves to be more widely grown. At Trinity College, Dublin was a specially good form of this species, and a youngster is doing well at Mount Usher. The milk-white bark has a smoothness and *creaminess* and purity unmatched by any other in my experience. Both *B. ermanii* and *B. utilis* are conspicuous also in the Heather Garden in Windsor Great Park.

White and cream are not the only colours given by the birches.

Several species are resplendent in bark of sienna brown and buff. My memory travels to Bodnant too, where, in that great dell so filled with beauty, two trees stand which for purity can hardly be matched. They are two birches, the one with yellowish bark and the other of soft coppery brown. This is *B. albo-sinensis septentrionalis*, the Western Chinese form of the species, but it is a satisfactory tree only in districts free from spring frosts. Another species of equally capricious growth in these drier parts of the country is the Himalayan *B. utilis prattii*, where it enjoys the conditions and is particularly beautiful in its warm ruddy colouring.

Lastly we have the Canoe or Paper Birch of North America, *B. papyrifera*. Of less beauty in other respects, this tree has the cleanest, smoothest trunk of all. The bark of this and other species have been useful in earlier centuries for making domestic vessels, having notable lasting qualities, and the wide sheets torn off the trunks provided the native races of North America and Canada with material for writing and for facing the framework of their canoes. It is not that the Paper Birch has whiter bark than other birches but that it does not give way to the great, black, corky excrescences at the base of the trunk. While it may be true that the black enhances the white in a grove of our native birches, yet to see a trunk one foot or more in diameter of the Paper Birch is to realize that the black and white effect can be surpassed by the smooth white of this species.

I must mention *B. nigra*, the River Birch. Fine young trees by the lake at Wisley show how this graceful tree does not shed its light brown bark but retains it in a furry mass round the branches. By no means noticeable as a birch, it is a tree of considerable beauty. A number of choice birches have been planted in the ever-growing gardens at Windsor Great Park. They thrive there in ideal conditions on well-drained soil. Among them I have been particularly struck with *B. grossa* (*B. ulmifolia*), with buff-cream bark. At Westonbirt Arboretum, Tetbury, Gloucestershire, and at Wakehurst, East Sussex, many species are thriving in totally different conditions, and this will suffice to prove that birches generally are fairly easy to please.

Conifers do not really give us much bark colour, but some of the Japanese species of *Chamaecyparis* have warm brown bark, and also the giant Wellingtonia and the Redwood. The Scots pine has been mentioned; to this I would add *Pinus pinaster* (*P. maritima*) with its trunks of lovely rose-brown streaked with black fissures in maturity, and the

Chinese Lace Bark, pine, *P. bungeana*. The former is a large, round-headed tree, with a fine trunk full of character, and quick-growing with a rather thin foliage effect, while the Chinese tree is slow and bushy as a rule, its bark peeling in large flakes revealing whitish patches. Its style is therefore that of the plane trees, than which there is no grander thing in our parks. They have a majesty and beauty apart from all other trees, but are much too large for the average garden of today. For one of the most inspiring sights of winter, stand at the foot of a plane tree's giant bole and look up through the flecked branches and tracery of twigs to the blue sky above. Such contemplation is free to everyone and is a recreation for the mind after harassed hours among the pettifogging details that make up one's daily routine. The London Plane is *Platanus* × *hispanica* (*P. acerifolia*), a hybrid, and is the largest growing plane, but *P. orientalis*, which does not as a rule make a tall stem, has equally good bark and more ornamental leaves.

The great Rose Family, so much to the fore in our gardens, does not forsake us in our winter search. The Bird Cherries give us *Prunus maackii* with smooth-polished, yellow-brown bark, while in the true cherries we have the superb *P. serrula* (*tibetica*); it is occasionally seen in cultivation and is renowned for the metal-like polish of its shining, coppery bark. There is nothing like it among hardy trees; the thin, almost transparent strips of bark peel off and are exceedingly tough against the grain. In flower both these cherries are inferior to their relatives, but are small trees of high value in winter. Although usually seen as tall-stemmed specimens, I always think that a specimen with several branches from a 4-foot stem gives the most beauty, and I shall certainly encourage my own specimen to branch low. The bases of the stems of almost all these trees grown for the colour of their bark usually become dark and corky. Therefore the more branches we have at eye-level the more we shall be able to appreciate their tints. As with all trees that have ornamental bark, it is vitally important to remove unwanted branches while they are quite small, so that the unavoidable scars will be as inconspicuous as possible.

There is one very valuable Mountain Ash, *Sorbus aucuparia* 'Beissneri' (formerly known as *S. moravica laciniata*), a slender tree of rather erect growth, with the usual flowers and pale, fretted leaves, and with bark unlike anything else in colour. It seldom fruits. In summer rather dull, by midwinter it becomes a warm coral-red. This is a most useful tree of dual purpose for average or small gardens, for its foliage is daintily cut into tiny lobes, and turns to pale yellow in the autumn.

Leaving the Rose Family temporarily, the 'Snakebark' maples give much interest in winter, and are unique in the colour they provide as youngsters. Their smooth green bark is striped lengthwise with white, and the most ornamental kinds, when growing vigorously, are of extreme beauty. *Acer davidii*, *A. grosseri hersii*, *A. laxiflorum* and *A. forrestii* are natives of China, and, like all other members of the group except one, have only been in cultivation since the beginning of the present century. They are all attractive in leaf, and the young wood of *A. laxiflorum* is brilliant red, an astonishing combination of colour with the old. They are small trees and grow well in these islands. Their relatives from Japan, *A. rufinerve* (which is almost synonymous botanically with *A. capillipes*) and *A. crataegifolium*, are less satisfactory, while the largest-leafed kind is an old friend, known since 1755 but still very scarce, *A. pennsylvanicum*, from eastern North America. This is our original Snakebark maple and has a wonderfully attractive form with vivid scarlet-pink bark, *A.p.* 'Erythrocladum'. It has the most brilliantly coloured bark that I have seen, beating the dogwoods and willows for intensity and clarity. In the first year they are scarlet, showing the white stripes from the second year onwards. There is nothing like it. Knowing so little about their ultimate merits as we do, it is difficult to make a selection among the species, but those I would certainly plant first are *A. laxiflorum*, *A. grosseri hersii* and *A. pennsylvanicum*. They vary somewhat in their bark quality and if a tree vegetatively propagated from a good form can be obtained it is wise to have it in preference to a seedling. They all have a peculiar beauty in leaf and habit; seeing them in the summer at Westonbirt and at Edinburgh one is struck with their airy lightness and admirable habit for the smaller gardens of today, and at Wisley, looking down on them in winter from the slopes of Battleston Hill, one realizes they have an assured future in our gardens.

This looking down is, of course, ideal for the appreciation of bark colour. In Surrey our prevailing winds are from the south-west, and this and the sunlight cleans the bark and gives the best polish possible. In planting for bark colour one must place the trees or shrubs so that they can be viewed from a southerly point, with the sun lighting their colours. The acers at Wisley have a dark background of woodland soil and rhododendrons, and this, with one's back to the sun, is ideal. Unfortunately, the beauty of the maple's bark is not retained for many

WATERCOLOUR PLATES

I. *Bergenia purpurascens, Elaeagnus pungens* 'Dicksonii', *Hedera canariensis* 'Gloire de Marengo', *Iris foetidissima* 'Variegata', *Arum italicum* 'Pictum' and *Mahonia* 'Heterophylla' (two-thirds actual size)

II. *Camellia sasanqua* and *Viburnum* × *bodnantense* 'Dawn' (actual size)

III. *Cornus alba, Perovskia atriplicifolia, C. alba* 'Elegantissima', *C. alba* 'Sibirica', *Leycesteria formosa* and *C. stolonifera* 'Flaviramea' (three-quarters actual size)

IV. *Rhododendron lutescens* and *Cyclamen coum* (three-quarters actual size)

V. *Helleborus kochii* 'Bowles' Yellow' and a dark form of the *H. orientalis* complex (three-quarters actual size)

VI. *Crataegus* × *lavallei* 'Carrierei' and *Iris foetidissima* (three-quarters actual size)

PLATE I

PLATE II

PLATE III

PLATE IV

PLATE V

PLATE VI

years. While it is still to be found on the younger branches, near the top of the tree, the trunk and main branches are, in most of the species, at their best from four to ten years, after which they tend to lose their white stripes and take on smooth and sober greens.

There is a most brilliant maple of the Japanese group (*A. palmatum*) of which the finely-drawn twigs take on a glowing coral-red colour in winter. This is a very beautiful small tree or large shrub which may well take pride of place in many a garden of the future, for its summer foliage is dainty and turns a fine pale orange tint in the autumn. For lack of a name until its botanical status has been determined, it is known as the 'Coral Bark Maple', or by its Japanese name, 'Sen-kaki' or 'Sangokaku'.

Coming to the waterside or any reasonably retentive soil, we have the willows and dogwoods to consider. As a group the willows have a wonderful variety of tints in twig and bud and leaf, and a thing of rare beauty at all seasons is the golden-twigged weeping willow. Botanically it is *Salix* 'Chrysocoma'. In most gardens and lists it appears under the name of *S. babylonica ramulis aureis*, while sometimes it is called *S. vitellina pendula*. With such abundance have the botanists christened the willow that is without doubt the most beautiful of our larger weeping trees! It can be a focal point for the whole garden. Contrary to the usual supposition, this and other willows mentioned here will all thrive in any good garden soil and do not need wet conditions; on the other hand, they link in one's mind with the waterside, and certainly no tree fosters so well the idea of water and its coolness as the weeping willow. The tresses of yellow twigs of the Golden Weeping Willow, hanging perpendicularly to the ground or water, create a picture only less beautiful than its March dress of exquisite greenery. This is a large tree, rapidly forming a big dome of branches 50 feet high and through, and it will grow much larger. A more erect tree is found in *S. × sepulchralis* (*S. babylonica × S. alba*), which inherits its vigour and hardiness from the second parent. The main stem frequently ascends to 30 or 40 feet, from which the weeping branchlets may reach the ground, but they lack the bright yellow colouring of *S.* 'Chrysocoma'.

Salix alba, the White Willow, a tree up to 30 feet or so, has another variety, *S.a. argentea* (*sericea* or *regalis*), which should be included in all mixed willow plantings; its silvery, silky leaves lighten the summer landscape, while in the winter the burnished red twigs give warmth.

They are not the most brilliant of the osiers, however; for these we must turn to the comparatively small-growing *S.a.* var. *vitellina* in yellow, and the glowing orange of 'Britzensis', which has long held the field as the best scarlet-barked kind. Either of these kinds creates a really rich effect in winter, or when large branches are brought indoors, to contrast with a cream wall. Where space is limited these willows are very effective when pruned almost to the ground every spring; their long, resulting shoots will be the more brilliant, and especially when seen in sunshine against a dark background, such as a clump of evergreens or a bank of dark cloud.

   S. acutifolia has dark purple bark covered with a waxen 'bloom' and both this and *S. irrorata* are described with *S. caprea* in Chapter 2, giving as they do their flowers in winter. The Chinese *S. fargesii*, a shrub of more modest dimensions than the foregoing, provides colour from its scarlet terminal buds throughout the winter.

   With the willows I like to grow the several dogwoods which require similar annual pruning to the ground to encourage long, straight and well-coloured shoots. The crimson-barked *Cornus alba* – so named on account of its pearly berries – is a wide-spreading shrub and one of the best groups I know is near the river on the Romsey road near King's Somborne, Hampshire. The warmth of the reflection in the cold wintry water needs to be seen to be believed. The white and yellow variegated leaf-forms of *C. alba* are available for those who desire such things for summer contrast; the white form sometimes produces small albino shoots at the base of the plants with no chlorophyll in the leaves, which are pure white. Similarly, the bark is of a really vivid scarlet and is most useful for indoor decoration in winter. Unfortunately, if propagated, these shoots have no constitution. In the majority of nurseries this *C. alba* is often grown under the name of 'Sibirica', but its 6- or 8-foot height and spread make it unsuitable for the average garden. In any case the variety 'Elegantissima', which has beautiful white variegated leaves in summer, is more often planted. The most desirable form is that known as 'Westonbirt' and correctly named 'Sibirica'. This is a much more compact shrub, having good autumn colour and a brilliance of bark unrivalled in the dogwoods or willows. It is reddish all the year, but by the end of November it assumes an intense scarlet hue. The large patches of dogwood in the Arboretum at Westonbirt are of ordinary *C. alba*; the special variety is not much in evidence, strangely, in that great planting. Rabbits eat with great enjoyment 'Sibirica' but not *C. alba*, which is why the former is not seen in the Arboretum. It is invaluable for cutting for the house in winter, as young foliage quickly grows, in clear contrast to the red bark. It is possible that this plant may prove to be a different species, perhaps closely allied to *C. stolonifera*, whose variety 'Flaviramea' is very useful with bark of a light yellowish-green. It is of similar height and growth to the Westonbirt Dogwood and the two when planted together create a most effective contrast. These two are more compact than the others mentioned, but will easily reach 6 feet. All these dogwoods can be cut to the ground every spring to encourage strong colourful shoots, but I think it better to let each growth last for 2 years, thinning out the older wood only, thus retaining the semblance of a shrub always.

One of the most brilliant winter effects can be achieved with the Westonbirt Dogwood in full light against a wall on which grows the 'black ivy', *Hedera helix* 'Atropurpurea', as recorded in my book *Three Gardens*.

One more shrub can be put to this annual coppicing treatment, and that is the rich grass-green *Kerria japonica*. The stems of this pretty Japanese orange-flowered shrub provide the brightest and fullest 'Hooker's green' in the winter garden, and groups of this and the various cornus and willows can be used with really brilliant effect.

The warm dark brown of the trunks of *Arbutus unedo* has been mentioned earlier in this book, but a spring flowering species, *A. menziesii*, has light brown peeling bark, revealing a wonderful surface of soft green. It is a small, evergreen, large-leaved tree with great bunches of small, honey-scented, creamy-green flowers, but the fruits are less conspicuous than those of the popular Strawberry Tree. During recent severe winters established trees of *A. menziesii* have proved more hardy than *A. unedo* in Surrey. At Kew the vivid red-brown bark of *A. andrachnoides* is a heart-warming sight in winter.

Various shrubs, like certain of the genus *Philadelphus* and *Stephanandra tanakae*, in red-brown, *Berberis dictyophylla*, with its bloomy shoots, and *Leycesteria formosa*, in pea-green, all help the garden in winter, and when one becomes alive to such beauty it will be seen that every shrub or tree has some attraction.

For our last we will sift the brambles for quality. They are coarse brutes to entertain. The three most distinct 'white-washed' species – *Rubus biflorus*, with creamy-white bark and yellow fruit; *R. lasiostylus*, blue-white bark, reddish fruit; and *R. cockburnianus* (*R. giraldianus*), more slender white stems and black fruit – form a striking ornament wherever planted, but they need a vast area to accommodate their 12-foot arching stems. *R. tibetanus* is rather less vigorous but spreads by suckers. The annual cutting to the ground in spring keeps them tidy, but they are rather useless in all but the largest areas. With them I should like to plant the *Rubus* species with dark mahogany polished bark, such as *R. subornatus melanadenus*, which was collected in Yunnan by Professor Te-Tsun Yü earlier in this century.

7. Foliage

There is no doubt that were the use, culture and development of foliage given the care and study that we accord to flowers, our gardens would be very much better. With many shrubs we have only foliage to look upon for eleven months of the year, the flowers being over in two or three weeks. The foliage may act as a complement during the flowering period, but, even with deciduous shrubs and plants, it lasts much longer in beauty than the blooms themselves. In winter, when flowers are more scarce out of doors, foliage comes very much into its own, whether it be the fresh grass blades, the heavy greenery of shrubs from warmer climates than ours, or the brown of the beech hedges and *Polygonum affine*. Theirs are the colours that make the winter landscape, together with the tints of lichens and mosses.

In the garden in general the variety of foliage that we can now command is infinite in shape and colour and tone, and the bronzes, greys, greens and yellows can all be used with very lovely effect, playing the glossy against the matt, and the small and finicky against the greater blades.

But quite so catholic a choice may not be ideal; there are certain tones that do not assort well with our garden of winter flowers. It seems to me that the warmer and more healthy tones should be used, if not exclusively, at least in preponderance. Lovely as the greys and blues of some shrubs and conifers may look in autumn, except on the sunniest of winter days they give a sombre and dull effect. Therefore, much as I value their colour at other seasons of the year, and elsewhere in the garden in winter, I would not place such things as *Senecio* 'Sunshine', *Atriplex halimus*, *Eucalyptus*, blue and grey conifers against my hamamelises and hellebores, crocuses and irises; rather I would use them in the approach to my winter garden. Thereby the change from their greyness to the rich greens and yellows around my winter plants would create an illusion of sun even on dull days. To these approaching positions would I relegate my favourite blue columnar cypresses, such as those varieties of the Mexican *Cupressus arizonica* – or *C. glabra* as it now perhaps should be called – usually found under var. *bonita*. Two forms have grown up since the last war. The most brilliantly glaucous and most shapely as a young plant has been taken to heart by most nurserymen; it is called 'Conica'. But it becomes untidy in maturity whereas the form known as 'Glauca', which is only slightly less brilliant as a youngster, retains its narrowly conical or columnar shape even as an old tree. There are good bluish forms of the Lawson's Cypress, *Chamaecyparis lawsoniana*: 'Columnaris', 'Pembury Blue' and 'Triompf van Boskoop', and also of *Chamaecyparis pisifera*, whose form 'Squarrosa' is only beaten in glaucous tint by the narrow compact 'Boulevard'.

A remarkable piece of winter colour can be obtained from the most glaucous forms of *Juniperus horizontalis*, which turn to a bright violet-blue with the advent of cold weather. This is quite prostrate and excellent for foreground planting, or the rock garden. There are, however, certain grey yet bright plants which I would include: *Dianthus* 'White Ladies' (the improved 'Mrs Sinkins'), for instance, or the trailing glaucous stems and leaves of *Euphorbia myrsinites*, which are admirable beside the varied shades of pink and madder of *Erica herbacea*. *E. rigida*, which most of us know as *E. biglandulosa*, is a bigger, taller edition of *E. myrsinites* and of the same colouring, but is not so hardy. Among shrubs there is the bright lustre of *Elaeagnus macrophylla*, mentioned also for its flowers, and the fretted blue-grey of *Mahonia fremontii* for sheltered walls. Rhododendrons are being given a chapter to themselves, so important are they in winter, and, indeed, throughout the year. *Daphniphyllum macropodum* (*D. glaucescens*) is often mistaken for a rhododendron in winter; it has something of the same poise and growth, and the rosettes of drooping, long leaves have reddish stalks. The clusters of these red stalks are sufficiently bright to be noticeable at a distance.

Where space is limited our foliage will of necessity be composed of those plants chosen for the value of their winter flowers, and certainly one could search for long and find few more worthy subjects for foliage than *Arbutus unedo*, *Mahonia* × *media* 'Lionel Fortescue' and *M. japonica*, camellias, and *Garrya*, which were discussed in Chapter 3.

The majority of greens should be chosen from those of soft general effect and richness of tone, such as *Arbutus*, *Garrya*, *Viburnum rhytidophyllum* – a giant with leaves in proportion – *Pieris formosa* for sheltered gardens, and many of the rhododendrons, and lovely things like the low-growing *Viburnum davidii*, and the skimmias for shade. Particularly would I recommend *Skimmia japonica* 'Rubella', whose foliage is no less good than the warm, mahogany-red colour of its large clusters of buds. It is a male form, but in common with other male forms its flower heads are large and their scent is very far-reaching in March and April. The bud colour from this *S.j.* 'Rubella' is one of the most satisfying things of all those we have chosen for the winter, adding warmth to the garden and also to small vases of winter blooms indoors. *S.* × *confusa* adds a ready fragrance of foliage to a handsome growth and fragrant flowers. All these shrubs have a soft quality and quiet green to serve as a foil for the winter flowers, berries, stems, and the more striking foliage.

Glossy foliage is much more common. There is first the sparkling holly – for no leaf has so much beauty as a prickly holly when edged with rime frost – and its several fine berrying varieties, which are given due space in Chapter 8. Particularly I must call attention to *Ilex* × *altaclerensis* 'Camelliifolia', a large dark-leafed towering variety of superb stance, with very small prickles, and also to *I. aquifolium* 'Argentea Marginata', the most beautiful in growth and colour of the white-variegated kinds, particularly attractive when bearing berries. Perhaps the darkest green of all comes from the small leaves of *Phillyrea latifolia*, a noble, glittering evergreen of considerable dimensions.

In spacious semi-woodland conditions the maligned Cherry Laurel, *Prunus laurocerasus*, can add great dignity if *P.l.* 'Magnoliifolia' ('Latifolia') be chosen, while for smaller gardens in any conditions I know of no evergreen that gives me so much pleasure in its foliage and horizontal line as the miniature variety *P.l.* 'Zabeliana'. This is a shrub which will reach to some 12 feet across in time while only 5 feet or so high, and the narrow leaves, 5 inches long but only an inch wide, make flat platforms to display the spikes of white blooms in spring. To those who have suffered from a surfeit of laurels it may seem strange that I should include yet another, 'Otto Luyken'. Messrs Hesse of Hanover, the raisers of this plant, must have known they had a real gem; it received an Award of Merit from the Royal Horticultural Society in 1968 and may thus be considered comparatively new. It has taken planters by storm and is to be found in every garden centre and is included in numerous planting schemes, private and municipal. We do not know how high it will grow, but it is difficult to stop a laurel and even though this is a compact form I shall be surprised if it will not achieve 8 feet and as much through. Its merits are a dense bushy habit, with semi-erect branchlets clothed in very dark green, glossy, erect, narrow leaves. The numerous spikes of white flowers in spring make a good contrast. Its green is of that same dark, even blackish tint found hitherto only in *Helleborus foetidus*. It makes a contrast to plants of almost any kind, shape or colouring and has an assured future in our gardens.

To these may be added all the mahonias that are hardy; they love the shade, and some, like *Mahonia repens*, will creep and cover woodland ground, while others, like that fine plant known as *M*. 'Undulata', will reach 6 or 7 feet in height. It has very glossy leaves, burnished in sunlight, and is a distinct horticultural clone, possibly a hybrid between *M. aquifolium* and another species. Another hybrid is *M*. 'Moseri', a slow-growing, very colourful plant whose green leaves turn to coral-red in late summer lasting through the winter, although it must be admitted that it lacks the usual shining leaf-surface of *M. aquifolium*. It should be planted with full exposure to the sun. A very uncommon mahonia is sometimes called *M. toluacensis*; its origin is unknown and it may be classed as *M*. 'Heterophylla'. Certainly the latter name suits it, for its leaves are of all shapes, very narrow, of thin texture, and glossy. It forms a loose, dainty shrub and the beauty after hard frost, when the glossy leaves have turned to plum colour, is of a very high order. It makes an admirable foil for other foliage through the year.

For lime-free soil well laced with humus are the shining camellias and graceful leucothoës. *Camellia japonica* cultivars usually have fine foliage and the varieties can be chosen with regard to their flower colour for later display.

Among leucothoës my favourite is *Leucothoë fontanesiana* (often known as *L. catesbaei*), but all are beautiful. They form colonizing thickets of arching stems set with curved, pointed leaves, and are admirable for ground-cover under the largest shrubs. In the sun, however, and in more exposed positions, they take on rich reddish tints in winter, an added advantage. For similar positions is that shrubby relative of the lilies, *Danaë racemosa* (*D. laurus*). Frequently taken for a dwarf bamboo, its thicket of stems is delightfully leafed in shiny, narrow blades, and for cutting in winter it is ideal. Prince of all this glossy-leafed group is of course *Magnolia grandiflora*, in whose variety named 'Exmouth' the best shape and colour is found. This is one of the finest of all foliage shrubs and will thrive in the open in the south, but must be given a warm wall in cold districts. There is a prodigious clump at Wisley.

The freshness and grace of the neater bamboos are very valuable to enhance the darker evergreens in winter. Tallest among our hardy species is that which we have known for years as *Arundinaria fastuosa*, now to be called *Semiarundinaria fastuosa*. Where a columnar effect is required, this giant with erect stout canes up to 15 or more feet is not too much of a spreader for the garden, and its leaves are of a bright green. Many other species are so rampant that they may become a nuisance in all but landscape gardens, although they are useful as an annual source of canes for staking. At the other end of the scale is the miniature *P. ruscifolia*, now to be known as *Shibataea kumasasa*. This is an erect yard-high plant of non-spreading habit but has not the grace of the greater bamboos. Among these I should have no hesitation of placing foremost *Phyllostachys nigra* var. *henonis*, in spite of the rival attractions of its black-stemmed species. These two have a grace before which all others are dimmed, and they have too from our point of view the priceless quality of holding their leaves in their fresh mid-green throughout the winter. Most become tarnished and tawdry by the spring, but in spite of this I would also reserve a place for *Arundinaria murieliae*, another very slowly spreading bamboo, for the sake of its grace and the enjoyable way it has of shedding its oldest leaves in November, turning to clear yellow. For larger gardens *Phyllostachys viridi-glaucescens* is of great grace and beauty and will make, with its widely arching stems, clumps of 30 feet across; a close relative is *P. flexuosa*, which is not so large, but none of these has the evergreen value so much to the fore as *P. nigra* var. *henonis*. Alas, it is not easy to find, being so slow to increase.

The hardy palm, *Trachycarpus fortunei* or *Chamaerops excelsa*, and *Cordyline australis*, more often seen gracing hotel lounges, may be added if a 'tropical' effect is desired. They do give at least a complete change from the usual lumpiness of evergreens. The palm is generally hardy in the less cold parts of this country, but the cordyline needs sheltered conditions. Three plants with sword-like foliage are also useful in this respect. They are the dark green, foot-high 'Gladwin', *Iris foetidissima*, useful also on account of its berries and invaluable in its creamy striped variegated form for decoration in winter, both indoors and also in the garden; pale green *Sisyrinchium striatum*, a freely seeding biennial; and the giant 5-foot *Phormium tenax*, or New Zealand Flax, in a variety of tints of soft green, purplish, or variegated. A particularly vivid yellow stripe is found in 'Williamsii'; a splendid purplish one with coppery edges to the leaves is 'Sundowner'. I have not found phormiums particularly hardy in the open field in Surrey, but in the shelter of gardens there is nothing else that can give so bold an effect among evergreens. 'Sundowner' is one of the several new hybrids between *P. tenax* and the shorter *P. colensoi*; all are of brilliant tints but as yet they are unproven for hardiness.

To return, the bamboos and *Sisyrinchium* have a soft, light green unlike most evergreens, and they further the idea of growth and freshness that prevails among the winter flowers. To them we will add those fresh green, small shrubs the Kurume azaleas, and especially 'Hino-Mayo', the brightest green of all. On a lime-free soil they are not difficult to please, and give generous reward in April and May with their abundant flowers. As a temporary plant while others are growing and filling up, the common yellow broom, *Cytisus scoparius* (now to be called *Sarothamnus scoparius*), has much to recommend it; the tall, rush-like, rich green twigs do give interest to the borders. Parsley is perhaps the very best of all plants for rich green leaves, and if the eye can greet it in its wider sense of a foliage plant, the utility side can be forgotten in contemplation of its virile green before the frosts spoil it.

Apart from the parsley, *Sisyrinchium* and *Iris*, there are few evergreen herbaceous plants for the winter garden. Doronicums, *Campanula latiloba* and certain hemerocallises have persistent grass-green leaves, and, in really sheltered gardens, the magnificent evergreen ferns, *Polystichum munitum*, with its broad, neatly divided leaves, and

Blechnum chilense remain green and fresh through the winter, as do numerous other ferns such as the Polypody and *Scolopendrium* or Hart's Tongue, in shaded places. Having passed some years under the revised name of *Phyllitis scolopendrium*, the Hart's Tongue has now been revised again and is called *Asplenium scolopendrium*. I would not have much in this way otherwise, for dead and dying leaves, however beautiful they may be – the various grasses for instances – do not capture the spirit of perpetual growth any more than the berries and seed heads mentioned on page 84. I would make an exception of *Polygonum affine*, however; this rather rampant spreader puts up numerous spikes of pink flowers from summer to autumn, and in winter is a 5 inch carpet of rich sienna-brown leaves. I know of nothing else, not even a beech hedge, with so warm a brown tone in winter. The new form known as 'Superbum' has the best-coloured flowers, and foliage as good as the type, while 'Donald Lowndes' is less hardy and less rampant. I imported 'Superbum' with some ferns and other plants from Messrs Hagemann of Hanover some years ago and it has quickly found favour, being superior in bloom to all other forms we grow.

The Megasea Saxifrages (*Bergenia*), those noble path-side plants with large, rounded, leathery leaves and heads of pink flowers in spring, are very useful for greenery in winter, and they have one species of special value; it is *Bergenia purpurascens*, and its plum-purple leaves with their red undersides can be seen from afar. On the Wisley rock garden it used to be noticeable through the winter, and was contrasted there with *Euonymus fortunei* 'Variegatus' of which there are several named forms, the most splendid being 'Silver Queen', while another good bergenia with more rounded leaves, but again of rich winter colour, is called 'Abendglut'. 'Ballawley Hybrid' *Bergenia* was raised soon after the last war by Mr Shaw-Smith of Dublin. This has more than exceeded the claims that were made for it. It has leaves 9 inches across in poor Surrey sand, and I know they are larger in better conditions. All the summer they are of a lustrous green, far more glossy than any other *Bergenia* of my acquaintance. When severe weather arrives, they turn to a rich plum-red, or mahogany-red, and remain so until the spring, when they suddenly – after a day or two of really warm weather – turn back to green. Then the magnificent red flower stems arise, carrying a graceful, large, drooping head of magenta flowers. But it is winter we are concerned with, and as garden furnishing it is excellent, only surpassed in a cut state indoors, where each leaf will last for a month, and provides a wonderful foil of colour for many other leaves and flowers.

At Sunningdale Nurseries we raised a batch of seedling bergenias and picked out one which not only had clear coloured flowers and good foliage, but whose leaves, firm and rounded, turned to a wonderful colour in the winter in the full exposure of the open fields. They turn, even in a nourished garden, to the same rich tint, and are as colourful as Ballawley's and much more weather-proof. There is a good colour photograph in my book *Plants for Ground-Cover*, Plate XIV B, which brings me to the point that, long suffering as bergenias are in almost any position short of a bog, they must be properly nourished and growing well. A starved clump is a poor sight. Fortunately they soon regain health if replanted with a little enrichment of the soil.

Lesser plants for bright fresh green in winter are the stoloniferous *Tulipa saxatilis* and the freely increasing *Muscari armeniacum*. Together with that rather terrible weed *Allium triquetrum* they appear in late autumn, though many weeks go by before their flowers open.

Many of the larger rock plants, such as *Cardamine trifolia*, have good evergreen foliage, too, and are invaluable for edgings to beds and borders, and odd plants of the golden-leafed 'Feverfew', *Chrysanthemum* or *Pyrethrum parthenifolium*, can be allowed to seed about, making little patches of bright yellow-green. A very striking contrast to this is found in the leaves of the autumn-flowering hardy cyclamen, *Cyclamen hederifolium* (*C. neapolitanum*), close on the ground and mottled in shades of grey-green; this foliage appears in October and November and lasts the winter through. A similar strange but welcome habit is found in *Arum italicum*, of which the garden variety 'Pictum' should be sought, for the spear-shaped leaves are most beautifully marbled with creamy and greyish-green. They are ideal for picking with Christmas Roses. *Arum creticum*, bearing yellow flowers in spring, also puts up its handsome green leaves in autumn. Completely different from anything else are the bunches of silvery leaves of *Celmisia coriacea*, a New Zealand white daisy. It is not usually a success in the south-east of England, preferring the cooler north, Ireland and Scotland.

My own favourites are found in the above paragraphs, but there is of course an endless wealth of green to choose from. For greens,

Hedera helix 'Arborescens'

therefore, let us look for those without too much gloss and glitter, and select those of as fresh a tint as possible, to mingle with the blossoms, reminding us that all is well in the garden even in the winter.

For walls there is a range of ivies; these much neglected plants have some beautiful things amongst them. What is more lovely than a trail of some fine-leafed ivy like *Hedera helix* 'Pedata' ('Caenwoodiana') as a finish to a bowl of fruit? And, accepted indoors, should it not be accepted in the garden? A stump or wall-buttress clothed with the great leaves of *H. colchica* in either its green- or cream-variegated form (*H.c.* 'Dentata Variegata') is a constant joy in winter; it is most effectively used at Spetchley Park on wall and garden house, and on the buttresses to the steps near the Temperate House at Kew. When the long stems of the latter grow out at the base and thread thinly over the ground amongst shrubs, their finest leaves are nearly all cream, and the same is equally true on shady walls. For sunny, sheltered walls the white and grey-green variegated form of *H. canariensis*, known as 'Gloire de Marengo' ('Variegata'), is successful. The large leaves are a mixture of ivory white, pale grey-green, and darker green, irregularly flaked and marked. The common ivy, *H. helix*, has varieties of similar colouring, the most handsome being *H.h.* 'Marginata Major', while tiny-leafed versions such as 'Adam' and 'Silver Queen' repeat this coloration in miniature, and 'Buttercup' (*flavescens*) upholds its name in a yellow tint. One that has leapt to popularity of late years is 'Gold Heart' whose name well describes it; I also favour 'Angularis Aurea' or 'Chrysophylla', two very similar varieties which present a varied amount of clear yellow leaves over the plant, especially where fully exposed to the light and sunshine. As a delightful cool, soft background to the mauve winter-flowering rhododendrons, such as *R. dauricum* and *R.* Praecox, there is nothing better than the grey and white of *Hedera h.* 'Glacier'. Ivies are so useful for ground-cover too. I have already cited *H. colchica* with its broad fragrant leaves; *H. helix* presents two small compact charmers in 'Little Diamond' and 'Sagittifolia Variegata', both clearly variegated in white. They make a first-rate contrast to the soft greyish-lilac winter foliage of *Cyathodes colensoi*, a lime hater from New Zealand. This has all the air of a dense *Erica* and is for frontal positions; it in its turn provides a lovely colour combination for *Iris reticulata*. Those who saw the Trial of ivies at Wisley in the late 1970s will know that I have barely touched on the variety of colour and size available; there are two which yet need to be mentioned. Their leaves turn to dark maroon-black in winter. They are 'Glymii' and 'Atropurpurea'. In summer they would not be noticed, but contrasted with Winter Aconites they produce an amazing effect. The same sort of winter tint occurs in *Euonymus fortunei* 'Coloratus' whose leaves, like *Rhododendron ponticum* 'Foliis Purpureis' and the two bergenias I have referred to, are rich in their dark plum colouring during the cold weather.

Even more neglected today than the climbing ivies are the so-called tree ivies. These are produced by rooting the bunchy, flowering stems off a normal climbing plant. Old plants some 2 or 3 feet high of the yellow-tinted kinds can be of rare beauty, with their glow of gold over the more exposed part of the bush. The arborescent form of *H.h.* 'Marginata Major' is one of the finest, and is particularly brilliant in its young foliage in June.

Two most handsome evergreen climbers or sprawlers are found in

Rubus flagelliflorus and *R. irenaeus*, both with large leaves of mid-green, felted beneath, oval in the former, nearly orbicular in the latter. Their flowers are cream and they produce edible fruits, but from a garden point of view their foliage comes first.

Although we have passed from plain greens to variegated-leafed plants, let it not be supposed that I advocate these whole-heartedly. Their bizarre tones can be very upsetting in the garden, however beautiful some of their leaves may be on close inspection. They are seen at their best perhaps when carefully placed amongst more sober greens, or to show up some brick or timber colour to great advantage. Few of them are much use as a background to any winter-flowering plant, but berries or coloured twigs can occasionally make a bright contrast. When I wrote this book first, in 1956, I wrote 'Variegation is often a thing of scorn these days'! Times change, and today a variegated plant is a sure seller in garden centres. There are however plenty of foliage tints available to give variety to the winter garden without having to resort to variegation. To bring warmth into the winter scene we need the rich olive greens and khaki tints of some of the hebes, such as *H. ochracea*, which used to be called *H. armstrongii*, and particularly its form 'James Stirling' which is an astonishing shade of orange-brown in winter. The dense-growing, hardy, small-leafed hebes are ideal for augmenting a heather garden but are in any case first-class front-line plants. A good yellowish green is *H. rakaiensis* (*subalpina*) 'Golden Dome', also 'Canterburyensis'. Rich greens are found in *H. rakaiensis* 'Edinensis' and *H. vernicosa*, while 'Mrs Winder' excels all others with mahogany-purplish foliage and is, like these others, perfectly hardy in Surrey. Among glaucous kinds is that gem *H. pinguifolia* 'Pagei', also *H. albicans*, 'Pewter Dome', and something quite different is the very small-leafed *H. glaucophylla* 'Variegata' whose general effect is silvery-cream. There is however no end to these excellent small New Zealanders; their merits and hardiness were brought to light in the Trial at Wisley after the severe winter of 1981/2 when almost all large-leafed cultivars were killed.

To return to *Elaeagnus*, already mentioned at some length in Chapter 3, the hybrid *E.* × *reflexa* of *E. pungens* is the most graceful for gardens or for cutting as an evergreen, and the reverses of its leaves are of a metallic-brown sheen. Those who enjoy variegation can find no grander shrub than *Elaeagnus pungens* 'Dicksonii'; it is far more brilliant and clear in its yellow tint than the commoner *E.p.* 'Maculata'.

Another variegated form is *E.p.* 'Variegata', which is not so prone to reversion to the original green as the two more brilliant forms mentioned above. The leaves in this form are edged with cream, Dickson's are edged with brilliant yellow, while those of 'Maculata' (or *aureovariegata*) have yellow in varying stripes in their centres. *E.p.* 'Frederici' is again quite different, and produces many leaf sprays of pale creamy-yellow, glossy and striking among the normal green. The most strikingly variegated of all elaeagnuses is 'Gilt Edge', which is a sport of *E.* × *ebbingei*. The edges of the leaves are a brilliant yellow and every now and again a shoot will be produced with leaves entirely yellow. These are a great luxury for cutting for indoors; this is no wastage as they cannot exist without chlorophyll on their own roots. *Elaeagnus* × *ebbingei* itself can be somewhat disconcerting in its green type: branches die and sometimes a whole plant will go. So far there has been no pronouncement upon the cause of this disorder, but I have not noticed it happening on shrubs on well-drained soil which have been allowed to grow unpruned. It is a hybrid between *E. macrophylla* and *E. pungens* and was raised at The Hague by the late S.G. Doorenbos.

Choisya ternata is a good, dark green, aromatic shrub with white flowers in spring, for sunny, sheltered places. In 1986 there burst upon us a remarkable 'sport' selected by Peter Catt, called 'Sundance' whose leaves are, throughout the year, a brilliant yellow, flushed with green if grown in shade. It is an eye-catcher which needs careful placing to reveal its full value.

As to the conifers, we have already cast aside the blue and grey varieties; the yellow varieties, of which none is brighter than *Chamaecyparis lawsoniana* 'Lanei' and *Thuja occidentalis* 'Lutea', may find a place here and there. These spires of brilliant colour grace many a garden but can easily be overdone. The golden variant of our native Scots pine *Pinus sylvestris* 'Aurea', which is normal green in summer but at the approach of winter assumes a buttery-yellow, is a slow grower and is usually seen as a shrub or very small stunted tree. I was in fact very astonished at the specimen at Castlewellan, County Down, which is a fine tree with a large round head some 30 feet high. It is inexplicably rare in gardens. For brilliance in winter it is now surpassed by *P.s.* 'Gold Coin' and also by *P. contorta* 'Frisian Gold', which will perhaps bring home to people the value of these unique plants. Forming a delightful dense bun-shaped bush is *P. mugo*

'Ophir'; this would be lovely in association with heathers. For small-sized trees there is *Thuja occidentalis* 'Rheingold', which slowly makes an elegant spire of coppery-orange and the compact little conical bush *T. orientalis* 'Aurea Nana'. In *Thuja orientalis* the leaves are all appressed in erect fans and, when crushed, have none of the fruity scent of other thujas. For the very front of groups on lime-free soils certain heathers are useful. I have mentioned my choice of these in Chapter 4. Many conifers in winter develop dull brownish or greyish tinting when they are not blue-grey, yellow or plum-coloured, but a few remain rich green such as *Thuja plicata* 'Atrovirens', *Chamaecyparis lawsoniana* 'Witzeliana' (not 'Wisselii') and *C. obtusa* 'Nana Gracilis'. The last two are suitable for smaller gardens.

There is generally so much to be done in a garden in winter and so few light hours to do it in, that one does not often get the chance of a quiet walk round, to appraise the value of plants. With the deciduous trees and shrubs all bare, new vistas are opened and any kind of leaf takes on an added importance. In fact, designing the garden can often be started afresh, so prominent and beautiful are the many fine evergreens which are obtainable today. A visit to an old garden like Westonbirt School, Tetbury, Gloucestershire, convinces one that our modern, rather flimsy, flowering trees and shrubs, mostly deciduous, cannot compare with the garden-making solidity of the great specimens of hollies, yews, rhododendrons and others which are such a definite foil for, and give such quality to, the splashes of colour during the summer months. The towering plants of golden yews at Westonbirt, and hollies, and the horizontal line of Dovaston's Yew have no peer in the garden today. Truly it is the leaf that makes the garden and luckily for us there are plenty of smaller evergreens awaiting our selection.

8. Berries

I will bring you berries
Dusty with bloom,
And berries like lanterns
To glisten in your room.

J. BUXTON

As we have decided to include no 'dead heads' in our search for colour in the winter garden, it may seem strange that a whole chapter should be devoted to berry-bearing plants. Berries, truly, are of the autumn, and few last into the winter; and while they do certainly provide colour in the so-called 'dead' months, they do not give quite that freshness and joy that we ask of a winter garden, the forerunner of the spring display. Many reveal their colour during October and carry on their display until hard frosts spoil them, but I think they should be grouped away from our present favourites. There are however, some trees and shrubs and an iris of more lasting quality, which can be relied upon to give bright colour, and all the following are at their best during November, December and onwards.

If there should be no hard frost before Christmas, *Malus (Pyrus)* 'Robusta' will keep its fruits, the size of large cherries, until well into the New Year. It is a hybrid between *M. baccata* and *M. prunifolia*, and is often called Red Siberian Crab, a name that rightly belongs to *M. baccata*. On one memorable day in early January I came upon two noble specimens at Kew heavily hung with fruits, near the Palm House, and their soft crimson-scarlet was a glorious sight, like one of the flowering peaches in April. It makes a small tree to about 20 feet and has a pleasing habit. There are not many other trees that we can consider here, but certainly a place must be found for *Crataegus × lavallei* 'Carrierei'; this, one of the best known of the thorns, makes a compact head of branches, and after its shiny, leathery leaves fall in late November the large fruits gradually deepen in colour until in December they become bright orange, and are held well and fresh into February in all but the hardest winters. This colour is a welcome change, for nearly all other fruits are some shade of red. *C. × grignoniensis*, a little-known but very worthy relative of *C. × lavallei*, has the usual red fruits, of a good size, and holds them also until the early year. The colour of 'Carrierei' is found also in an uncommon though easily grown and beautiful evergreen shrub up to 9 feet or so, *Euonymus myrianthus*. This is the right name for the species that, until it flowered, was known as *E. sargentianus*. It is not spectacular in the display of its fruits, which appear in early autumn, but when they have fallen the angular yellow husks remain on the bush and in midwinter turn to a warm orange colour. The pink and orange fruits of our native Spindle Tree, *E. europaeus*, are most unusual in colour and last well into the winter.

Birds are, of course, the main trouble with these berrying trees and shrubs, and it is useless to expect a lasting display where they abound. They can, however, be tricked; they seldom touch the yellow- or white-fruiting Rowans or the orange- and yellow-fruited pyracanthas, to be mentioned later. Presumably they do not expect fruits to be ready for their beaks until they are highly coloured! The common Rowan is so well-known and so thrifty in a variety of soils and positions that its very ubiquity has probably kept some of its beautiful Eastern relatives in the background. The yellow-fruited variant that I mentioned is *Sorbus aucuparia* 'Fructu Luteo', and the white is *S. hupehensis*. For many years the latter was known in gardens and nurseries as *S. wilsonii*, but this name should refer to a red-fruited species. Good pink forms of *S. hupehensis*, once called *S. oligodonta*, have been given several names 'Rosea', 'November Pink' and 'Rufus'; all have soft greyish colouring of leaf that tones well with the fruits. When the leaves have fallen I know of no better sight for a November day than the clusters of pink or white berries on reddish stalks, contrasted above one's head by the dark stems and blue sky. It is an exquisite picture not excelled at that time of the year even by the Autumn Cherry.

Several of the Rowans retain their fruits well into November if not removed by the birds, but the majority are givers of colour during September and October rather than November and December. *S. esserteauiana* (*S. conradinae*) is a splendid species for late colour, and its wide clusters of dark red berries frequently hang on the tree

Cotoneaster lacteus

through December and January, at which time it is among the most handsome of trees. Its yellow form, *S.e.* 'Flava', is no less good. A Rowan of late growth, flowering and fruiting, is *S. commixta* 'Serotina'; this gives the joy of the common Mountain Ash to the month of November. It is a native of Japan.

Another large shrub or tree which the birds do not usually rob is the half-evergreen *Cotoneaster frigidus*. It is of course one of the best known of cotoneasters, in fact it is this species which has given so much impetus to the cult of the berried shrub during the last fifty years or so. But it is of gigantic proportions, growing to 20 feet or more in good soil, and is totally unsuited to the average garden. It does provide, however, a feast of colour in the autumn and sometimes well into the New Year, the birds often leaving the berries severely alone. With species of the *salicifolius* group it has produced several fine hybrids, one of the best being *C.* × *watereri* 'John Waterer'. Almost evergreen, it makes a rounded shrub some 12 feet high and 18 feet wide. 'St Monica' and 'Cornubia' are similar, and very lovely in the young state, but on sandy soil at least (not the cotoneaster's favourite medium) tend to develop into rather ugly shapes after a few years. Yellow berried cousins are 'Exburyensis' and 'Rothschildianus' while 'Inchmery' and 'Pink Champagne' are salmon-pink.

The weeping *C.* 'Hybridus Pendulus' (*C. frigidus simmondsii*) is very beautiful while in full colour, but unfortunately it holds its berries long after they turn brown and shrivelled, and a tree in February or March is a sorry sight. On the other hand, when it is grown as a prostrate shrub the damage is not so frequent. The late Walter Bentley had about 15 to 20 feet square of ground covered with the green of this hybrid, and the berries nestling among the leaves created a fine effect. The plant is so prostrate that it can either be grown as a carpeter in this way or top-grafted on a stem of another cotoneaster, when it forms an umbrella-shaped head, incongruous but not without interest.

There are several evergreen cotoneasters which are truly winter-fruiting: *C. lacteus, serotinus, pannosus, harrovianus* and *conspicuus*. *C. lacteus* makes an enormous dense mound in time, 20 feet across; this handsome-leafed shrub has been rapidly increasing in popularity since it was introduced by Forrest in 1913. The very dark green leaves, borne gracefully upon wide-spraying branches, are always well-fruited, and fortunately this handsome bush goes on fruiting freely even when lopped severely to keep it within bounds. Both this species and *C. serotinus* do not reach their full colour until mid-November; *C. lacteus'* berries usually vanish by Christmas, when the birds find them ripe. Those of *C. serotinus* hang on in full colour until March or April. This large shrub is open, rather erect, but still of very graceful growth, and the glossy, rounded leaves, pale beneath, are very elegant on young shoots. *C. pannosus* is a shrub to put behind others, as it is a rather spindly thing, but its ultimate arching sprays of tiny green leaves make a soft foil for the downy, orange-red berries. These become polished with the winter rain and wind, and shine brightly by Christmas.

Our next species, *C. conspicuus*, is a comparative newcomer, raised from seed collected in 1924 in South-east Tibet by Captain F. Kingdon Ward. There are two forms in cultivation, of which one makes a dense, rounded shrub up to some 6 feet in height, like a slightly larger-leafed variant of the untidy growing *C. microphyllus*. At Nymans I have seen berries on *C. conspicuus* still bright and attractive in June, among the azaleas, but it is a large, rather overpowering shrub in its stronger forms. Low growing, semi-prostrate forms (sometimes erroneously called *C.c.* var. *decorus*) are much more useful for the

Cotoneaster serotinus

Cotoneaster conspicuus

garden of today; they are excellent for foreground planting and to cover banks, where a dense cover is needed, and the berries have the same lasting power.

A little plant for the rock garden or bank is *C. microphyllus* var. *cochleatus*, with exceptionally large berries studding its hummocks of green; the berries can usually be relied upon to provide colour in December. The birds' taste in berries varies from season to season. I have known *C. lacteus* despoiled in October, and until the last three seasons another species, *C. salicifolius* var. *floccosus*, has been cleared of berries in autumn regularly. In many winters, the berries, which become brilliant scarlet in October, stay on the branches until March. In such a season this species is without rival in its class, and its value as an evergreen and shrub of beautiful habit really warrants its inclusion in Chapter 7. *C. harrovianus*, less well known than these others, is nevertheless a graceful and pleasing shrub, and its berries, like those of *C. pannosus*, do not reveal their polished colour fully until December.

Both *C. horizontalis* and *C. simonsii* are deciduous and well known and in some winters the birds leave them entirely alone. *C. horizontalis* is as useful for ground-cover as it is for training on walls; its flat fish-bone-like spreading branches display its berries to advantage and it is best in cooler places. On hot sunny walls it is apt not to thrive. *C. simonsii* has particularly bright berries on a rather stiff upright growth and a few of its leaves keep the berries company through mild winters.

Returning to the large evergreens again, we have the showy stranvaesias, now to be called *Photinia*; *S. davidiana* with erect growth and *S.d.* var. *undulata* of more horizontal growth are the most distinct. Their shining foliage makes a noticeable contrast to the unusual fruits, which are not glossy but of matt finish, and particularly beautiful on this account. The heavy clusters of scarlet are part of a picture of extreme beauty, for it is seldom that there is not a scarlet or yellow leaf here and there as well. In addition to the usual red-berried type, a yellow-fruited form is grown. Again they are not polished and are most admirable for cutting in winter.

The pyracanthas, or firethorns, are often grown on walls, but these are first-class shrubs for general planting as well. The majority are autumn-fruiting, but three distinct species are suitable for our list. The most noble of all, with large, dark leaves, is *Pyracantha atalantioides*, which most of us used to know better by the name *P. gibbsii*. This has the finest foliage and the largest flowers and fruit of all the kinds. There are several distinct forms in cultivation; one is superlative, with extra broad leaves and large fruits. The flowers produce a snowy display in May and by December the fruits – black-eyed berries – are a brilliant red. It is a very vigorous erect shrub up to 10 or 15 feet, while *P. crenato-serrata* (*P. yunnanensis*), equally vigorous, is low-growing, almost horizontal, and I know of few finer things for banks or crowning a bluff of rock. Its berries are small and do not colour until December, but they hang in lacy clusters and are of a peculiar soft coral-red tint. *P. angustifolia*, an admirable hedge plant, is also good as a shrub or on a wall. Possibly not quite hardy, especially when loaded with berries, it is exceptionally beautiful as late as January or February, when its slowly maturing fruits, greeny-yellow in autumn, take on a ruddy orange, and show up well amongst the small, neat leaves.

Of recent years I have been more and more impressed with the excellence of *P*. 'Watereri', a seedling which originated in the famous Bagshot nurseries of that name. This is certainly the best *Pyracantha* for small gardens, for it makes a dense bush prettily covered with small, dark leaves, and the prodigality of its flower display is a foretaste of the splendour of its berries, which are more numerous and more densely cover the branches than in any other shrub I know. 'Waterer's Orange' is another good one. Some American hybrids deserve appraisal as they become better known; the following carry their fruits, as a rule, well into the winter: 'Mohave', 'Shawnee', 'Navaho' and 'Teton'. All of these keep their fruits until well into December if the birds allow it.

It is not generally appreciated that when a shrub is bearing a heavy crop of fruits it is liable to damage by prolonged frost. It is presumably drought, not cold, that affects it at such times. With the effort of producing berries, it cannot stand curtailment of the normal flow of moisture from the roots. As a consequence instances may occur of these late-maturing fruiters being severely spoiled in long periods of frost after Christmas. *P. angustifolia* is one which is particularly prone to damage, and the common holly another. No doubt the removal of the berries would enable the plant to carry on safely, but neglect to do so often results in the plant losing its leaves in spring and taking a season or two to recover. The common holly, being a plant that fruits irregularly, is only affected in isolated instances when a tree in heavy fruit is caught by a prolonged frost.

Although generally speaking the 'heps', or 'hips', of roses do not last until the winter, many being taken by the birds or destroyed by early frosts, there are a few which may find a place in these pages. *Rosa* 'Andersonii', that fine hybrid of our English briar, and the Sweet Briar (*R. rubiginosa*, *R. eglanteria*) with its 'Penzance Hybrids', are very conspicuous from October at least until Christmas, and I have noted *R. gallica officinalis* and *R. damascena* 'St Nicholas' carrying crops for a similar period. Dr Hurst's hybrid 'Cantab' has large, red heps which last through the winter, and some climbers, like 'Allen Chandler' and 'Cupid', together with the Hybrid Musks 'Wilhelm' and 'Will Scarlet', are equally noteworthy. 'Penelope' is unique among roses that I know, the heps retaining a 'bloom' throughout the winter, giving their soft green and coral-pink a subtle charm. Perhaps the most distinguished of all for large, colourful, lasting heps is Wilhelm Kordes' 'Scarlet Fire', introduced in 1952 under its German name of 'Scharlachglut'. It is trained on a wall at Sissinghurst and normally creates a glow of scarlet well into the New Year.

Leaving now the invaluable Family of Rosaceae, which embraces all the plants in the foregoing paragraphs except the *Euonymus* and the holly, we will return to the latter, one of our most regular of winter performers.

The holly as an evergreen has been considered in the last chapter, but here I want to mention a few regularly fruiting kinds, for our loved Christmas emblem should certainly find a place near our winter flowers – nor should we forget the yellow-berried variety *Ilex aquifolium bacciflava* (*fructu luteo*), whose tint to my mind is far better than the red to crown the Christmas pudding, as it matches the rum-and-butter sauce! *I.a. heterophylla* ('Pyramidalis'), which also has a good yellow-fruiting form, is a form that can be relied upon to fruit regularly, and by itself too, as it is monoecious, while the common holly has the sexes on separate plants. It is difficult to pick out one regularly berrying holly from among the many green forms and hybrids, but my choice would be 'J.C. van Thol'. This seems to have every possible asset: free berrying, leaves not excessively prickly and an elegant growth. It is again monoecious and is far less prickly than the common kind. Hollies are not outdone when it comes to variegation; two regularly berrying kinds are *I.a.* 'Argentea Marginata', with white edges to the leaves, and *I.* × *altaclerensis* 'Golden King', with leaves margined with deep yellow and few prickles. Under the name of 'Barterberry' a fine fruiting holly was shown to the Royal Horticultural Society in February 1983; it has good leaves and berries and is fairly certainly another *I.* × *altaclerensis* cultivar. It was found in a Wiltshire hedgerow. A deciduous, compact holly from eastern North America, *I. verticillata*, often produces numerous red berries; in fact it received an Award of Merit in November 1962. A special selection, reputedly free-fruiting, is 'Xmas Cheer'. Like many North American plants it will not tolerate excess lime in the soil. 'Nana' is a useful dwarf.

While thinking of Christmas, the Mistletoe (*Viscum album*) comes to mind. Although a parasite, it has sufficient beauty to make the keenest gardeners grow it on some old apple or lime tree, which, it is said, it eventually permeates and overruns with fatal effect. It is a slow but interesting process raising plants from berries stuck on to the host branches, but its sexes are on separate individuals, so that berries cannot be guaranteed. For indoor decoration it is most useful *in water* with other winter things.

Among the smaller evergreens we have the bright berries of the skimmias and the soft, unusual tints of pernettyas. Skimmias are very confusing and confused in gardens. *Skimmia japonica* needs a male plant among a group of females to ensure berries setting, but I would not bother with this, as there are other good kinds with perfect flowers which will berry unaided. These are all compact evergreens with leaves of dark, soft green, not glossy; the smallest-growing is one called *S. reevesiana* (*S. fortunei*), much used in London window-boxes and by florists. The narrow, pointed leaves have pale, hard margins, and the trusses of berries are borne well above the leaves. Of the taller berrying kinds *S.* × *foremanii* has long held an honoured position, but its exact status is in question; *S. japonica* 'Nymans' is extra vigorous and has achieved some 6 feet in the garden of that name and is brilliantly berried every winter. The birds seldom touch the berries of this genus. *S.j.* 'Rubella' is mentioned on page 73.

The pernettyas from the Magellan region of South America provide a new tint. The type species *Pernettya mucronata* is very variable and names have been given to a number of distinctly coloured forms. The soft, glossy fruits follow in great clusters the tiny, white bell-flowers and last well into February, and forms in every colour from white through pink to dark rosy purple may be obtained. There is a beautiful pure albino with rather smaller green-white fruits (not to be confused with the handsome blush-white variety), but all these need a male or two with them to ensure fruiting. Their suckering red stems and dense yet lax habit with tiny prickly dark green leaves make them admirable for planting in large drifts and stretches amongst other taller shrubs, for they do not mind a certain amount of shade; they are, however, intolerant of lime and do best in a soil that contains humus and is not too heavy.

There is a valuable kind called 'Bell's Seedling' which will fruit unaided; the fruits are a great size and of a rich mahogany-red. We are fortunate also in having that self-fertile race 'Davis's Hybrids' in a fine range of colour forms. These were raised by Mr Davis of Hillsborough, County Down, and received much recognition from the

RHS, being awarded several First Class Certificates around 1882; they are today still in the front rank of fertile forms, in colours from blush-white to pink and crimson and lilac. The 'Butcher's Broom', *Ruscus aculeatus*, like *Pernettya mucronata*, normally needs plants of both sexes to ensure fruits, but, again like our former example, hermaphrodite forms have been selected and propagated. They are all spiny, horrible shrubs to deal with, not at all what one would expect from a member of the Lily Family, but are useful for growing under trees and especially on poor chalky soils. There the spiny mass of shoots, up to a yard or so high, is reasonably pleasant to look upon when set with red berries. *Danaë racemosa*, on the other hand, a most beautiful plant to my mind, has qualified for inclusion among the foliage plants, on page 75, and it also occasionally produces red berries.

Before passing on to the deciduous shrubs we may as well pay tribute to our native evergreen Gladwin Iris (*Iris foetidissima*), whose orange-scarlet seeds in the buff pods lie amongst the dark green sword-like leaves. (A white-berried form is recorded but I have not grown it.) This is an even more accommodating plant than most irises, for it will thrive in dense shade as well as sun – in fact I think it prefers it. The form 'Citrina' is the most ornamental in flower, and it is recorded in Lynch's admirable volume, published long ago, *The Book of the Iris*. And in waste spots in full sun, where there are yards of room for its running roots, may be planted physalis – Chinese Lanterns, Cape Gooseberries, Winter Cherries, call them what you will; their tiers of orange-red 'lanterns' will light the ground on stems 2 to 3 feet in height. The most lavish and resplendent species is *Physalis franchetii*. It is a native of various countries from south-eastern Europe to Japan, whereas the true Cape Gooseberry (*P. peruviana*) is found in yet warmer parts. Quaint dwarfs and monstrous-fruited forms are for those with a taste for such things.

The deciduous shrubs do not provide us with many kinds retaining their fruits until December. At Christmas one favourite table decoration of mine is a combination of the flowers of *Prunus subhirtella* 'Autumnalis' with fruits of the best pink Snowberry – *Symphoricarpos* × *chenaultii*. This little-known hybrid between *S. microphyllus* and *S. orbiculatus* is a very graceful, tiny-leafed shrub, and its white fruits, the size of large peas, are so densely dotted with madder on the sunny side that they appear to be rose-pink. Contrary to the usual theories, symphoricarposes fruit best in full sun, although the common *S. albus* (*S. racemosus*) runs wild in dark hollows on chalky ground. The great, white, snow-like fruits of *S. albus* var. *laevigatus* (*S. rivularis*) are very beautiful during early winter, hanging in rope-like clusters on the over-weighted branches. They are all very easily grown shrubs and are apt to become a nuisance, since they tend to spread by suckers.

The late Mrs Constance Spry purchased many years ago at the Aldenham sale the entire stock of a seedling Snowberry. This is superlative in vigour, size of berry, and length of fruiting spray; 'ropes' over one foot long arching with their weight are common on good stiff soil. This was subsequently named 'Constance Spry' and distributed for the first time in 1959, and may probably be considered as a particularly good form of *Symphoricarpos albus* var. *laevigatus*. *S. orbiculatus* is rather dull, with twigs thickly clustered with crimson-purple fruits, but it is one of the species used by S.G. Doorenbos of The Hague to produce several valuable compact bushes of upright growth and few wide-ranging suckers, known as *S.* 'Doorenbos Hybrids'. 'White Hedge' describes itself by its name and will achieve 5 feet; 'Magic Berry' is much shorter, with rosy-lilac berries; 'Mother of Pearl' comes between the two in colour. Together the several kinds mentioned bring new tints, like those of the per-nettyas, into a field usually dominated by scarlet.

One of the most handsome combinations of berries is the white of the best Snowberry with the shining black of the Common Privet, *Ligustrum vulgare*. They are both found in quantity on our chalk hills, with the Spindle, Dogwood, 'Old Man's Beard', and viburnums. This Common Privet is a better plant, therefore, for chalky gardens than the much more commonly planted Japanese species, *L. ovalifolium*. Even this, when allowed to grow into a shrub, can be very noticeable on a winter's day, loaded with duller black berries and perhaps leafless on account of poorness of soil. Equally handsome is the uncommon *L. compactum* (*L. yunnanense*), again with dull berries of indigo or maroon colouring. All berrying shrubs are more prone to fruit heavily when somewhat starved and unpruned, although the health of the bush may thereby suffer.

A shrub that provides red currants in winter is *Ribes fasciculatum*; the transparent scarlet fruits stud the stems and can be attractive with the sun through them, but it is by no means a first-class shrub. For sheltered, semi-woodland conditions the violet-berried *Callicarpa*

Celastrus scandens

bodinieri (often called *C. giraiaiana*) is very beautiful; the tight clusters of small berries are something quite different from any other shrub and it is of small growth, up to some 6 feet, with lovely autumn colour of rosy-violet and bronze tinting. Among the several species of *Callicarpa*, some of which are tender, *C. dichotoma* does well at Kew, but I have not grown it. It has a similar beauty to *C. bodinieri* and like that species fruits well in certain years when fully established.

Those who admire the silvery beauty of the Traveller's Joy or Old Man's Beard on our chalk hills in winter should find a place for that superlative Chinese species *Clematis tangutica*, selecting *obtusiuscula*, which has stronger growth and plentiful flowers. The fluffy seed heads last well and are of a silkiness unknown in our native species. This is a fairly rampant climber, bearing yellow, bell-shaped flowers in July and August, while the *Celastrus*, our only other winter-fruiting climbing plant, has no beauty in flower. There are two principal species, *Celastrus orbiculatus* (by far the best) and *C. scandens*, for both of which two separate sexes are needed to ensure fruiting. *C. orbiculatus* has fortunately produced a hermaphrodite form. They are relatives of our native Spindle Tree, *Euonymus europaeus*, and have the same beauty of form in their fruits, the lobes yellow in the *Celastrus*, opening to show the orange-red seeds. These plants are vigorous twiners and the large trusses of berries remain in colour throughout the winter, on stump or tree or fence.

Elsewhere in these pages I have given my reasons for not using dead heads in this winter review. A possible exception might be found in the hydrangeas, mainly the Hortensia varieties of *Hydrangea macrophylla* and also *H. paniculata* with its variety 'Grandiflora'. The Hortensia varieties present wonderful tints in sheltered places, late flowers dying off in palest green and shot-shades, and the fully ripened heads remaining in fair condition through the winter in buff-brown. *H. serrata* 'Grayswood', one of the open-headed or normal types, is remarkable for the dark crimson tints of the ray-florets. But they do, of course, smack of the autumn and a dead or dying season and therefore should be used carefully and only occasionally with winter flowers. The same applies to all the other items in this chapter except those whose foliage may also be counted as a useful foil and adjunct. The berry is, after all, the crowning achievement of the season, and as such is perhaps well entitled to be included in a book of winter colour. The colour, the brightness, and the sense of completion of the year's efforts all add to what may be described as one of our main seasonal delights.

9. Rhododendrons

Flowers gather'd in this world, die here; if thou
Wouldst have a wreath that fades not, let them grow,
And grow for thee.

HENRY VAUGHAN (1622–1695)
from *The Garland*

No genus of plants has had so profound an effect upon the trend of gardening during the last eighty years as the rhododendron. In the days when labour was cheap the great garden owners planted hundreds of them, which now cover many acres of Surrey, Sussex, Hampshire, and sheltered areas from Cornwall to the north-west of Scotland. Now, when only the few can employ a gardener, the rhododendron, since the discovery of almost the entirety of its variations in the wild, has in many ways proved to be the most useful and valuable of all woody plants. To put its values in a few words, this genus provides us with tiny creeping shrublets to giant shrubs, even trees, and among them will be found species and garden forms which flower at different times from January to July and August, and also compete in beautiful leaves and bark with the best of the shrubs described in this book. A chapter to themselves is the least, therefore, that can be given them.

Although there are one or two species that can thrive on limy soil, it may generally be understood that a lime-free or acid soil of sandy, stony, or even a heavy loamy texture will suit them well so long as it is well laced with humus – be it bracken-peat, leaf-mould, very old well-rotted manure, granulated peat or garden compost. The drainage must be good, the soil never be bone-dry or waterlogged; the plants mostly enjoy sunshine broken by a light canopy of trees in our south-eastern counties at least, and appreciate shelter from cold winds. But they are not difficult to please so long as they are planted carefully. Their roots lift with a ball of soil, which should not be broken, but should be put in the allotted position, taking care that it be not deeper than in its original station. Many troubles, even death, may arise from planting too deeply. In dry, windy areas I prefer to plant 3 or 4 inches lower than usual, leaving a shallow basin above the plant to collect moisture and dead leaves – in fact this method will be found beneficial in many ways and on all of the drier soils.

The great company of large-flowered garden hybrids does not concern us here, for they flower in May and June and only a few are noted for interesting foliage; nor the hosts of garden azaleas, which are simply rhododendrons with five instead of ten stamens, and which flower at the same time and are mostly deciduous. Once again for our winter garden, we are confronted with just those wild shrubs of other countries which will best fit in with our semi-woodland or naturally arranged garden where the light shade of Autumn Cherry is the very thing for *Rhododendron leucaspis*, or the protection afforded by the equally thin covering of bare oak twigs will shelter *R.* Shilsonii; or, again, the wide verges of winter heaths in full sunshine will provide contrast and ground-cover for sun-lovers like *R.* Praecox.

During the last hundred or more years new species and geographical forms of rhododendrons have poured into this country, mainly from the Himalayas and allied mountain ranges of China and Tibet, providing us with the greatest influx of useful garden material we have ever known. Those who have been fortunate enough to see a large plant of *R. thomsonii* – or a group of them growing in natural grandeur as at Wisley and Leonardslee – will know their value when in winter their leaden green leaves contrast so well with the smooth 15-foot stems, softly coloured with bark of *bois-du-rose*, peeling in papery layers. Or later, when spring is coming, and, hung with translucent bells of fiery crimson, their colour seems to *sound* through the garden, so clangorous is this sudden awakening to the full tones of the dazzling garden year. Also with beautiful bark of similar colouring are several tender species such as the magnificent *R. griffithianum* (*R. aucklandii*) and *R. auritum*; considerably hardier are some members of the Barbatum Series, and especially *R. barbatum* itself, which I shall mention again on account of its early flowers.

But it is as foliage plants in particular and flowering plants as a secondary consideration that rhododendrons enter into these pages and, indeed, into any garden. Their value is immense, not only in their varied attractions but also because of the solidity of the bushes, which at once places them right in the forefront of useful evergreens, along with bamboos, laurels and camellias, with which they make pleasing contrasts.

The species rhododendrons, by which term I intend to embrace also the newer hybrids closely related to them, give us many with foliage richly aromatic. Most of them are little bushes of 1 to 4 feet in height and as much or more wide, covered with a dense array of small leaves which in winter take on grey, purple, bronzy and other tones to their soft green, and may be dull or glossy. *R. saluenense* has forms which combine purplish colouring with a glossy texture and are very interesting when contrasted with *Erica herbacea* 'Springwood White' or the glaucous trails of *Euphorbia myrsinites*; while grey-green is found in *Rhododendron hippophaeoides* forms, specially that known as 'Haba Shan' or 'Sunningdale'. Good forms of *R. impeditum* turn to dark violet-grey. These are all for the sunny foreground and the colour they give later is as rewarding as anything in the garden; their names will be found mainly under the Saluenense and Lapponicum Series, and their flowers range from white through pale yellow to rose, plum, purple, violet and lavender-blue, a galaxy of tones and shapes from flowers borne singly and in tiny trusses from March to June. With them I would grow the evergreen Kurume azalea, 'Hino-Mayo', for its greenery of almost lettuce-freshness, and the Kirishima azaleas (*R. kiusianum*).

Rather larger are several of the Sanguineum Series such as *R. dichroanthum apodectum*, whose glossy leaves, 2 to 3 inches long, are arranged in close rosettes. The unique *R. lepidostylum* is at its best in summer, when the young leaves are a remarkable, almost turquoise-tinted, grey-green, and each is edged with a regular neat array of short hairs. Much of this pristine beauty wears off by midwinter, but enough colour and interest remain to remind us of its extraordinary beauty. The Thomsonii Series gives us some fine foliage plants, mostly showing the rounded, grey-green, smooth leaves of *R. thomsonii* itself, with palest green undersides; fortunately they are in the highest class for flowers later and among them are numbered such famous shrubs as *R. callimorphum*, *campylocarpum*, *caloxanthum*, *wardii*, *soulei* and the much smaller *williamsianum*. A species in the Fortunei Series, but still in the same style, is *R. obiculare*, with wide discs of grey-green, waxy smooth. *R. fortunei* itself is much larger, with attractive purple leaf stalks and buds. With these may be grouped the larger yet slender wiry bushes of *R. cinnabarinum*, and *R.c.* var. *roylei*, and the related *R. concatenans*, the best form of which is from the original collection of Kingdon Ward. All bear small, rounded, grey-green leaves and are in the Cinnabarinum Series.

R. concatenans with *R. lepidostylum* are my two prime favourites in this special grey-green beauty class. Another unique Fortunei Series is *R. vernicosum*, a shining 'varnished' type whose surface is a splendid contrast to the waxen or matt finish of the majority. Some very slow-growing species of the Taliense Series, *R. roxieanum* and *R. pro-teoides*, are quite hardy and are of great beauty; their under-felting alone gives them a special interest. Compact bushes with small leaves are found in the Glaucophyllum Series; among them I would choose *R. charitopes* for its beautiful later flowers and the white undersides to the aromatic leaves.

Few would recognize *R. ponticum*, often naturalized in our native woodland, as the donor of distinguished foliage colour, yet it has through closely related species and even a variety a claim for inclusion. The variety is the purple-leaved *R.p.* 'Foliis Purpureis'. This, at Kew, in winter, is an outstanding plant and is as rich in tone as *Bergenia purpurascens*, with its dark plum-coloured leaves. It amazes me how this plant can have existed unnoticed in our leading garden without recognition of its undoubted value for our winter plantings. I have had a plant for many years and have recently given away grafting scions and cuttings to enthusiasts. It is interesting to note that in 1895 William Paul of Cheshunt, the famous rose grower, received a First Class Certificate for *R. ponticum foliis purpureis*. Presumably it was the same plant. There are several forms of the Ponticum Series such as *R. degronianum, hyp-erythrum* and *makinoi*, whose rolled – or quilled – leaves in winter have a special contrasting value. *R. makinoi* crossed with *R. discolor* has produced 'Ninette'; this was raised by J. B. Stevenson and is not in general cultivation, but on going round the wonderful collection at Tower Court with my friend James Russell, whose insight into these species is remarkable, I was struck by this plant's decorative quality. The yellow twigs and yellow leaf stalks seemed to merit consideration, for they were as noticeable as those of a *Daphniphyllum* at the 'dead' season of the year.

Most of the Tower Court Collection has been planted in Windsor Great Park and the change of soil and greater space given to each plant provides the rhododendron student with a wonderful picture of this great genus. For in Windsor Park the broken canopy of foliage and the

resources at command provide conditions for creeping species such as
R. repens, in rich green, through the types I have mentioned to the
great-leafed species of the Far East. Species with very long leaves are
found in the Fortunei Series; *R. calophytum* has grey-green blades a
foot in length, and *R. sutchuenense* leaves slightly less. With
R. auriculatum they provide us with some of the most handsome of
evergreen shrubs or small trees, with interesting bark colours and a
line and poise of unequalled quality among the inhabitants of our
gardens.

The size of a paddle, the enormous leaves of *R. sinogrande* and
R. falconeri are almost unbelievable. A related species is *R. fictolacteum*
– both Forrest's fine form with the orange indumentum beneath the
leaves, and Kingdon Ward's with fawn indumentum; the latter has
now been given specific rank with the name *R. rex*. These are the
hardiest of the big-leafed species and can be tried with likely success in
most gardens. *RR. basilicum, hodgsonii* and *macabeanum* are other notable big-leafed species, all with their own special character and poise,
the last named being usually the first to flower. They are notable not
only for their leaves but for their often lustrous, purplish bark. It is,
unfortunately, only those with sheltered woodlands in Surrey who
can grow these successfully; for their true grandeur we must go to
richly wooded Sussex, or better still, to the coombs of Cornwall,
Ireland, and the luxurious west coast of Scotland. Nothing that we can
grow in this country short of a tree fern, palm or hardy banana, can
give quite such an overpowering, exotic touch as these wonderful
trees – for they can scarcely be called shrubs – their blades of lustrous
or leathery texture hanging at a gentle angle in great rosettes. Looking
down upon them is a privilege accorded to few of us, but I cannot
imagine anything more satisfying, especially when each rosette is set
with a great crown of milky or pale yellow blooms. But we can all
look up to them, and then a further beauty is apparent: to reduce their
transpiration these lovers of moisture cover the undersurfaces of their
leaves with a thick indumentum, mentioned above, in some of grey-
white and others a rusty brown.

But we cannot, many of us, find room in our gardens even for one
of these giants, and it is comforting to know that this third great
attraction is found also in many smaller species. I would choose the
best type of *R. fulvum*, whose undersides are of vivid red-brown
and soft as a piece of chamois leather; or perhaps the 'Knap Hill'

R. campanulatum, *R. fulgens*, glossy *R. bureavii*, and the neat *R. mallotum*, while that other treasure *R. yakushimanum* is nearly white in its covering beneath, later turning to cinnamon brown.

And so we find beauty of bark and leaf, coupled with a variety of tones on the surfaces of the latter, all at our command although we are only considering them in winter. How much greater are their attractions when the young leaves appear, often encased in scarlet bracts, and unfolding from a grey-white shuttlecock growth, in such marked contrast with the dark leaves of the previous year!

The above paragraphs record at least my own favourites among the species for stem and leaf effect in winter; many others are of equal though perhaps less striking beauty.

In mild weather from Christmas onwards we may expect the early-flowering rhododendrons to start opening their blooms. Flowering as they do during the first six months of the year, they should be considered as spring-flowering rather than winter-flowering, but many are constant to the first two months of the year and, so I feel, merit inclusion, although their tender petals are destroyed by a few degrees of frost. Luckily they all open well and last in water, and at the approach of frost a few sprays or twigs will add cheer to winter indoors. I find it well worth the risk, however, to grow *R. dauricum* and *R. mucronulatum* for their frail blooms. The former is of rather upright and slender growth and is partially evergreen, while the latter is more rounded but deciduous, and both bear small, magenta–pink blooms singly or in clusters of two or three, making an airy display. I should choose *R. mucronulatum* on account of its better habit and larger, more freely produced flowers; in fact it is one of our very best winter-flowering shrubs. Two excellent forms have been selected at Windsor; both have received a First Class Certificate from the Royal Horticultural Society at January or February shows; they are *R. dauricum* 'Midwinter' and *R. mucronulatum* 'Winter Brightness'. They are of good bushy habit, free flowering and of rich colouring. Both species have white forms which contrast well, and from Cornell University in the United States comes 'Cornell Pink', a selection of *R. mucronulatum* with flowers of clear bright pink. This has also been accorded a First Class Certificate and was raised from seeds collected in Japan. Belonging to the Dauricum Series, all of these are good, thrifty garden plants for sun or shade.

R. dauricum has united with *R. ciliatum*, giving us the hybrid *R.* Praecox, one of the best of early March-flowering shrubs, but often opening in February. The glossy, fragrant leaves are borne freely, and it makes a splendid hedge. All these reach up to some 6 feet in time, but are very effective while small and are comparatively slow-growing. A few weeks earlier we may expect 'Olive' to flower (*R. dauricum* × *R. moupinense*); it is like *R.* Praecox but is taller with larger paler flowers and larger leaves – a useful companion for Witch Hazels.

R. Praecox and its parent *R. ciliatum* are perhaps rather late-flowering for our purpose, but the latter has given us another excellent garden hybrid, *R.* Cilpinense, a cross, as its name suggests, with *R. moupinense*. Cilpinense, as usually grown, is a very free and pretty shrub up to about 4 feet high and wide, with glistening flowers of

Rhododendron dauricum

Rhododendron Praecox

white, tinted pink in the bud. But it may very well be raised again, using one of the most richly rosy of *R. moupinense* forms, in which case a range of colouring may be expected. These are all suitable for sheltered positions, delighting in thin woodland, and are among the most beautiful of early flowers. Here I will include the showy hybrid 'Tessa' (*R.* Praecox × *moupinense*) which was raised at Tower Court, and charmingly unites its parents into a good compact and free-flowering shrub, producing masses of frilly lilac-rose blooms, and inheriting the coppery bark of *R. moupinense*. *R.* Multiflorum is a free-flowering hybrid between *R. ciliatum* and *R. virgatum*, with the latter's growth, and soft blush-pink flowers freely studded along the young shoots.

Although *R. moupinense* is not in the same series as *R. ciliatum* there is a distinctive family resemblance, I feel, between the two, and also with *R. leucaspis*. They all have glossy yet ciliate leaves and glistening, mainly white, but often pink-tinted blooms, while *R. moupinense* has also provided us with a beautiful rosy-pink form. *R. leucaspis* has great

Rhododendron moupinense

character and its chocolate-brown anthers – tubular-shaped as in all rhododendrons, and from which the strings of pollen exude at a touch when ripe – are not the least of its attractions. The dome-shaped bushes, 3 or 6 feet across in sheltered gardens, are well covered with medium-sized, dark, brownish-green leaves, and the flowers, wide open, of creamy-white, are usually generously displayed in February and early March. The late Lord Aberconway raised a series of dainty rhododendrons of the above species together with *R. valentinianum* and *R. chrysodoron*. They bear hybrid names but are little known at present, and I have no first-hand experience of them; they are rather tender. *R. leucaspis* has, however, given us a very free and pretty hybrid, with *R. moupinense*, named 'Bric-a-Brac', and this embodies the crystalline white and dark anthers of the one with the rich tinting in the bud of the other parent. It is likely to become popular. Another, 'Silkcap', raised at Windsor is equally desirable. A Cornish hybrid, 'Golden Oriole', is a hybrid of *R. moupinense* and *R. sulfureum*; the result is a brilliant yellow flower, opening in February as a rule at Windsor; it has the added attraction of richly coloured bark.

One of the most regular of early species is *R. parvifolium*. An old plant in the Botanic Garden at Cambridge attained nearly to 3 feet, although its conditions were hardly congenial. It grew in full sun for

Rhododendron parvifolium

many years, in soil which, though originally peaty, must have become impregnated with lime, and made a twiggy little bush with small, dark, aromatic leaves. The small, dark magenta blooms appeared regularly in January and February and it should be borne in mind that they are fragrant. A white form is also recorded. This little shrub might well become better known if its values were better understood; it is the only early-flowering member of the Lapponicum Series that I know, apart from the dense, dwarf *R. intricatum*. This studs its dull grey-green hummocks in February and March with cool, pale lilac blooms, and is a miniature suitable for the rock garden and similar positions.

Many species of the Triflorum Series are among the most hardy and free-flowering of all, and I need only cite *R. yunnanense*, which surely has a very certain future in our gardens, for an example. *R. lutescens*, its close relative, is hardy in many forms, but the Exbury variety, which received a First Class Certificate in 1938, needs a little more shelter, such as that afforded by thin woodland. From February to April, according to the season, its primrose-yellow butterfly-like blooms may be expected in quantity, and it gives a dainty spring-like effect on a shrub both wiry and open in growth, semi-evergreen, up to 6 or 8 feet high and wide. 'Bo-Peep' is a charming hybrid midway in flower (palest yellow) and foliage and growth between its parents, which are *R. lutescens* and *R. moupinense*. Another small flowered hybrid is 'Crossbill', uniting the good points of *R. spinuliferum* and *R. lutescens*. Giving bright pink from clusters of strange little tubular blooms are *R. scabrifolium* and *R. spiciferum*. The latter is the more brilliant and hardy, but both are rather far removed in quality of bloom from what we expect from the genus, although reliable in so far as their freedom and time of flowering are concerned.

All the above are shrubs of light appearance and lack the heavy layers of foliage which are so apparent in the older, well-known May- and June-flowering garden hybrids.

Fortunately for our present purpose there are a few species and near crosses of the heaviest calibre, but all need, and in fact deserve and demand, some shelter. I well remember visiting Tower Court and Exbury in a favourable February and being astounded by the brilliant spectacle given by early *R. arboreum* forms, towering aloft in leafy pyramids, splashed with vivid crimson and pink flowers to 30 feet or more. In many a western garden – at Killerton, Devon, and in Cornwall, at Muncaster and in Western Scotland, to say nothing of Ireland where Lady Londonderry's avenue at Mount Stewart comes to mind, and at Castlewellan – these great Arboreum Series rhododendrons dominate many a fine vista early in the year, as few other shrubs can. But they need the shelter of neighbouring trees; here in Surrey they are only a success in very sheltered conditions and are better in the great favoured gardens of the Sussex Weald. Also in the Arboreum Series, *R. rirei* gives a pleasant change of colour; the trusses of soft purple flowers are very effective.

The Barbatum Series provides species of even more brilliant colouring. The giant *R. barbatum* itself and the smaller *R. smithii*, together with *R. strigillosum*, are both very rich in their intense red, glistening trumpets and dark hairy leaves. These again need the shelter of woodland.

Perhaps the most majestic and sumptuous of these tall-growing, early-flowering red rhododendrons is *R. thomsonii*. We have already given it high marks for foliage and bark; its blooms are of a waxy, dusky red of quite indescribable intensity, hung with a lovely poise among the lead-green, smooth, rounded leaves. Truly is this a shrub of majesty, up to 12 or 14 feet, and as such deserves every care in its placing. Fortunately it is hardy in Surrey in woodland areas and I know of few more satisfying sights than its blooms when lit by the sun. And even when the great red bells have fallen, the fascinating pale green or flesh-coloured calyces stare at one with all the impudent air of flowers that know very well they are *not* flowers! But the plants have a very long season of floral beauty thereby, and Thomson's rhododendron has transmitted this useful trait to several of its progeny. Even more intensely coloured is *R. hookeri*, bearing equally good leaves with characteristic curved barbs or bristles on the veins underneath. It is less hardy, but both this and *R. meddianum* flower earlier than *R. thomsonii*, while another near relative, *R. cyanocarpum*, is, in its best form, pure white; all have the beautiful lead-green leaves of Thomson's species.

Rather smaller-growing are two woodlanders in this series, with yellow flowers. *R. stewartianum* and *R. eclecteum* both vary from pink through white to this welcome spring colour, and personally I should always set aside others in preference to a good yellow. They reach to 7 feet in height and their foliage is in pleasing contrast.

Fortunately *R. thomsonii* has produced some fine hybrids; with *R. barbatum* it gives us *R.* Shilsonii, which leans heavily to the beauty of the first parent, and 'Cornubia', 'Red Admiral' and 'Alix' are equally fine plants and grew well at Exbury; they are the result of crosses with allied species. Unfortunately, their parentage does not permit them to be hardy everywhere. Very startling in its brilliant red was 'Choremia' (*R. arboreum* × *R. haematodes*) at an early February Show, while 'Titness Park' (*R. barbatum* × *R. calophytum*) is an outstanding deep rose.

Two species in the Fortunei Series which I noted for the grandeur of their fine long leaves are *R. sutchuenense* and the magnificent *R. calophytum*. Both of these flower in February and March, having trusses of blush-white or pale lilac fragrant blooms. *R. fortunei* itself and *R. oreodoxa* and *R. fargesii* are three others of these cool-coloured large shrubs or small trees with strikingly poised leaves. Here I must mention the beautiful hybrid Carex (*R. irroratum* × *R. fargesii*), a handsome shrub with fine foliage and blush bells fading to white and spotted with chocolate inside.

These noble rhododendrons have all set new standards among the specialists of the genus in recent decades. Their striking foliage, the arrangement of the flowers in loose trusses, and their often waxy or glistening texture, set them well apart from the accepted floral style of ordinary hybrid varieties which are seen in quantity in our parks and gardens in May and June. It is, however, good to know that this last group, deriving their stamina almost entirely from species of the Ponticum Series, have something to show us in the very early year. *R. caucasicum* when crossed with *R. arboreum* gives us the Nobleanum family – rosy-red in that known as 'Coccineum', a clear and lovely pink in 'Venustum', and 'Album' white, opening from pink buds. They all bear dull green leaves backed with brown, denoting *R. arboreum* hybridity; need sheltered or semi-woodland conditions and slowly reach 6 feet or more. Crossed again with *R. caucasicum*, this same hybrid produced *R.* 'Jacksonii', a very useful and free-flowering hybrid with rosy-red flowers and low bushy habit; in the Savill Gardens Nobleanum types have been used freely to give warm colour to the Autumn Cherry, and seldom a January or February passes without their adding rich colour to the glade.

Two other pretty named forms which belong here are 'Christmas Cheer' and 'Rosa Mundi', and both produce blush-pink blooms in tight trusses over domes of dull green leaves, slowly spreading and reaching to 5 or 6 feet. Both of these and *R.* 'Jacksonii' are perfectly hardy in the open here and regularly greet us with flowers during February, or as soon as the weather permits.

I have done little more than make a cursory survey of rhododendrons that appeal to me, and no doubt there are many others that deserve attention. However, in the foregoing paragraphs will be found, I think the bulk of the earliest-flowering species and hybrids and the few words of description accorded to each will possibly lead some gardeners to delve more deeply in the quest for colour in January and February, although in backward years and districts many may not open until March. All the plants I have mentioned are hardy in sheltered woodland conditions and many of them thrive in the open in Surrey; my area is a hard and inhospitable place for many of these children of humid mountain-sides, where the undergrowth and trees create a sheltering company which it is hard to imitate in an open garden, subjected as we are so often to perishing winds in spring and torrid heat in summer.

The flowers of rhododendrons are among the most beautiful of all that we grow. They have charm in their often nodding shape – for I always feel that a nodding flower has much more charm than one that looks one in the face with a bold upturned eye. Their glistening texture – even in the most modest of them – is something that is rare in flowers, and the dainty spottings and rich colour in the throats of some of them are extremely winning. Often dark-coloured anthers give a distinctive contrast. Very few of these early species have any fragrance; but there is a fragrance of a rare order in later-flowering species; in fact some have both the scent and the shape of lilies: little more could be asked of them.

Yet with all their glory the greater rhododendrons' prime value in the garden is in their leaves; as I have mentioned, they are among our most telling and heavy evergreens for shaping the garden. All those fortunate gardeners who have suitable soil and conditions have such a variety to choose from that the task becomes at times very involved. During this century hundreds of packets of seeds from our famous collectors abroad have been raised, adding species to species and form to form, until, were it not for the industry of the Rhododendron Association – now merged into the Rhododendron Group of The Royal Horticultural Society – and their admirable handbook, it would be bewildering indeed to make a choice. The handbook, revised in 1980 through the industry of Dr Alan Leslie at Wisley and taking full account of work done at Edinburgh, does, however, solve many problems and elucidate many parentages and pedigrees. We thus have a great genus well sorted and organized, ready to face the whole-sale hybridization which is going on today. In time to come the records of these early crosses will assume a greater significance. It only remains for the public to be adamant in their quest for plants propagated vegetatively from only the best stock.

With the welter of hybrids being raised it is a comforting thought that only some of them will equal their parents in general excellence. They may, however, be steps towards a horticultural ideal. We may often be greatly struck with the beauty of a new seedling only to realize its shortcomings when assessing its values over the years. This does not apply only to rhododendrons, and we plant-lovers, on contemplating a species, must often be ready to hand the palm to Dame Nature.

10. Herbaceous Plants

I praise the tender flower,
That on a mournful day
Bloomed in my garden bower
And made the winter gay.

ROBERT BRIDGES (1844–1930)

Our title is somewhat ambiguous, for very few of the plants in this chapter are what one would expect to find in the modern herbaceous border, but it must obviously stand. We will allow it to embrace evergreen and deciduous plants excluding bulbs and corms and tubers, but including a few woody alpines and tiny shrubs.

Seldom a November passes without frost, but when a few weeks of mild weather do linger with us the violas, particularly the brilliant yellow 'Bullion', the winter pansies, and sometimes violets appear. The most floriferous of this breed is *Viola florariensis*, that pretty little naturalizer which is named after the late Henri Correvon's garden near Geneva. It is a fixed hybrid of *V. calcarata* and, seeding itself about rock garden or border in any light soil, is in flower from March to December. Every 'face' has an expression of its own. I have not seen it for many years and should like to acquire it again. The winter pansies, in many good seedsmen's strains, are lovely velvety things in a variety of colours and need no special care beyond good cultivation. Among native violets the pale 'St Hélèna' and that charmer in soft rosy colour 'St Anne's', may be planted amongst the common *V. odorata* and its dainty relative in white *V. alba* from South Europe at the foot of hedges and amongst deciduous shrubs, where the low winter sun will warm them in sheltered spots. Their occasional late blooms will be followed in a mild February by many more.

The winter garden is an appropriate place for colonies of wild primrose and the hybrids of the 'Juliana' class, for the latest and earliest days of the year seldom pass without odd blooms poking forth from the mats of knobby buds and leaves. One of the most constant is the

Primula edgworthii

well-known 'Wanda', and also *Primula acaulis sibthorpii*, the eastern European pink variant of our common primrose; it is often found labelled *P. altaica* or *P. sibthorpii*. This is a bright little plant which flowers at odd times in November and during mild spells onwards, but its main flush is in March and April. Then its multitudes of light lilac-pink blooms are a real delight.

Presuming that a lime-free, cool slope of the rock garden is within reach of our planting space, we must pay passing tribute to the Himalayan primulus, harbingers, like our own primrose, of the spring, but frequently producing early blooms in February. Chief among these is *P. edgworthii* (formerly known as *P. winteri*) whose white-powdered pale green leaves form such a perfect rosette-foil for the rich lilac blooms with white and yellow eyes. A varying combination of rosy mauve and pale green runs through the species; *P. bracteosa*, *P. boothii*, *P. gracilipes*, and *P. wightii* are all worthy of the best care and attention, and with them I would try to place *P. edgworthii* 'Alba' for the sake of its pure and beautiful flowers, dead white with a dark yellow eye. They cannot tolerate excess of wet in their crowns in winter and depend upon good loam and humus for their well-being. *P. megaseifolia* may be tried with them for the sake of its rich lilac-crimson tubular cowslip blooms. But these are all, I repeat, to be cosseted in the south and cannot be relied upon for general garden embellishment. They are queens of the primrose tribe and as such deserve all homage, when growing well out of doors. In the south of the country this is not often possible; they love the cool, damp air of the West and North, where whole banks and borders are covered with them in the gardens of their devotees.

While dealing with these oddments we must remember chrysan-themums. Some of the very old garden favourites are a wonderful sight in November and can be relied upon year after year to flower well in between the frosts, but the same cannot be said for the Korean varieties, which seem to be only half perennial. At the same time I feel that, flowering though they do within the period we have set for our winter, they are so reminiscent of autumn that they are not quite at home. Much the same may be said of the Michaelmas Daisy *Aster pilosus* var. *demotus* (*A. tradescantii* of gardens). This is a genuine November-flowering plant and for garden or room decoration I know of few plants of greater delicacy, yet sturdy and independent of winds. The stems are exceptionally wiry and support a gypsophila-like cloud of tiny pure white daisies with yellow eyes in fine sprays. It is a woody little plant up to 4 feet in height and increases very slowly. For a November group in the garden a few clumps of this with some bright berrying shrubs can be very satisfying. *Ionopsidium acaule*, an annual plant which, if sown in autumn, will cover its 1-inch high greenery in mild winters with multitudes of tiny pale lilac stars, is most at home in a sheltered nook on the rock garden.

For late autumn we have *Polygala chamaebuxus* var. *grandiflora* (*P.c.* var. *purpurea*), an alpine shrublet forming a neat dome of box-like leaves, some 6 inches high, studded all over in November and April with typical milkwort flowers of dark yellow and magenta; a strange combination to some eyes but very common in nature. The floral beauty of this little plant is not of great garden value, but its scent reminds one of gorse and vanilla. It likes a cool humus-laden soil such as one would provide for rhododendrons.

Another plant which fits in well with the above is *Liriope muscari* (also known as *Liriope graminifolium* var. *densiflorum* and *Ophiopogon muscari* and *Dracaena graminfolia*), a Japanese plant frequently seen in conservatories. Not one whit abashed by the bounty bestowed upon it by the botanists, this little plant, some 12 inches high, grows well out of doors in Surrey in warm sunny places and its spikes of tightly packed violet flowers emerge from the grassy tufts in November. There is a charming variegated form whose leaves are striped with cream. At Wallington this is used as a pot plant to bring indoors in autumn. Near these I should group another Japanese, the remarkable *Saxifraga fortunei*, whose lovely fleshy lobed leaves are tinted with browns and reds and contrast strongly with the delicate panicles of tiny cream flowers. Highly susceptible to frost at flowering time, this plant is worth waiting for yearly in the hope that its blooms will remain unhurt. It thrives best in half shade with plenty of humus. Fine forms are available.

The saxifrages form an accommodating family and if a trough garden can be happily placed near our winter flowers let *S. kellereri* be planted generously upon it. This is, year after year, the first saxifrage to flower, usually in January, and its croziers of pink blooms on sticky 3-inch stems above the grey rosettes are a very beautiful sight. Though now placed in a separate genus the saxifrages of the Megasea group are noble relatives of these little alpines and in our foliage chapter *Bergenia purpurascens* has been extolled. There are others with even more handsome foliage, though not so richly coloured; and among these I would choose the Western Himalayan *B. ligulata*, seldom without flowers in February, and the fragrant garden hybrid *B. × schmidtii*, a much hardier and more common plant. Among its big leathery 9-inch leaves are found the heads of light pink, fragrant flowers, often in January. The Himalayan is smaller, having blush-white golden-eyed blooms arrayed with great charm in rosy-red calyces. These are best grown among shrubs for shelter.

Towards the end of January the pulmonarias raise their hairy stalks from the woody mass of winter buds on the ground, and give us vivid blue or pink blooms to greet the forsythias. These Lungworts in some kinds have spotted leaves and flowers of varying tints (both in regard to the variety and the age of each flower) from salmon-rose to dark blue. In many January and February days I have had *P. saccharata* (*P. picta*) and *P. rubra* in flower. The former has pink and blue crozier heads of flowers and its early display is followed by long, spear-shaped, magnificent bristly leaves, heavily blotched with grey-white

Saxifraga kellereri

– a treasure for foliage effect for the rest of the growing season. The common species, *P. officinalis*, also known as 'Soldiers and Sailors' and 'Spotted Dog', has more distinctly heart-shaped leaves, less spotted, and is inferior in garden value. *P. rubra* has, like *P. saccharata*, long narrow leaves, but of plain fresh green, while its flowers are of bright coral-pink or terracotta. These all are thrifty, spreading plants for cool, shady positions, where the soil remains just moist without being wet. In these conditions good foliage may be expected through the summer and autumn until really hard frosts arrive. They are of such simple needs that they may be confidently planted under any deciduous tree, where they will be more or less evergreen.

No chapter on these plants would be complete without reference to that dreadful weed *Petasites fragrans*, a Coltsfoot with running underground ramifications such as would break the spirit of any tidy-minded gardener. Even so, before its large, rounded leaves cover all the ground in a dense shade, the hairy, short flower stems do bear

Petasites fragrans

charming daisy blooms in soft mauve and cream tints, beset with stamens and with a fragrance which justly has earned it the title of Winter Heliotrope. It is best to get a neighbour – at least three doors away – to grow it for you! If February is very mild *P. japonicus* rears its round heads of cream daisies from the bare soil surrounded by a toby-frill of palest green bracts. It has enormous umbrella-like leaves later, but is a running, coarse plant and not easily kept in check: a smaller relative is the species *P. albus*. It is a pity our native Coltsfoot (*Tussilago farfara*) is such a vigorous weed; in late February or early March there is no more beautiful roadside patch than its clusters of brilliant yellow, small dandelions on their short stalks. Unfortunately it can only be trusted in the wildest parts of the wild garden.

This brings us to Ranunculaceae, that most diverse of families for our gardens. The celandines belong to this family, likewise hepaticas and hellebores. The Lesser Celandine – to differentiate it from the Greater Celandine, a totally distinct plant belonging to the Poppy Family – bespangles the ground during February and March with its shining, starry yellow flowers and clumps of rich, fresh green leaves. It is a pernicious weed in many a garden and a delight, as often as not; and may often be found in copses and hedgerows where the ground is reasonably moist. I would not mention it here except for its varieties *Ranunculus ficaria* 'Aurantiacus' and 'Primrose', in orange and lemon respectively, and some double forms, which may merit inclusion for the sake of their present rarity. These special forms do not spread themselves with anything like the prolificity of the native species. Their larger relatives the adonises are very early starters, too, and *Adonis volgensis* annually appears on a shady slope of the Wisley rock garden in February. The glazed yellow buttercup blooms are prettily set in very much divided foliage.

Adonis volgensis

Hepatica nobilis

There is a sweet charm about all hepaticas; perhaps it is their meek little blooms, nodding at night, nestling under the leathery leaves of last summer. Of the anemone persuasion, the leaves may be rounded or lobed like an ivy's. The clumps, thriving best in shade in retentive soils with a cool root run and greatly fostered by lumps of stone on the surface, throw up quantities of leaves on their 3- to 4-inch stalks, and seldom a February departs without a few blooms heralding the main display in March. *Hepatica nobilis* (*Anemone hepatica*) gives us blooms in pastel shades of blue, pink and white, and doubles also in these tints. The double pink is a fairly common plant, the double blue far less often seen, while the white is a great rarity, but I cannot say that any have the beauty of the singles, with their tufts of powdery stamens. *H. nobilis* is a native of some parts of Central and Northern Europe, and has white filaments to its stamens; *H. transsilvanica* (*H. angulosa*) has blue filaments, toothed involucre, and more elaborately shaped leaves, and grows wild only in Hungary. Again available in the three colours, this is a larger-flowered kind and various special forms are offered, but I do not think it is so amenable in cultivation. The most lovely of all is the late Ernest Ballard's *H.* × *media* 'Ballard's Variety', a hybrid between the two above species and superior in vigour, foliage and size of flower, without having lost any of the charm or beauty of its parents. The wide, powder-blue blooms are borne on 5-inch stalks and last well in water. This is a most beautiful plant and thrives in sunless corners. It lasts in flower for many weeks and is unsurpassed in its bland, cool tint by any flower of spring.

My attention has been drawn by Professor W.T. Stearn to an amusing little point among the welter of botanical matter surrounding the nomenclature of the *Hepatica* breed. It appears that the correct name of the *Angulosa hepatica* is *Hepatica transsilvanica*, and the old combinations *Anemone* or *Hepatica angulosa* are now obsolete. 'Angulosa' was a descriptive name published in 1783 by the botanist Lamarck; his description, it was found later, was based upon a Herbarium sheet bearing a flower of the common blue *Hepatica nobilis* and a leaf of *Cortusa matthioli*!

Another member of Ranunculaceae is *Pulsatilla vulgaris*, better known as *Anemone pulsatilla*, our native Pasque Flower. In the majority of its forms, passing through all colours from white to pink, to purple and pale lavender, it flowers too late for our purpose. But my cherished plants of the Budapest form, a kind gift of the late Hew Dalrymple, flowered more or less regularly in February or very early March. This is a stately form reaching a foot in height, set with the characteristic downy hairs on finely divided leaf and stem; the flowers are large and starry, opening flat, and in the best tinted forms are of a clear, spode blue, offset by yellow stamens. Truly this is a plant which will be much sought when it becomes known, for it is at home on rock garden or border so long as the drainage is good. Every year I feel it to be one of the supreme moments when its exquisite blooms greet the pale sun. This was written for the first edition of this book. Alas! I have lost my plants and have not seen this lovely form since; it is the spode-blue or even forget-me-not colouring that has gone, I fear, and needs introducing again.

Lastly, the hellebores form by far the largest and most handsome group of winter-flowering herbaceous plants. Throughout the genus there is a wonderful quality of sculptured perfection and classic poise both of leaf and flower. They are conveniently grouped into two main sections, the one whose flowers and leaves grow annually from the

Helleborus niger

base, and the other in which they are borne from a woody stem produced during the previous summer. All kinds like a little shade and shelter from wind, and they will also thrive in sunless positions. They are gross feeders and amply repay a generous dressing of old manure in late spring to help them to build up again for the next flowering season, for they all flower from December to April.

Usually the first, frequently opening in late November, is the well-known old garden favourite the Christmas Rose, *Helleborus niger*, a native of Southern European and Western Asian districts. This stalwart belongs to the first section and the big, dark green, fingered leaves on their red stalks lie around the rising stems in the centre of the clump, each of which bears a sumptuous, pure white bloom with a cluster of yellow stamens, green nectaries, and stigmas in the centre. This, I suppose, is our prime winter flower and it withstands the frost as well as any. It is very difficult to ascertain which is the finest form to plant. I do not recall seeing any form that could not be considered beautiful, but some do undoubtedly have very large flowers with broad, overlapping segments, often tinged with pink outside, and these I believe should be called *H. niger*. Thousands of the species are raised annually from seed by nurserymen and very good strains are usually obtainable. 'St Brigid' is a famous old variety, found many years ago – so the late George M. Taylor recorded – in an old castle in County Cork, Eire. Mr Taylor, a noted authority on these plants, raised a form of great excellence from 'St Brigid', which he named 'St Margaret'; I wonder whether either are still growing in any gardens in the north. *H.n.* var. *macranthus* (*H.n.* var. *altifolius*) is another fine form, which has very large flowers often rosy-tinted outside. The leaves stand well aloft in this form from Greece and Italy. All kinds of *H. niger* have very dark green leaves.

Personally, I should like to select my 'Christmas roses' in flower, and should endeavour to pick those with the delightful, warm, rosy flush on the outside of the flowers which are frequently found. The best forms bear two or even three flowers on one stem when established. Perhaps the finest, with noble pink-flushed flowers, was raised at Cambridge and named 'Louis Cobbett'.

The next best-known hellebore is the 'Lenten Rose', generally known in gardens as *H. orientalis*, whose varied flowers of dusky greens and wine colours, creams and rosy tints, are borne on branching stems up to 18 inches. But before discussing the garden varieties let us look at some botanical variants.

A very uncommon hellebore, sometimes described as a variant of *H. orientalis*, but by other authors given specific rank, is *H. kochii*. This is certainly very near to *H. orientalis* from the gardener's point of view; the leaves are similar but more coarsely toothed, and the flowers are of similar shape and borne in the same graceful sprays, but open much flatter, like a saucer instead of a cup. It is the unique colour and the flowering period, however, that matter most to me, for they are almost yellow and appear in January as regularly as the Christmas Roses. A clump a foot across is a lovely sight; dozens of buds in palest green open to a soft and delicate pale yellow-green, almost primrose colour. My own introduction to this plant was over fifty years ago and I call my particular plant 'Bowles' Yellow', after the donor. Sir Cedric Morris introduced and raised some good creamy yellows and lately Mrs Helen Ballard of Colwall, Malvern, has raised a mass of superb forms and hybrids including yellows. With *H. kochii*, soon after

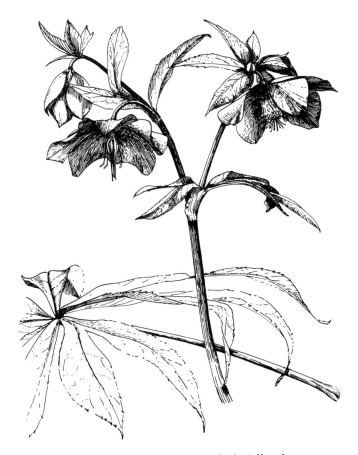

Helleborus kochii 'Bowles' Yellow'

Christmas, flowers a deciduous plant (otherwise all the plants called *H. orientalis* are more or less evergreen) known in gardens as *H. atrorubens*. This is believed to be one of the plants which gives the dark colouring to the Lenten Roses, but it does not set seed in our gardens, though it is a hearty good plant. Another very richly coloured parent is *H. abschasicus*. Then there are Lenten Roses whose floral segments are freely spotted inside with crimson or purple; this is a character found specially in *H. guttatus*. Those with large creamy-white flowers are usually attributed to *H. olympicus*. *H. caucasicus* has greenish flowers. These species and their progeny have given us the *H. orientalis* hybrids of our gardens, a mixed lot if ever there was one, but seldom do we find ugly variants. At the same time the specialists have by selection produced some superlative, large, sumptuous flowers. In the past many were given special names, but the plants take some time to settle down after division and are best raised from seeds and the desired colours selected and kept. Miss E. Strangman of Washfield Nurseries, Hawkhurst, Kent, has an excellent strain.

In pure green and belonging to the same group are the native *H. viridis* and the far more elegant *H. cyclophyllus*, but except in very mild seasons they cannot be expected to flower before March. *H. purpurascens*, a miniature in flower, holds the prize for most unusual interest; its flowers, small bells on 8-inch stalks, are of an indescribably leaden purple, softened with a hint of green and bright green inside. They flower in February and March, but are for the connoisseur only, and not for general garden planting, though quite easy to manage in the cool conditions desired by all kinds. I believe the mysterious *H. torquatus* belongs here. These and other hellebores are easy to raise from seed if it is sown as soon as it is ripe, but the first leaves will not usually appear until the spring.

Once settled in the garden they grow from strength to strength, producing sheaves of blossom, which unfortunately are tricky to use as cut flowers. All have a graceful poise, their nodding blooms adding to their charm; long-lasting qualities. They like the same conditions as *H. niger*, but it is astonishing on how meagre and rooty a diet they will thrive if they are given the half-woodland conditions they love, and are left alone. This group of hellebores is one of the very finest for trouble-free ground-covering, delighting us with an annual display of bloom and good, lasting foliage for a very minimum of attention. Of all the herbaceous plants here mentioned they may be expected to thrive under the most diverse conditions, in dense shade or even in sunshine, on heavy or light soil.

Turning to the shrubby section – those which produce leafy stems during the summer, at the apex of which branching clusters of flowers appear the following spring – we have first to consider that elegant native *H. foetidus*. From the point of view of form alone it stands pre-eminent in the elegant race – the divided, dark green, leathery leaves clothe the base of the green pyramid, bearing at its summit those gradually lengthening pale green stems set with pale green bracts, supporting the bells of green rimmed with maroon. The 'Stinking Hellebore'! Could a more evil name be chosen for a noble

Helleborus lividus

plant? Its somewhat heavy odour is only for those who bruise and sniff it, but in any sun-forsaken spot its good temper and annual reawakening should be a source of joy to all true gardeners.

The home of *H. foetidus* is over a wide area of Western Europe, but its two closest relatives, *H. corsicus* from Corsica and Sardinia and *H. lividus* from the Balearic Isles, are very limited in their distribution. These are particularly lovely plants. The Corsican in good well-drained soil will form great mounds, a yard across and 2 feet high, with pale green stems and crowns of large pale green holly-like leaflets; from every crown arises the symphony of pale green stems, bracts, and blooms, all alike in this delicate vernal tint – the globular cups nodding until fertilized and then, in common with all these plants, opening wide to the sky. The stamens fall first, then the nectaries, followed by the floral segments, and lastly the pod-like achenes gradually enlarge with the swelling seeds.

H. lividus has similar beauty; the leaves are darker and even more beautifully veined and pointed, and the blooms with classic poise take on a strange, rosy tint over their leaden green. But it is not such a hearty plant in the garden as *H. corsicus*. Grown under glass in a cold house, this plant will scent the air with its sweetness, and the rosy tint becomes enhanced as the days lengthen. With the idea of producing the rosy blooms on the magnificent pile of foliage given by *H. corsicus*, I hybridized the two some years ago, and the progeny certainly have sufficient merit to warrant 'selfing' and selection. The pink tint on the undersides of the leaves of *H. lividus* has been given to the stalwart growth of *H. corsicus* and the flowers are tinted too. It has been named *H. × sterniana*, although I was the first to exhibit it! They are all so beautiful, these two species and hybrids, that a large area can be given to them without any regret.

H. × nigericors is the name given to a very beautiful and striking hybrid between *H. niger* and *H. corsicus*, raised by J.E.H. Stooke of Hereford; the cross received a botanical certificate from the RHS in 1931. This grew well at Wisley for some years prior to the Second World War, producing excellent foliage and rich creamy flowers in erect clusters with a maroon flush on their exterior and stalks. The same cross has been made by several enthusiasts, including Miss Strangman who has named hers 'Alabaster'.

It can be readily understood that all our winter flowers will do best in sheltered positions, but of none is this more true than of these three hellebores with persistent stems. I have seen the branches of *H. corsicus* blown round about like a clump of Pampas Grass leaves, and often in a strong gale the stems may be wrenched from their hold. In enclosed gardens this does not of course, occur. These, like the species and varieties earlier mentioned, appreciate rich feeding; the Niger and Orientalis races seem most at home in a retentive soil and nearly complete shade, while these sub-shrubby kinds seem to prefer a stony, drained medium, with plenty of sunshine.

I mentioned earlier how diverse are the members of the great Buttercup Family, Ranunculaceae. It is a family of great quality in its many branches. Take, for instance, the *Delphinium* and the Monkshood (*Aconitum*), the peony, *Ranunculus*, *Thalictrum* and *Clematis*, *Aquilegia* and *Eranthis*; to what extremely high quality and lasting garden value these attain! Scent is not so outstanding as in some other families, but stance, fine foliage and interesting shapes abound, and the garden that contains a good share of these noble plants will never lack interest. In comparison with any of these the hellebore holds its own in finely chiselled and aristocratic line, and for longevity has no rival.

11. Bulbous Plants

Little brown bulb, oh little brown brother,
Are you awake in the dark?

OLD SONG

There is nearly always a bulb in flower somewhere in the garden, and it is also always bulb-planting time. This great group of resilient small plants, seasonally reminding us of their annual awakening and repeating thereby the message of the first aconites and snowdrops even in the heyday of summer, needs careful watching to ensure that planting and transplanting are carried out at the right period. For some bulbs this is immediately after flowering; snowdrops and aconites profit amazingly with such treatment, catching hold at once of the new ground, absorbing its fresh goodness, and storing it in the bulb for the next flowering period. I believe many bulbs are best treated so, but it might be argued that the resting period which occurs in all bulbs, whenever they flower, during the spring, summer, or autumn months, is safest. This resting period as a rule coincides with dry weather in their native countries, when the bulbs 'ripen' as it were, ready for the thrusting of roots into the warm earth after rain.

Although morphologically a bulb is quite different from a corm, and a tuber is distinct from both, for our present purpose I propose treating them as a whole, and not allowing these differences to arrange our procedure. It is difficult to know when the bulb year starts. Some might say with the first snowdrop, but there are snowdrops that flower in October; crocuses have an even longer span, many of the earliest starting in September or even August, and at this time the cyclamens also flower. Then there is that tiny *Leocojum autumnale*, part of a spring and summer race of larger species; this appears in August and September too.

The harvest months do indeed seem to start the bulb year – one reads how in the desert tiny bulbs push up two days after the autumn rains have started – and many of the September- and October-flowering kinds linger in flower until November.

For warm, dry borders, getting the benefit of all sunshine, *Zephyranthes candida* from the banks of the La Plata River may be tried; its many white, crocus-like blooms with yellow stigmata, among its tufts of rich, green, grassy leaves will generally be produced from September until the frosts. The Persian Lily of the Fields, likewise reminiscent of the crocus, also flowers at the same time and likes the same conditions; the narrow-leafed species, *Sternbergia sicula* (*S. lutea* var. *angustifolia*), generally is the most free-flowering. They are of really rich and lovely yellow and are strongly contrasted by the ribbon-like leaves in dark green. This is the best and most reliable of sternbergias, but those craving for variety should try *S. cretica* (*S. graeca*) and *S. maroccana*, which are respectively smaller and larger forms, and the glaucous-leafed *S. macrantha*, flowering well into December. Also for the sunniest, best-drained spot, preferably at the foot of a south wall, there is the gracious *Nerine bowdenii*, a South African whose papery bulbs need shallow planting on the soil, and do not produce their strap-like leaves until after the flowers have appeared. Few flowers have a more elegant outline than those of *N. bowdenii*, and their colour, a warm and lovely pink, is also beyond reproach. Reaching to 18 inches or more, the stalwart stems bear as many as twelve flowers from October onwards, each flower like a tiny lily with crimped and reflexed segments. A specially fine form is known as 'Mark Fenwick's' or 'Abbotswood' variety. This is larger and more robust than the type species and should be planted in preference to it whenever possible.

Also from South Africa are the Kaffir lilies, species of *Schizostylis* and related to *Gladiolus*. *Schizostylis coccinea*, the most common, usually flowers in September together with 'Mrs Heggarty'. These plants have erect, mid-green, grassy leaves clasping the stems to a height of a foot or so, above which the spikes of flowers are borne. Each bloom, standing out from the stem on alternate sides, is an inch-wide silken star, in *S. coccinea* a rich, dark red, and in 'Mrs Heggarty', a warm, salmon-pink. A variety 'Professor Barnard' is mid-way between these two in colour, with a beautiful dusky sheen; this is well worth searching for, as also is the superlative, large-flowered red form *S. coccinea* 'Major'. With flowers nearly twice the size of the ordinary red one, this has lost no grace or charm and is in consequence a very desirable

Schizostylis coccinea 'Viscountess Byng'

plant. Under Eric Smith's care it produced a sport or seedling of clear pink colouring and special excellence; 'Sunshine' is its apt name.

In late seasons these may last into November, but the most valuable for our purpose is 'Viscountess Byng', a stronger plant, up to 2 feet, with the same silky blooms in pale, clear pink. Of course, an early frost will spoil the blooms, as it will the zephyranthes and sternbergias and nerines, but it is well worth the gamble for the good cheer that a clump of these elegant flowers can provide, and only in occasional years do we get a frost to upset them in October and early November. The conditions they require are a well-drained soil that is never dry but which gets the maximum amount of sunshine. There they should thrive, spreading by underground stolons, and throwing up quantities of grassy leaves. When the clumps become congested they sometimes cease to flower, but dividing and replanting in spring with a handful of bone-meal scattered through the soil will usually result in fine stems again for the autumn.

Apart from crocuses, colchicums, and the Algerian iris, this brings us to an end of the late autumn bulbs; the crocuses and irises have chapters to themselves, but colchicums must be dealt with here. These are strange plants whose crocus-like, rosy mauve blooms spring nakedly from the gound in September and October, followed by a crop of leaves in many species as vigorous and luxuriant as the finest *Aspidistra*. Such kinds we can leave behind and come in, as it were, in November, on *Colchicum bifolium* (*C. szovitzii*), one of Admiral Furze's introductions from Turkey; 2 to 3 inches high, the pink or white blooms are produced for many weeks. Like the early autumn kinds this prefers a warm, well-drained soil, and given such is reasonably easy to keep.

Turning the year, we come to several species whose blooms may appear during January and February and into March. They are *C. ritchii*, *C. doerfleri*, and *C. kesselringii*. The latter often has slender, pointed segments of white striped on the outside with purple or lilac; some forms are rosy mauve. *C. hungaricum*, while by no means showy – none of these are – is a useful little plant of 4 inches or so in mauve-white, or more really pure white, enlivened by black anthers, and flowers for a long time in the earliest months. One species stands out from all the others, as it is alone in the genus with yellow flowers. In flower sometimes at Christmas-time, this little plant, *C. luteum*, is very cheery, and loves a warm, sunny spot to remind it of its Afghan home. None of these little species is common and they are best suited to the specialist's garden, thriving in a cold frame or alpine house.

The merenderas are sometimes classed, I believe, with the colchicums, in spite of their segments being cut to the ground and forming no crocus-like tube in lieu of a stalk. A most interesting explanation of the derivation of the name is given us by Mr Bowles: the word *merendar* in Spanish and Portuguese means 'to lunch', and has given rise to a number of words connected with food, the feeding of animals, and pastures. So when the autumn rains start the flowering of merenderas, colchicums and crocuses, the profusion of these lovely flowers warns the shepherds that the time has come to quit the upland pastures, and they call them *quita meriendas*. The rosy lilac *Merendera sobolifera* can be quite a good sight in February, but I should be misleading my readers if I were to suggest that any of these species have the beauty, charm, or refinement of the crocuses. So alike in many ways, these colchicums are not members of the *Iris* Family, but belong to the lilies, having six stamens, not three; their corms are, in addition, coarse and unshapely like their foliage, and have none of that neat attraction of a tunicated *Crocus* corm.

In June the amazingly fragrant little *Cyclamen purpurascens* (commonly known as *C. europaeum*) heralds the long displays of these hardy treasures, which, like the irises and heathers, almost span the year with their flowering seasons. They are members of the *Primula* Family, with dark corms of various sizes, which are their only passport to inclusion in this chapter. They should be widely grown, for they have a notable longevity, are easily managed if their few requirements are understood, and give sweet cheer to any garden scheme. I would go further and say that few plants give such a settled air of distinction to a garden as these little gems of the Mediterranean Region, hardy miniatures of our popular florists' forms. Our greenhouse plants have been bred from *C. persicum*, a refined species of wonderful fragrance and delicate charm, an inhabitant of hot, rocky hillsides in the Eastern Mediterranean region and North Africa, but like several other small species from these warmer areas it is not hardy in the open.

Having known for many years the handful of hardy cyclamens which are grown outdoors under their accepted names, it comes as something of a blow to find that there has been a great upheaval of nomenclature in the genus. Several experts have been at work and new combinations of names will be in use among botanists be_ore long. I will try to give a few synonyms in the vast tangle, but the nomenclature is so confusing that it seems doubtful if the old botanists' names will ever be reconciled and sorted out, since many students of the genus subsequently have added to the early rather unscientific confusion by giving new names, regardless of the originals given to distinct species, and some which were species are now considered to be varieties.

This confusion is unfortunately not confined just to cyclamens, and many old garden plants are due for revision; many reputed to be species may be found to be garden hybrids; for to set matters right it is

Cyclamen coum

generally best to refer to pressed specimens from collectors' original herbaria, or to import plants or seeds from their native habitats.

And so, in a brief review of the several hardy species, we have to say that *C. purpurascens* (forgetting the names *C. europaeum* and *C. repandum*) appears in flower in June, and there may even be a few flowers as late as October. The best-known of all these hardy species is *C. hederifolium* (*C. neapolitanum*), but its flowers, including those of its beautiful white form, are normally also over before November, although its exceptionally lovely leaves appear in October and remain in beauty until the following spring. This plant has the strange habit of producing its roots from the crown of the corm, and is thus dependent on the late summer rains to start it into growth. It is well worth examining the flowers of all these little plants; the petals spring from the nodding stem, forming a transparent dome over the stamens and stigma, then reflex with a decisive fold to form the shuttlecock flower so well known to us all.

From our present point of view, the most important cyclamens are those we know as *C. vernum* and *C. coum*. The botanists group these together, though *C. coum* usually has leaves of plain green while *C. vernum* (which we have known in the past as *C. ibericum*, *C. orbiculatum*, *C. hiemale* and *C. atkinsii*) has leaves marbled with grey, much as in *C. hederifolium*. They both have tubby little flowers held just above the leaves and may both be expected to flower in

December and January during mild spells; it is certainly a time of excitement when one first finds those points of bright cerise or crimson-purple among the dark leaves. Both have forms with pale or white flowers.

These two cyclamens are so small – although so sturdy – that they really need growing in some choice corner of the rock garden, or at least in an area given over to miniature bulbs and plants. It is not until we have plenty of youngsters to play with that we can be bold enough to use them as ground-cover under shrubs. They do well in shade but will also thrive, like *C. hederifolium*, in warm, sunny corners.

Those who garden in very sheltered districts may like to try *C. libanoticum*, for February and March flowers, but this is by no means as hardy as the above species. It has very beautifully marked leaves and fragrant flowers of good size and more elongated in shape than those of *C. coum*, and of a clear, almost salmon, pink, with a bright crimson spot at the base of each petal. There are several other species from the Mediterranean region which are scarcely to be trusted out of doors except in the most favoured localities; even *C. purpurascens* has died, apparently from frost, in my garden.

In the garden the hardy species are usually easy to grow when once they are established, and this is when, of course, their wants are understood. *C. hederifolium* – although it is not a winter-flowering plant it must be grown in our winter garden on account of its beautiful leaves – is sometimes difficult to establish, but often this is because its rooting methods are not understood; others fail perhaps because they are not planted at the right time. August is a resting month for the species we are discussing here, and small corms may be planted then. They are easy to raise from seed and their strange little spherical capsules on their spring-coiled stalks are fascinating to examine, but the seedlings do not flower for three or four years. When, however, the plants are thoroughly established and at home, they will quite likely seed themselves, and few natural regenerations can give more satisfaction and pleasure. Success in establishing them is more or less assured if pot grown youngsters are obtained. Dried corms are much less responsive.

Let us now look at regular January flowers again. It is seldom the month goes by without a mild day or two to entice the yellow Winter Aconite from its toby-frill of green. The little knobbly brown tubers, loving woodland soil under deciduous trees, send up what is perhaps the freshest green of its season, in these flat round frills, on strong stalks, starred with yellow cups in their centres. But 4 inches high, this little member of the Buttercup Family is to some of us of greater importance at the dawn of the year than the first snowdrop.

Eranthis hiemalis is the commonest and is naturalized in numerous gardens; its yellow cups dot the bare ground usually in January or early February. The specialist may like also to grow *E. cilicica*, with a brown-tinted, much more delicately lobed toby-frill and rich yellow cups, and the handsome stalwart hybrids between the two, *E. tubergenii*, of which the finest has been named 'Guinea Gold'. There is also a white-flowered species from Japan *E. pinnatifida*; it has blue stamens but is very small. Strangely enough while a white snowdrop is acceptable as a symbol of winter days, to my conservative mind a white aconite is but a cold thing and an oddity.

In a normal year, the scillas, chionodoxas, and muscaris all flower too late for our purpose, although I have seen them in flower with *Crocus tomasinianus* at the end of February in an exceptionally mild year, and no sight remains more loved in my memory than that carpet of blue and mauve covering some rose beds in a green lawn. But those wanting as much variety as possible can well include one of the grape hyacinths, *Muscari schliemanii*. I have not grown this species, but Mr Hadden wrote that for some years after he had received it from Dr Lemperg 'it flowered regularly in December and January, but of recent years it has waited till the spring, when it is rather over-shadowed by better blue species'. *Hyacinthus azureus* is also an early riser, in clear china blue, a dainty little spire of blossom, but this little plant now has to be called *Pseudomuscari azureum*. True blue is pro-vided by *Scilla bifolia* var. *praecox*. This will grow at the sunny base of a hedge, where the warmth of the January or February sun will cause its four or five starry blooms to open, a bright and unique tint of violet-blue in our winter garden, considerably larger and brighter than *S. bifolia* itself. *Scilla tubergeniana* (*S. mischtschenkoana*) bestirs itself equally early in the year, and its palest blue flowers, with a turquoise central line to each segment, are produced abundantly. The flowers at the top of the stems open first. It is a native of Iran.

Blue and its allied shades are always sought in gardens and an onion-relative *Ipheion uniflorum* starts to flower in mild Februaries and continues until early summer, especially in warm dry corners. 'Wisley Blue' is a good form but 'Froyle Mill' verges onto rich violet-blue.

This occurred as a sport or seedling in the garden of Mrs Olive Taylor-Smith in Hampshire. I should not know which to choose, and botanists have been equally hesitant over the genus as a whole, for it has been called *Triteleia*, *Brodiaea* and *Milla* at different times but now seems settled under *Ipheion*. A place in some shade from a bush, but nestling at the foot of a south-facing wall seems to suit *Arisarum vulgare*. The neat, dark green, triangular leaves are only a few inches above ground but over them stand quaint little arum-flowers, white striped with brown and with a long, brown, overhanging 'tail'.

There are a few little *Narcissi* that we must include. One is that miniature of miniature daffodils, *Narcissus asturiensis* (*N. minimus*), a Spaniard unique in having a corona or trumpet which contracts before it opens at the mouth into a tiny puckered frill. The little nodding

Narcissus bulbocodium romieuxii

Narcissus × dubius

flowers need the soft carpet of an anti-splash plant to protect them from February showers, like all these little bulbs. The other is an exact replica of those multitudes of yellow trumpets that star the alpine meadow at Wisley in March, *N. bulbocodium*, the Hoop-Petticoat Daffodil; this January-February form, *N.b. romieuxii*, from North Africa, is soft citron-yellow in colour, the flowers last an astonishing time, and are exceedingly frost-resistant. *N.b. riffanus* flowers with it; it is similar in colour but has narrower trumpets. It is unfortunate that *N. clusii* (*N. bulbocodium monophyllus*) is not very hardy. The tiny crystalline-white flowers are of similar outline to the Hoop-Petticoats, but this has an even shorter and wider trumpet. *N. watieri* is another tiny; again in white, this has flowers more the shape of a Jonquil, with a flat crown in place of a trumpet. Rather taller is *N. × dubius*, a

Narcissus hedraeanthus

Jonquil-type in soft yellow and very fragrant. The latest arrival is from one of Peter Davis's collecting expeditions, and is named *N. hedraean-thus*. This tiny has the colouring of *N. romieuxii* and a shape even more elementary – a simple cone, upturning with a puck-like air on a 2-inch stem, and the minutest of perianth lobes around it. All the above delight in a warmer, more gritty soil than the average daffodil, but in common with them should be planted by September, or moved immediately after flowering, and a carpet of some tiny alpine is important to keep them fresh and clean in rainy weather. They are ideal for growing on a cold frame in pots, so that they can ᴗe transferred indoors for greater enjoyment of their flowers. While we find it fairly natural that these very small species, being of an 'alpine' nature, should flower in the depth of winter, January and early February if the season be mild, it astonishes visitors to see in my garden a full-sized daffodil in flower in January. But so it is: 'Rijnveld's Early Sensation' is a sensation indeed in January. I am told that it is cut for market in the Cornish fields as early as January 6th. I have had it in flower once on January 10th but it usually a week or two later. Its name was registered in 1965; the raiser was F.H. Chapman of Rye, Sussex. It is amazing that it has not become well-known by now; it was selected for trial at

Wisley when I exhibited it a few years ago. It is followed by one of the most exquisite of all Alec Gray's exquisite hybrids, 'Jana', which is depicted in my book *Three Gardens*, along with 'Cedric Morris', a miniature which is usually in flower on Christmas Day. The origin of this remarkable plant is recorded in my book *Three Gardens*. 'Forerunner' and 'Ard Righ' (High King) are two typical yellow daffodils which can be in flower in February, and 'February Gold', a hybrid of *N. cyclamineus*, is a dainty thing to be relied on for early flowering. But I have forgotten our native Lent Lily, *N. pseudonarcissus*, which follows close onto the flowering of the Welsh native, *N. obvallaris*, the Tenby Daffodil. The former is a dainty charmer and seeds itself freely; the latter, noted for its extra glaucous foliage, is taller and in my experience increases well, but produces no seedlings. Its flowers are of a clear uniform yellow and last a month in bloom.

At Wisley I have noted on more than one occasion, during frosty spells, that 'Bartley', another splendid *N. cyclamineus* hybrid, will stand unbowed after a night's hard frost, while others may be laid low. From these examples I think we may hope that there are other early daffodils within sight, and this is a welcome thought. I always find great delight in early forms of well-known flowers, although late ones, which might equally be claimed to lengthen the season, quickly pall during the pageantry of bloom. For such is a gardener's year: the seasons pass so quickly that to be ready to appreciate the week's joys one must be ready to forget those that have passed.

12. Crocuses

It is strange how, throughout horticulture, certain plants have cap-
tured the popular imagination and left others, just as amenable and
beautiful, unrecognized and alone in the botanic gardens. Thus it is
with crocuses. To the ordinary man in the street (or garden) crocuses
are represented by the yolk-yellow Dutchman, and also by the even
larger purple, mauve and white and striped kinds, all forms of *Crocus
vernus*, that flower a week or so later. The yellow crocus is a horticultural triumph, for from an original bulb raised over two hundred and
fifty years ago, all the Yellow Dutch crocuses are descended, and they
show no signs of that diminution of vigour usually prophesied from
intensive vegetative propagation. This garden form, probably a seedling from *C. aureus*, is a sterile plant, giving no seed.

Crocuses, therefore, do not jump to the average mind when speaking of winter flowers, like the snowdrop and the aconite, yet they have
an even greater claim than either of these genera for inclusion in this
book. *Crocus* species are legion and their botanical groups are many,
but from our point of view it will be best to leave such studies to those
who wish for them. That noted authority on these plants, the late E. A.
Bowles, in his valuable *Handbook of Crocus and Colchicum*, treated them
in a horticultural manner, so I feel we shall be in good company if we
do the same.

We must leave that trio of beauties, *C. zonatus*, *C. speciosus* and
C. sativus, for generally they are all over before November, with
several other species. The pure lavender-blue rounded blooms of

C. speciosus globosus, *C.s.* 'Oxonian' in dark lavender-blue, and also *C. sativus* var. *cartwrightianus*, whose flowers have the doubtful advantage of remaining open in dull weather, are rather later and may linger until the eleventh month, together with *C. longiflorus*, a pure lilac, globular flower, with orange throat and scarlet stigmata, and *C. banaticus* (*C. byzantinus*, *C. iridiflorus*) with its strangely short inner segments. The type is one of the best crocuses for October and November and thrives in a shady, well-drained position. Some forms of *C. cancellatus* from the Asiatic end of its habitat, varying from mauve to white, are also useful at this time of the year.

From farthest east in the Greek Archipelago comes *C. tournefortii*, of similar colour and flowering in November, so really these are the two first species to earn a rightful place in these pages. It is a satisfying and lovely flower, and bravely furnishes leaves with its flowers, most of the autumnal species producing their flowers before the leaves appear. A little white species with yellow throat may often be seen in flower with it; this is *C. ochroleucus*, from the Eastern Mediterranean.

Possibly the best of all these late autumnal species is *C. laevigatus*. This is a freely increasing plant, making a lovely carpet of colour, the general effect being lilac, touched up by the yellow stigmata and orange throat. They are exceedingly fragrant. I remember seeing thousands of these in flower in November in R.D. Trotter's Surrey garden. The outside of the outer segment is more or less feathered with rich red-purple. A good deal of variation occurs; var. *fontenayi* might almost be mistaken for a form of *C. imperati*, so striking is its external marking on a buff ground. *C. korolkowii*, the Afghanistan form of which is the most vigorous and has starry yellow blooms veined with purple and brown on the exterior, usually appears by December, when also *C. vitellinus* may be seen, a bright orange little fellow, marked with brown in some forms.

There are several midwinter species. *C. heuffelianus* spans the seasons, putting up its well-proportioned purple flowers freely; there is also a lovely solid white form, *C. niveus*, of this plant, with a yellow throat and scarlet stigmata. Another useful white is *C. nevadensis*. But, truly named, *C. imperati* lords it over all. For this is a crocus in a regal cloak. In the bud these fine blooms are of soft buff, distinctly feathered or streaked with very dark purple, but on a sunny day open wide, showing the warm, rich lavender and contrasting scarlet stigmata. There are lovely but rare white forms. There is a very dainty,

Crocus fleischeri   *Crocus sieberi*

tiny-flowered, white species, *C. fleischeri*, from Asia Minor, for
January and February; the slim little blooms are of papery whiteness,
so frail that the scarlet stigmata can be seen through their segments
while in bud. For all its delicacy it is a good hearty grower.

They are joined by other February species, the globular, orange-
yellow *C. ancyrensis* from the Levant, purple-flushed outside, and
stout little *C. sieberi* in bright lavender-blue with orange throat and
remarkably wide leaves, from Greece and Crete. 'Violet Queen' and
'Hubert Edelsten' are two noted forms, increasing well. 'Bowles's
White' is a remarkably handsome form, selected at Myddelton House,
and noted for its intensely coloured stigma. They take no notice of
snow, and severe frost turns them to a navy blue colouring, immediately to revert to their cool lavender at the return of mild weather.
Truly is this a valuable winter flower.

And then on some grey day in early February the battalions of
C. tomasinianus are upon us. The frail, slim, grey buds open with the
first sun, and suddenly the ground is spangled with lavender, starry

Crocus tomasinianus

blossoms set with orange parts. These are hardly flowers for picking but a mixed bowl of snowdrops and crocuses can be a delight for several days, and it is not until the crocuses open on the table, close under one's eyes, that the miracle can be fully appreciated. That such a frail tube can support no less frail a flower during early February weather is in itself a marvel, but in addition the silken sheen of the inner segments and their bland, exquisite tint cannot be surpassed by the best the seasons give us. This is indeed a plant for everyone; it is cheap to buy, it increases almost too freely by offsets and by self-sown seeds, and the annual beauty of its blooms is a welcome reward to the chilly gardener.

It is, perhaps, the most freely increasing of all crocuses, thriving in a variety of soils so long as they are reasonably drained, in sun or shade, but preferring full sun. The later blooms often get crossed with some big garden crocuses and it is amusing to pick out these enlarged hybrids. Two very good forms have been named *C.t. pictus*, in a pale tint, touched with rich purple at the apices of the outer segments, and the rich 'Whitewell Purple', probably owing its size and colour to a form of *C. vernus*. Two other excellent vigorous forms are 'Barr's Purple' and 'Taplow Ruby'. The latter is a particularly fine, richly coloured, red–purple form, but these variants or hybrids do of course lose the exquisite charm of the species in becoming 'grandifloras'. A very unusual type which occurs occasionally in self-sown colonies is a rosy-amethyst form, coloured wholly with this tint and lacking the grey exterior; some exceptionally warm rosy seedlings appeared at Myddelton House and in my own garden.

In early February, the earliest forms of *C. chrysanthus* bring to the crocus beds something unique. This species from Asia Minor is, to my mind, with the *C. biflorus* hybrids, pre-eminent amongst the winter- and spring-flowering kinds, and brings to the collection a touch of quality and interest which finds its parallel in the *batalinii* × *linifolia* hybrids found amongst the Tulip species in March and April. When *C. chrysanthus* is raised from seed an amazing amount of variation may be expected. Very often with a rich yellow throat, which is not trumpet-shaped, but forms a globular cup below the open segments; these may vary from dark or pale yellow to white or lilac, and the orange-red stigmata and anthers are shown up by the black barbs of the latter. A rich fragrance is noticeable as with nearly all these

Crocus chrysanthus var. *fusco-tinctus*

crocuses, and it is a scent with all the warm promise of spring in its qualities. *C. chrysanthus* is a short, bunchy species, the tight clusters of flowers of established clumps pushing each other over with their wide shapes. Usually the first to appear is *C.c.* var. *fusco-tinctus*, whose rich yellow blooms are heavily flushed or pencilled on the outside with warm brown. (It is here, among some of these tiny bulbs, and particularly with the yellow ones, I like to grow that strange little evergreen *Ophiopogon planiscapus* var. *nigrescens*. In spite of its long name its grassy leaves are only a few inches long, of almost black tint. The flowers are insignificant; it increases by underground stolons. The leaves need colour to augment their dark tint).

My favourite among the varieties of botanical status is *C.c. pallidus*, whose soft, creamy, sulphur-yellow is particularly satisfying. But apart from this my admiration goes out to that superb series of hybrids raised by E.A. Bowles and named so aptly after our birds. 'Yellow Hammer' tells us its colour and so does that persistent charmer 'Snow Bunting', feathered outside with purple. 'Warley White' is even more striking but of similar colouring. 'Siskin', yellow without and white within. 'Canary Bird' and the fine 'Zwanenburg Bronze' are of the *fusco-tinctus* colouring. The prince of the clan is undoubtedly that glorious plant raised by the Zwanenburg firm and named after E.A. Bowles, in rich butter-yellow, a fine plant in colour, form and stamina. Apart from these excellent forms, newer kinds include 'Goldilocks', with deep yellow, fine blooms, purple-shaded in the cup, 'Jester', in lemon-yellow, feathered with purple stripes outside, 'Lady Killer', maroon and white, and 'Blue Pearl' in forget-me-not blue. These show the influence probably of one or more other species as parents and particularly of our next species.

Of the 'Scotch' crocus – a foolish name for *C. biflorus*, which is an Italian species – there are many varieties again, and the flowers have almost that same lovely globular shape, but in miniature, and with more pointed segments. The most usual colour is white, with bronze throat and orange anthers and stigmas, striped in the bud with indigo-purple. This type is sterile but increases rapidly from the corm. The variety *C.b.* var *weldenii*, the Dalmatian variant, brings us to the highest quality of form and colour, and is well able to assort with the *C. chrysanthus* varieties in pure quality. This is again a variable type, but the solid white blooms are flushed or flecked (not striped) outside with grey, blue, indigo, or lavender. Selected forms like 'Fairy' are

Crocus biflorus var. *weldenii*, blue form

gems of the first water, while there is the occasional wild form such as that known as *C. alexandri*, which is flushed all over with dark indigo-blue and has a fine large flower. The species has, then, reached a new pitch of perfection. When these forms hybridize with *C. chrysanthus* we get some of the most beautifully coloured crocuses in existence. To my mind there is no more lovely crocus than a hybrid of this type with soft, creamy sulphur segments widely open, show-ing the globular throat in a deeper tint, set about with the bright orange of the stamens and stigma; next to them is an unopened flower with the contrasting soft indigo tinting outside. Truly a wonderful combination. Their fragrance is another compelling factor.

The tale of these two grand species, so very amenable, too, in a light friable soil on sunny slopes, should not close our eyes to other Febru-ary species. I have already mentioned the Dutch Yellow crocus, usually regarded as a form of *C. aureus*, but the species itself must not be overlooked, for it has the same lovely colour, but is of neater form and suitable for association with the other species. There are charming paler forms too. Little *C. susianus*, the 'Cloth of Gold' crocus, and *C. balansae*, in richest orange-yellow, are rather later-flowering. The latter species has the rounded, globular flowers of *C. chrysanthus* and in some forms the buds are of dark mahogany-brown, a very telling

Crocus balansae

contrast in colour. *C. versicolor*, 'Cloth of Silver', is a white after the nature of *C. biflorus*, equally robust but inferior in quality. *C. olivieri* resembles *C. balansae*, but is normally of pure orange-yellow colour; both are chubby little fellows with rounded blooms. 'Jamie' is one of the most free-flowering forms of the latter species and a very desirable garden plant; 'Zwanenburg' is of rich orange with dark brown stripes on the outer segments. One large garden crocus must be added before we leave the field to the spring species and all the *vernus* forms, and that is 'Vanguard', a fitting companion to the Dutch Yellow, in soft grey-lilac; it is a fine large flower and the greyish exterior suggests that *C. tomasinianus* may have been the influence prompting its early appearance.

Perhaps the best way of growing crocuses is in grass, where the green will form a background to the flowers; while the autumn species and all the spring species do produce leaves with their flowers, they are seldom sufficiently large or plentiful to be seen when the flowers are wide open. This aesthetically, as well as practically, is not satisfactory. One needs green above all colours in the 'dead' months and especially in the awakening year. The grass prevents rain-splash to a certain

Crocus olivieri

extent and provides support for those frail kinds on their long perianth tubes. Most crocuses keep their corms some inches below ground, thrusting their roots downwards, their spears piercing any verdure. Strictly speaking, no stems arise above the ground, as the flowers are borne on the tube formed by the united segments, down which travel the pollen grains to fertilize the ovules, to ripen eventually as orange or other coloured seeds just on the ground. The smaller species, however, are unsuitable for the thick turf formed by grass. *C. speciosus*, *C. sativus*, *C. luteus*, *C. aureus*, 'Vanguard', and other vigorous kinds will be happy in it, but the tinies like *C. laevigatus*, *C. fleisheri*, *C. balansae*, *C. biflorus*, etc. need a neater, thinner carpet. Fortunately, with an occasional exception, all the species like the soil and conditions given to the better-class rock plants and our problem is thereby easily solved. For what could be more effective on the slopes of the rock garden than a carpet of *Antennaria tomentosa*, whose grey leaves contrast well with the mauve and purple species, or a dark green carpet of *Helianthemum alpestre* 'Serpyllifolium' for the yellow and white kinds? The crocus leaves do, indeed, cause annoyance to some tidy minds, but no bliss comes into this world unadulterated and the leaves are gone before midsummer.

As with other bulbs, they can be safely moved when in flower or immediately afterwards, and the planting season, from dry corms, extends from June until October. Mice and birds are their great enemies; the first eat the corms and the others, especially the sparrows, want only to peck at the yellow and some other kinds. Tightly stretched black cotton on thin stout wires is the best deterrent, and is not unsightly if carefully done. As to the mice, planting the bulbs in parcels of very fine-mesh plastic netting will ensure the safety of the most precious bulbs. A corm is a strange thing, for each year the new corm grows above the old one and thus the plants gradually reach the surface, unless the contractile roots succeed in pulling them downwards. Mowing machines are thus sometimes the cause of the disappearance of a group of crocuses in a lawn and frequent division of clustering kinds is necessary before the increasing bunches of bulbs thrust themselves out of the soil.

The Yellow Dutch crocus is, very naturally, the most popular of all the varieties and species obtainable today, and it may frequently appear in splashes of yolk-yellow during February. I always find its colour rather harsh and startling by itself against the bare earth and my happiest planting has been among small green things like violets and *Waldsteinia* at the foot of a clump of Red Dogwood. The combination of colour is really vivid, especially if one plants the best Westonbirt Dogwood, as described in Chapter 6, and is hardly surpassed for brilliance by any grouping of summer flowers.

13. Irises

Daily they grow, and daily forth are sent
Into the world, it to replenish more;
Yet is the stock not lessened, nor spent,
But still remains in everlasting store.

EDMUND SPENSER (1552–1599)

No matter what its climate, position, or style, no garden in this country could be made where an iris or two would not thrive. They flower in their several ways from September through winter and spring to July; the various species come from boggy lowlands and from dry hillsides and so will grow in a variety of conditions in the garden, but as a general rule they do best in full sunshine.

Several species come within the scope of this book and we will start by considering one of our most precious winter flowers, *Iris unguicularis*, often known as *I. stylosa*, or the Algerian Iris. This is the species which raises the floral standard in September on hot banks or along the foot of a south or west wall; particularly does it like the foot of a chimney-stack where a fire, indoors, is kept going through the winter. Where the drainage, already sharp, has been amplified with old mortar rubble, and where the sun strikes mercilessly in summer, this species will thrive, at least in our southern and eastern counties. It does not really like heavy rains after June, but in very dry springs it is advisable to give it an occasional soaking with weak liquid manure, and for prolific bloom, a pane of glass can be supported to ward off summer, autumn, and winter rains. But these are counsels of perfection. The plant is easy to grow, tolerably hardy, and normally flowers and does well if *left alone* in the position it likes. Transplanting the thin rhizomes with their wiry, apparently lifeless roots can be done in spring but August is usually best, when new roots are being made.

The big clumps of grassy leaves, 2 feet high in the more vigorous forms, may look untidy, but forbearance is rewarded when the flowers appear, in autumn and during mild spells until April. They

Iris unguicularis

appear in three days in mild weather from their sheath of green and are usually ready for gathering on the third, about 9 inches high; for this is essentially a flower for cutting, although it often flowers freely enough to make a display out of doors. It is particularly galling, when flowers are so scarce, to find the slim, dagger-like buds, which shoot through the tangle of leaves, sometimes are eaten through before one can pick them. The damage to the buds may be done by snails or cutworms, and for this reason the tangle of leaves should be kept clean and all old leaves removed as soon as they turn brown.

The flowers would be a joy at any time, but especially so with their sweet fragrance in winter. It is generally recognized that the pale form known as 'Lilacina' is one of the first to bloom, but by November most of the forms will be in flower, including the white from Greece, which, though not so opulent as the coloured ones, is very beautiful and useful. There appears to be only one white form in cultivation.

The blooms of all are of an extreme quivering delicacy; three beautifully arched standards, or upper segments, between which are the three out-curving styles – hiding the three stamens – and the three broad down-curving falls. The soft, clear lilac or lavender-blue of the several forms is accentuated by darker veining on the falls around the white ring which again surrounds the orange blotch disappearing down the throat. One form, called 'Marginata', has a paler edge to the falls. Other names such as 'Agrostifolia', 'Altaflora', and 'Kaiserin Elizabeth', etc. cover no doubt equally beautiful forms, but it has not been my good fortune to see them. 'Walter Butt' (commemorating a noted gardener) made its debut in 1957 and has proved to be a splendid grower and free flowerer; its flowers are of very pale lilac and their only fault is that their standards are inclined to flop open. Among still newer forms, or forms that have never become well-known, is a pink one; but this must only be whispered at present. Most of these forms flower through the winter, but I must make special mention of *I.u.* var. *speciosa* 'Lindsayae', whose sumptuous purple flowers do not appear usually until February and continue through March into April. Each bloom is of an amplitude not found in others, and the falls have a coppery tint around the striking white and orange blotches; the standards are creamy grey outside. Fortunately this fine form has shorter and narrower leaves than the majority and holds its flowers well above them. One clump only of this was found growing wild in 1939 near Toulon, by Nancy Lindsay, but it has proved very slow of increase in my garden. The *speciosa* forms have as a distinguishing mark a little knob at the top of the perianth tube at the base of the floral segments. Another of them, 'Ellis's Variety', was shown at Vincent Square in 1949 and is again richly coloured and shapely, being of a definite blue-purple, but it is not free flowering as a rule. I find the most free flowering of the dark purples is 'Mary Barnard'. It is rather small and weak in its floral parts but this is not so important as its garden-worthiness. It was found in Algiers.

It is interesting to read in Dykes's *Genus Iris* that the distribution of this species, which extends from Algeria to the other end of the Mediterranean and onwards, appears to have a bearing upon the width of the leaves, for those approaching the eastern habitats have the narrowest leaves and the broadest are at the Algerian end, with one exception, *I.u. lazica*, from districts near the Black Sea, which has the shortest and broadest leaves of all. Mrs Gwendoline Anley grew this and told me it is rather insignificant and fugacious in flower, and of mid-purple colouring. From the Algerian giant with leaves 2 feet long, they scale down to a few inches, and are interesting but less valuable for our purpose. The narrowest-leafed forms, with some good flowers in miniature, come from Crete. A very pretty little plant, covered with flowers annually, is a Cretan form I have seen at Kew under the name of 'Oxford'. The flowers are very delicately marked in tones of white, grey, lilac and purple. The leaves scarcely overtop the flowers which are 4 inches high.

It is quite a big job, tackling the genus Iris, even for so restricted a purpose as ours, but we are helped by the winter-flowering kinds resolving themselves easily into groups. The well-known Bearded group, or June-flowering irises, do not enter at all. The big section called Apogon (beardless irises with rhizomes, or running, tuber-like roots on the surface of the soil) has been disposed of with *I. unguicularis* and we are left with the Juno and Reticulata sections.

I always consider the Junos to be some of the most handsome of irises. They have a bulbous base beset with fleshy roots and throw up their arching, glossy leaves in one plane from opposite sides of the short stem. In the axils of these leaves are borne the flowers. The best-known representatives of this section are *I. bucharica* and *I. orchioides*, which carry the flowering period into March and April; a similar yellow-flowered species, *I. caucasica*, may be expected in February.

One of the truest winter species, *I. planifolia* (*I. alata*), is of little use for the open air in this country. It needs an exaggeration of the conditions prescribed for the Algerian iris, and it is a fact that they all appreciate this, though not necessarily the wall, liking nothing so much as a pane of glass over them from June till October. This is to ensure a complete rest and drying-off of the roots, such as they would get in their Southern European homes, from the shores of the Mediterranean away east to the Himalayas.

But to return to *I. planifolia*, this is a beautiful lavender-blue or purple flower veined on the falls, and has the strange character of all the Junos: the standards are very small and instead of being held aloft, above all the other parts of the flower, project horizontally from the base of the flower and hang down between the falls. Their place is taken by the crests of the styles, those wing-like additions to the apices of the stigmata. The falls, too, are remarkable in several of these species, for they have wing-like extensions (hence the name 'alata') clasping the styles. At first glance this and the next species might be taken for members of the Reticulata group, were it not for their standards, for they are so short when in flower that their stems, mode of branching, and leaves are scarcely noticed.

I. persica is another fickle garden plant. It has an unusually beautiful and variable colouring; often the palest blue-green styles are contrasted by the maroon patches and yellow ridges of the falls. Both these species should be given a light friable loam in a sunny frame, where they will flower once from imported bulbs, but are very difficult to keep going. If only one could raise seedlings their vigour might be doubled. *I. persica* gives us several different colour forms, which are more robust than the type, such as the rich violet-purple *I.p. tauri*, with even darker blotches on the falls. Others are *I. stenophylla* (*heldreichii*) in pale mauve-blue, with falls of darkest violet edged with the paler tint and a white beard; *I. purpurea*, red-purple, touched black and orange on the falls; and *I. sieheana*, in a pale tint heavily veined. But these I have not grown. Perhaps the most notable of this type is *I.* 'Sindpers', a hybrid with *I. sindjarensis*. A good illustration appears in the *Flora and Sylva* for 1904. This freely increasing plant has a variety of colour forms and all are beautiful, and the hybrid is a fairly stable plant for well-drained rock garden positions in full sun. The azure-blue flowers are tinted with sea-green and orange markings. *I. persica* has been known in this country since Parkinson's day and is found wild in Iran and Asia Minor; *I. sindjarensis* grows in Syria. It is also known under the name of *I. aucheri*. These all flower in February and March, but we must not leave the section without reference to another January-flowering species, *I. rosenbachiana*, from Turkestan, and its variety, very rare in this country, *I. baldschuanica*.

I will not go so far as to say that *I. rosenbachiana* is the most handsome of the Junos – one cannot forget the claims of the March-flowering *I. warleyensis* and *I. bucharica* – but it is certainly one of the best of the dwarf early-flowering species. The standards are white and larger than in most species, and the falls, which open broadly, of a rich and brilliant red–purple with white hafts. Unfortunately it cannot be relied upon in the open garden, but must be given the cosiest and best-drained bed or be grown in a frame.

The Reticulata section gives us some real gems for the rock garden;

Iris histrio var. *aintabensis* and *Scilla tubergeniana* (S. *mischtschenkoana*)

they are hardy little mites, with sturdy flowers very resistant to gales and rain, except the rare and seldom obtainable *I. vartanii*. They thrive in a well-drained, sandy loam mixed with leaf-mould, preferably on the slopes of a rock garden, or along narrow borders in company with other small plants, and mostly increase freely. I think they all like to get their thong-like roots, which proceed from the fibre-sheathed bulb, into something more substantial and I recommend a few knobs of heavy loam to be mixed some 8 inches under the surface.

December usually brings us the earliest of the Reticulata section, *I. histrio*. This and all the other species grow in the countries clustered round the eastern end of the Mediterranean. The spearing, angular leaves, eventually a foot or so high, rather spoil the effect. The flowers are smaller and of the same sprightly, angular, general shape of *I. reticulata*, but the general effect is lilac-blue, with white, violet-margined blades to the falls. *I.h.* var. *aintabensis* has a pale china-blue flower and is longer lived and a better garden plant. It is certainly a neater plant, for the leaves do not grow up until after the flowers are over, and, as its lasts several weeks in flower and increases freely by the basal clusters of tiny bulbs, one can forgive its lack of scent. More shapely is the delightful *I. vartanii*, but its blooms are frail and it is not an all-weather plant; this uncommon species hails from Palestine and has almond-scented, slaty-blue flowers. Little *I. danfordiae* in bright yellow strikes a new note, but is not very permanent out of doors. After flowering the large bulbs divide into several small ones which take some years to reach flowering size, during which time they are often lost or devoured. In recent years a more vigorous triploid form has been introduced.

I. histrioides, flowering usually in January and February, and *I. reticulata*, carrying on into March, are by far the most generally useful members of this group and good sound perennials. They are amazingly resistant to snow and frost and winter storms.

I do not know a flower more lovely than *I. histrioides* 'Major' or 'G.P. Baker's Variety'. This was most beautifully portrayed by Mr Bowles's brush and appeared in the RHS *Journal* for 1933. Here the lovely spode-blue colour is faithfully reproduced, together with the beautiful veins and spots of dark navy blue with the orange blotch. These fragrant, sturdy, ample blooms, with their large standards and horizontally jutting falls ending in a round blade, appear before the leaves and especially need a carpet of greenery as an anti-splash. Their leaves, appearing later, do not run the enervating risk of being frozen in full growth as do those of the more precocious *I. histrio*, and hence the stamina of the plant is greater. It increases freely in any sunny, sheltered, well-drained position. Besides the lovely types mentioned there was also a form named after Lady Beatrix Stanley in white and blue, and one cannot leave out little *I.h.* var. *sophenensis*, only half the size but with an equal amount of charm in a soft grey-blue, tinted with sea-green on the styles.

I. reticulata, the type species of this group, is a very good garden plant, usually appearing in early February; the spiky, grey, angled leaves stand erect like soldiers' bayonets guarding those purple gems in their midst. Many of the irises described are fragrant, but the sweet odour of violets exhaled by *I. reticulata* makes it at once dear to the gardener's heart. The rich purple form that we know best, with its slender erect standards and conspicuous orange-yellow 'eyes', is

Iris histrioides 'Major'

apparently not the most common in nature. This position is held by that known as *I.r.* var. *krelagei*, which frequently occurs when seedlings are raised. It is often the first to flower in February and has a rich, warm, wine-purple tint, with the usual yellow zone on the falls. 'Hercules' and the finer 'J.S. Dijt' have this same rich colouring but are larger and more sumptuous. Several other forms have been propagated and are becoming generally available; there are larger forms of the purple type: 'Wentworth', in rich, royal purple, 'Harmony', 'Royal Blue' and 'Gigantea' are nearer to blue; all four forms have good, large flowers; 'Violet Beauty' is perhaps the most splendid, a good uniform colour, while 'Springtime' is a blue-purple with a large white blotch. Last but not least, there is that lovely thing of Mr Bowles's, 'Cantab', in cold, pale china-blue; all these have the characteristic orange-yellow marks on the falls. One which combines this paler colouring in the standards with violet-blue falls and white blotch is 'Clairette', but for garden value I think self-coloured flowers are generally best. Another species, closely related to *I. reticulata*, is *I. bakeriana* in vivid wedgewood-blue, with a creamy spotted area around the yellow zone; the lip of each fall is of darkest violet-purple. It is an interesting species, particularly as its leaves have eight sides instead of the usual triangular section of this group. It is slow of increase and rather tricky outdoors, and is a native of the upper reaches of the River Euphrates.

Planting time for the Reticulata irises is in late summer and early autumn; they are easy to raise from seed and if after flowering well a bulb misses fire for a season, it will usually be found that it has 'spawned' into a cluster of tiny bulblets, which should be carefully lifted when in leaf and given less crowded positions. *I. histrio* and *I. histrioides* thrive best if given a complete rest in summer by the simple expedient of placing a pane of glass flat on the ground after the leaves have died down, until early autumn. *I. danfordiae* should be grown in a frame, where such conditions can be enforced, with the rare and beautiful *I. winogradowii*.

I have left till last an iris of special appeal, raised by Bertram Anderson and named 'Katharine Hodgkin', a hybrid whose parents were stated to be *I. danfordiae* and *I. histrioides* 'Major'. It received an Award of Merit in 1969 and a First Class Certificate in 1974; its vigour thus is proved. The standards are greenish white veined with blue, the falls similar flushed with greenish yellow, and the crest yellow, surrounded by blue spots. From this prosaic description little can be gained as an image of a flower that is so exquisitely transcendent. And it is a good garden plant, increasing freely. 'Frank Elder' is similar, less exquisite and later flowering, and 'Tantallon', again of similar colouring, is less good, a hybrid this time between *I. winogradowii* and *I. histrioides* 'Major'; Christopher Brickell considers the first two are of the same parentage and not concerned with *I. danfordiae*.

14. Snowdrops and Snowflakes

Together with the violet and the aconite, the snowdrop is well known among the earliest of the year's flowers, even by those who do not profess to be gardeners. But it is not generally realized how many different species there are, varying in stature and foliage more than in any striking difference in colour, and flowering from October until April. Certain growers find that the salesmen at Covent Garden pay handsome prices for the really fine varieties, when sold as cut bloom, and the growing of four or five selected large-flowered varieties in areas where they thrive would seem to be a profitable commercial venture. And yet who would think that this meek little flower could rise to such heights – or sink to such depths – of commercial dignity?

All the forms of our common snowdrop – and several other species too – are at home in thin woodland conditions, where the sheltered swards of moss and grass provide just the right conditions for them. Loving the more retentive soils on chalk or sand, they make a particularly happy contrast to the trailing ivy and rich green box which thrive with them. My own special ideal for association with snowdrops would be aconites and *Pulmonaria rubra*. I never fail to have a little bowl of snowdrops mingled with the yellow of the aconites and the coral-pink of the Lungwort at the end of January, provided the weather be open. And as a rich, dark contrast I like to plant *Bergenia purpurascens*, whose leathery green leaves turn to metallic purple-brown in winter with rosy red reverses.

The first snowdrops appear, as I say, in September, *Galanthus reginae-olgae* being the group name that embraces the forms known as

G. *elsae* and G. *rachelae*, but these and the plant one finds under the name of G. *octobrensis* flower too early for our purpose. The Corfu snowdrop, G. *corcyrensis*, follows these in November, and unlike them, produces its leaves with its flowers; G. *cilicius*, with distinctly marked inner segments, often flowers in December. These are all from the Mediterranean and appreciate warm, sunny conditions in the garden. With them may be grown the January-flowering G. *graecus*, unique on account of its twisted leaves; it is an easily satisfied little plant and generally increases freely. These are all relatives of the commonest species, G. *nivalis*, which is a naturalized alien or native of this country, and occurs in sheets of thousands together in its favoured districts in February. And although it rather upsets our chronological progression in its many forms, we will consider these before returning to the other late autumn- and winter-flowering snowdrops.

G. *nivalis* is the one snowdrop we can all afford to plant in quantity and no flower of the season speaks so strongly of winter; the meek blooms, sensibly shaped against the weather, the colour of the flowers and leaves, all seem to me to fit in so well with dark days and cold winds. Yet what a charm lies in their delicacy. This old favourite of our childhood and noted flower of winter is to me most dear in its double variety G.*n.* 'Plenus'. Double flowers, especially double monocotyledons, do not generally appeal to me, but the scent – found in many snowdrops – and the delicate tinting of green in the well-filled centre enclosed by three or four large white segments, are very friendly and sweet. Rare and lovely is the double form with yellow central segments, 'Countess of Elphinstone'. The green form has been hybridized with G. *plicatus*, and the results that I have seen at Wisley raised by H. A. Greatorex of Witton, Norwich, are handsome (but not more charming) and have been given names such as 'Ophelia', 'Hippolyte', and 'Jacquetta'; and 'Dionysia' with a mass of dark green central segments.

It is a strange thing that the so-called yellow snowdrops occur habitually in Northumberland; I have not been able to distinguish between G. *nivalis* 'Lutescens' and 'Flavescens'; they both have a yellowish-green ovary and yellow markings in the flower instead of the usual green. They are interesting variants but have little garden value. The scarcity of hardy flowers in the depths of winter tends to sharpen our appreciation of such variants, however: variety is never more welcome. And so we must also grow that strange little form

Galanthus nivalis 'Plenus', *G.n.* 'Magnet', *G. caucasicus*, *G.n.* 'Straffan',
G.n. 'Scharlokii'

G.n. 'Scharlokii', which has green tips to the three outer segments, and the little green spathe, or sheath, that encloses the buds is divided into two long segments which stand up above the flowers like ears. *G.n.* 'Poculiformis' is another strange form, occurring from time to time, and in this the three short, inner segments of the flower are devoid of the usual green markings. Another is 'Viridapicis', denoting that it has green markings on the ends of the outer segments as well as inside, as usual.

Among forms of greater garden value, belonging to this species, are several very fine snowdrops. *G.n.* 'Atkinsii', a splendid garden plant with grey leaves and pure white January flowers, can make a handsome group. On closer inspection, however, it will be noted that few of the flowers are perfectly formed and the white outer segments lack the rounded beauty of most others. 'Magnet' is a well-known variety, tall-growing, with well-proportioned flowers on extra long flower stalks. They are the less able to withstand the vagaries of the weather. 'Galatea', 'Melville', 'Neill Fraser', 'John Gray', 'Augustus', 'Mighty Atom', 'Hill Poë', and other fine, large-flowered forms are also to be sought. One of the most beautiful is 'Straffan'. This probably has relationship with *G. caucasicus* or *G. plicatus*, and it produces, when growing well, two flowers from each bulb, a most valuable characteristic, prolonging the flowering season. It is one of the latest of this group to flower and frequently lasts until the end of March, and increases fairly satisfactorily.

One February years ago, I made a special pilgrimage to see the collection of snowdrops at Hyde Lodge, near Chalford in Gloucestershire, where Brigadier and Mrs Mathias had gathered many kinds together. It was my first sight of the form 'S. Arnott' in quantity. It is an exceptionally fine seedling which almost died out and was brought back into health by the late Walter Butt, the previous owner of Hyde Lodge. The splendid quality of the flowers, their full and rounded shape, large size, and upstanding, stout stems and good leaves made me feel that here indeed was the finest snowdrop for general garden cultivation. It increases regularly. I am glad to see it occurring in catalogues containing these delights.

By Christmas several of the bigger species are appearing, and one of the most handsome is *G. plicatus*, which is known as the Crimean snowdrop, for it occurs in quantity in that country, and, as Mr Bowles has recorded, several forms came to our gardens straight from the trenches after the Crimean War. The leaves are long, dark green, and folded back at the edges. *G. byzantinus* has similar, but more grey, leaves, an equally stalwart plant; the inner segments of the flower have either an upper and a lower green mark, or the marks are fused so that the segment is wholly green, except for a narrow margin. The variety 'Warham' is generally considered to be the finest of the *G. plicatus* forms, while 'Merlin' is a really splendid hybrid with, probably, *G. elwesii*.

1. *Prunus mume* 'Benichidori'. A fragrant Japanese Apricot which flowers soon after Christmas. The flowers are remarkably frostproof

2. *Hamamelis mollis* 'Pallida', the brightest of the fragrant, frostproof Witch Hazels; for lime-free soils. Photographed in January at Wisley

4. *Mahonia × media* 'Charity', photographed in November

3. *Lonicera × purpusii* in flower in early January. Extremely fragrant small flowers cover the bush

5. The Heather Trial at Wisley, photographed in January. Those in flower are cultivars of *Erica herbacea (E. carnea)* and *E. × darleyensis* both of which tolerate some lime in the soil. Those in the distance show the remarkable colours given by the foliage of cultivars of *Calluna vulgaris*

6. The contrasting tints of *Cornus alba* 'Sibirica' (red) and *C. stolonifera* 'Flaviramea' (yellowish), photographed at Wisley in winter

7. *Mahonia × moseri* showing its winter colour

8. The rare *Rhododendron ponticum* 'Foliis Purpureis' whose leaves are bronze-green in summer and the colour of a copper beech in winter, if grown in full sun. It is compact growing with the normal lilac-coloured flowers

9. *Cotoneaster* 'Cornubia' (red) and 'Rothschildianus' (yellow). Two strong-growing hybrids photographed in early February at the Savill Garden

10. *Rhododendron* Praecox in early February with *Erica carnea* 'Springwood White' in the background

11. *Rhododendron* Nobleanum 'Venustum' flowering in January. Successive crops of buds open from late autumn onwards during mild spells

12. *Primula vulgaris sibthorpii,* in flower in January. It is the pink representative of our common primrose in the Caucasus

13. *Narcissus* 'Jana', a cultivar which regularly flowers in February

Galanthus 'S. Arnott'

The most handsome snowdrop in foliage is G. *elwesii*; the leaves are up to 1 inch in width, of a distinct glaucous green, and beautifully shaped. The flowers, borne on stems up to 9 inches or so, are to my mind of poor form, but exhibit considerable interesting variation in the green markings on the inner segments, and G.*e.* 'Whittallii' is greatly treasured, being one of the most heavily marked and handsome forms. Some forms have green spots on the tips of the outer segments as well. G. *caucasicus* is a variable species with similar leaves to those of G. *elwesii*, but they reflex at the tip; it is a good garden plant with one green mark on the inner segments. Another fine snowdrop with broad leaves is G. *allenii*, but in this species they lack the beautiful glaucous colouring, and the inner segments of the flowers have only the usual one green mark. There are times, when it is growing well, that I consider this the most beautiful of all snowdrops in quality of flower.

Apart from the differences noted above, between the usual rather

Leucojum vernum

blue-green leaves of the common snowdrop and the attractive grey of *G. elwesii*, there is a group of species with shining rich green foliage. One that we have long known as *G. latifolius* or *G. platyphyllus* has now to be called *G. ikariae latifolius*; it has a small flower, but *G. ikariae* itself is larger with rounded segments, and is one of the latest snowdrops to flower, usually in March. Also with shining but narrower dark green leaves is *G. rizehensis*, whose flowers are again small but very rounded, appearing in January. This is a prolific plant.

Allied to the snowdrops are the snowflakes, among which is a charming little August and September flowering species, *Leucojum autumnale*. The early spring *L. vernum*, naturalized here and there in England, is a very stalwart plant; in January and February its broad dark green leaves clasp the sturdy stem, which bears one or two blooms in snowdrop style, but they are broader and more ample. Each of the six equal broad segments of the flower has a clear green spot at its tip, changing to yellow in the form *L.v.* var. *carpathicum*. A specially fine form is called *L.v.* var. *wagneri*, often bearing two blooms on each stem. All these are deliciously redolent of violets.

These spring snowflakes are of particularly generous proportions and are well fitted to withstand the weather, but slugs love them. They seem to like cool positions best, such as may be found to the north of rocks or shrubs, and will thrive in quite damp, humus-laden soil, such as one would give to trilliums, meconopsises, and the like.

Snowdrops and snowflakes come into flower at a time when their blooms are most welcome so it is not surprising that gardeners have segregated many forms and gathered species from many countries. In fact, so long ago as 1891 the Royal Horticultural Society held a conference about them, when dozens of varieties were discussed and shown; and I am glad to find many keen gardeners today are growing little collections of species and garden forms, thus preserving and increasing them. Small bulbs are so very prone to die out from neglect, or from an impatient fork or unwary spade, except where they settle down and spread in their thousands. And this, when well suited, the best snowdrops will do.

15. Some Notes
on Cultivation

This book does not aim at discussing the rudiments of gardening, but it would not be complete without at least a reference to the importance of thorough *preparation* of the ground before planting. Deep digging is so beneficial that it cannot be stressed too often, and thorough eradication of all perennial weeds is essential if we aim at planting all our new shrubs and other things permanently. It is galling in the extreme to have to lift a shrub which has perhaps just established itself because some insidious couch-grass or gout-weed has become entangled in its roots, or to find that a dock or dandelion, in spite of frequent removal, persists in reappearing in the heart of a plant.

There has been much publicity given to new ideas about cultivation of late years – such as that digging and hoeing are no longer necessary. I have myself pointed to this delightful prospect on page 5, but it is only true after the border has been prepared and the shrubs and plants are established.

No amount of afterwork will make up for lack of initial preparation; if an entire border is not to be planted, no hole or holes can be too large or deep – in moderation, of course! – for a plant or shrub. I must add that the preparation of 'holes' is seldom as satisfactory as the preparation of an entire area for new plantings. Holes, according to the nature of the soil, tend either to dry out or to collect water in extremes of weather, whereas the greater area, having been deeply dug, prevents undue drying in hot weather, and helps moisture to find its own level quickly.

In digging, an important point or two must be borne in mind. One is that subsoil should not be brought to the surface, so that if your good soil is shallow it is best to do your digging in two levels, digging and turning over the lower or subsoil and serving the top 'spit' the same way, but not mixing them. Most good text-books on gardening will give a diagram of this, and it is usually termed 'bastard' trenching. 'Double' trenching, or merely trenching, is preferable on soils where the dark colour of the top soil extends to 2 feet or more in depth.

Another important point is not to touch the soil for digging or planting when it is too sticky, if it happens to be of a clay-like consistency; temporary waterlogged conditions in winter may easily bring about this state on otherwise well-drained soils.

A third counsel is to make sure that trees are adequately staked at planting time. In the spring, when those dry windy spells occur, every tree and shrub, and some of the plants, may need a firm treading to ensure that the now drier soil is consolidated around their 'necks'.

When trees and shrubs are purchased from a nursery, the nursery-man usually sends them out as soon as he can after receiving the order. As is usual in a seasonal occupation, a great rush of orders is dealt with during the critical months and delay may occur. And then when the consignment is sent by rail, sometimes severe frost and even snow may have occurred before the plants arrive. Good nurseries pack their bundles and containers adequately, and little damage is likely to occur, but difficulty may be experienced in dealing with the plants on arrival. During the winter nearly all nursery stock is more or less dormant, and if a frost-proof outhouse or cellar is available the bundles can be stored in them until a thaw comes. On the other hand, if storage in a frost-free yet unheated building is not possible, it is seldom that the ground is so deeply frozen that the crust cannot be broken, and the roots of all hardy stock can then be 'healed' in the unfrozen soil beneath and planted properly when conditions improve. Well-packed nursery stock can survive several weeks in a packed state, but should anything appear to be suffering on arrival when unpacked, it is best to soak it for twenty-four hours in cold water, or to bury it entirely in the soil for twice as long or longer, after which it will usually become plump and fresh and will survive its ordeal.

It should also be borne in mind that the nurseryman's November rush is occasioned by purchasers, all demanding their goods at the same time, whereas nearly all deciduous trees and shrubs can be moved with perfect safety from the time their leaves fall until spring reawakens them, while evergreens are mostly best transplanted during September and October, or April and May, provided the ground is moist and the icy winds from the east are not prevailing. Herbaceous plants may be planted during the same months as the evergreens with every prospect of success; fuller details are given for all these categories and bulbs in the tables on pages 184–200.

The above two paragraphs were written for the first edition of this book in 1957. The suggestions still apply where nursery stock comes from a faraway nursery. Today we tend to pick up our plants by car, grown in containers, making transplanting easy at almost any time. The pitfall in late spring is that some plants have only just been put into their containers and will suffer if the soil falls off their roots during planting.

The only way to avoid work in the garden – and most of us who make it a hobby have to do so – is to prepare the ground thoroughly first; then to choose those plants which will be likely to thrive in our conditions, and which will grow with a minimum of attention. And above all to place all humus and manure *on* the soil instead of *in* it, and to plant carpeting plants and low-growing, ground-covering shrubs wherever possible, even under taller things, thus aiming at prevention of weed growth. For the first few years after a border has been planted it will need hoeing during the summer, and it is a good maxim to put in the trees and larger shrubs the first year and not to plant smaller things and bulbs until a year or two later. In this way we can make sure that the ground is really weed-free, and wield the hoe efficaciously for a season or two, and then put in the small fry, after which it is usually possible to keep the border weeded by hand until the ground-coverers and the mulching do the work for us. I am a firm believer in putting all humus and manure *on* the ground rather than *in* it. It is nature's method and has worked very well over a period of over twenty years in my own garden on light soil; anyone who needs further convincing could not do better than read *Ploughman's Folly* and other similar books by E.H. Faulkner.

My final advice is that there shall be no bonfires except for prickly and other prunings which will not rot in a heap with the help of one of the proprietary brand of humus-aids. The heap which will slowly accumulate from all soft clippings and dead herbaceous tops, and all soft vegetable waste from the kitchen, should be turned periodically as a counsel of perfection, but we do not all have time for this; it will prove an invaluable top-dressing material in time; weed seeds are usually present but the mulch of humus dries quickly and moving it about on the border on a hot day speedily kills the tiny seedlings, while if they get bigger they are very much easier to pull out of humus-covered soil than from ordinary soil.

It should be remembered that planting permanent things is an important long-term policy and, therefore, adequate initial preparation is necessary, and nature's own feedings with decaying vegetation is the best insurance we can give our new plants for their future. Especially is this true on hungry soils like those over sharply drained gravel, also those over chalk which dissolves humus almost faster than we can provide it.

The planting of the wild types of plants, as outlined in my introduction, and to which nearly all the trees, shrubs and plants mentioned in this book belong, calls for gardening quite different from the usual digging-and-hoeing type. By mixing our bulbs and plants with our shrubs, some in the open and some under trees, we are deliberately copying nature. By making a careful choice, we can, with periodical overhauls and occasional replantings of unsuccessful ventures, make a varied covering of our ground which will give us interest throughout the year, with a very minimum of trouble.

16. Planning the Winter Border

First follow nature, and your judgement frame
By her just standard, which is still the same.

ALEXANDER POPE (1688–1744)
from *Nature and Art*

The following plans of imaginary borders are fitted into this book with two objects in view. One is to show as well as possible what I have been suggesting about covering the ground with plants to prevent weeds and save cultivation, when once the initial deep digging is completed, and the other to indicate the different sizes and values of plants and shrubs in the composition of the border-picture. The various specimens have been given the amount of space they may be expected to occupy in a few years, although it will be obvious that species collected from all over the world and then placed in one border cannot all grow to perfection. Some will thrive magnificently and others will merely exist, and it is best for anyone unversed in this type of gardening to consult not only books and catalogues but to obtain the advice of a local gardener who has grown such things in the local conditions and will be able to judge their possibilities. Gardening being the paradox and varied sport that it is, I feel I must add here that one's own dearly bought experience is far more acceptable than the advice of another, and also that there is no spice of garden life like pleasing oneself in one's own garden!

Plan I is of an imaginary border and Plan II is exactly double the size. The same sort of planting is employed in each and it will be apparent that to achieve the ground-covering and to make the most of the area, three layers of growth are employed. First, the trees or large shrubs; second, the low shrubs or carpeting plants; and third, the bulbs. As envisaged in Chapter 15, the initial preparation of the ground would be followed by the planting of the trees and bigger shrubs. The following autumn, having watched the soil for pernicious weeds meanwhile, the smaller shrubs, ground-cover and bulbs would be planted. For the first three years or more much vacant ground will need mulching with fallen leaves, moss-peat, sawdust, or chopped bracken – all of which are almost free of weed seeds – or compost, which is often abounding in weed seeds. Another good nourishing mulch is made by laying out to rot (helped by sulphate of ammonia) bales of soft barley straw. Temporary plants such as cistuses and brooms, tree lupins and various herbaceous plants may well be used as 'fillers' while the shrubs are growing.

Plan I is of a border 20 feet long by 8 feet wide, backed by a wall or fence to the south. Thus this fence or wall will shade the back of the border, creating a cool root-run for the *Daphne*, *Viburnum* and *Rhododendron*, and the hellebores. The last-named will eventually benefit also from the shade of the *Hamamelis*. The white *Daphne* is given the dark, purplish background of the *Mahonia*, while the big, creamy leaves of the ivy will enliven the *Viburnum* and the *Rhododendron*. These two shrubs and the *Hamamelis* will dominate the border, with *Helleborus corsicus*, *Polystichum* and *Sarcococca* being of secondary importance, while the *Iris* and *Bergenia* will break the swards of heathers with striking foliage.

In the event of this border facing the other way, with the shelter of a north wall behind it, the sun would, of course, strike on the plants from the front. Hellebores would not then be so happy in front of the *Hamamelis* and could be replaced with more heathers; *Rhododendron mucronulatum* might suffer if the soil were too hot and dry, and the Laurustinus might well be planted instead. The fern could be replaced by *Hebe ochracea* or other sun-loving low evergreen, for daphnes are frequently gaunt in growth and look best when their tops appear over something more solid. *Skimmia reevesiana* would be replaced by *S. japonica* 'Rubella', as this variety, while equally tolerant of shade as far as growth is concerned, gives its best bud-colour when the sun shines fully on it. With the sun at our backs, as it were, giving an opportunity to plant a shrub for bark colour, I should want to put in the Westonbirt *Cornus* instead of the Fragrant Guelder, and under it to have some Yellow Dutch crocuses instead of 'Vanguard', to create a more richly coloured contrast.

In the gaps along the front, small bulbs of every kind can be planted, with some tiny, ground-covering plants like the variegated or golden-leafed aubrietas, together with creeping thymes and *Ionopsidium acaule*. These will suit whichever way the border faces, and a few clumps of daffodils 'Rijnvelds's Early Sensation' and 'Jana' will be useful for January and February colour among the heathers and bergenias.

Turning now to Plan II, we will again presume that a wall or fence prevents the sun's rays from drying the back portion and thus the shaded soil would help the shrubs and plants chosen. Athough we again have a deciduous, dominating specimen on the left, it can be much larger, and the Autumn Cherry has been selected, casting shade, in time, over a large area, sufficient to contain several mahonias, hellebores and low plants. The grassy effect of the iris again provides that invaluable contrast to enhance the broader leaves of other plants and shrubs. Once again climbers at the back will give contrasting colour and shapes of leaf with specimens in front of them. Through the branches of Witch Hazel in the foreground, beset with its yellow flowers, would be seen the reddish stems of the Dogwood, while in summer the latter's white, variegated leaves would add light relief.

Once more taking our alternative, the accommodating Fragrant Guelder, or its hybrid *Viburnum × bodnantense*, both of which will thrive in sun or shade, may be used instead of the Dogwood, and the *Rhododendron* left out in preference to a sun-loving shrub, as, for instance, *Arbutus unedo rubra*, *Lonicera × purpusii*, or *Mahonia lomariifolia*. We would change the skimmias as in Plan I, and try *Helleborus lividus* or colchicums, early daffodils or *Rhododendron intricatum* or *R. saluenense* in place of *Helleborus niger*. *Saxifraga fortunei* would likewise have to be replaced. The variegated ivy under the cherry should give untold joy, threading its way through other things and displaying its great, creamy leaves to advantage at all seasons; it would, however, need the knife when fully established, for it is vigorous and invasive. In this border a great variety of small plants in the frontal gaps will form anti-splash covering for many groups of snowdrops, aconites, cyclamens, irises and crocuses.

Now we must consider those who garden on limy soil, for the above plans have presumed an acid or at least a neutral soil, where rhododendrons and camellias will thrive. No change need be made to the heathers, for, as explained in their own chapter, these winter-flowering varieties are tolerant to an amazing degree to almost all types of soil. But the rhododendrons will not be worth the attempt to make them thrive. It is better, far, to plant something else, such as viburnums, cotoneasters, loniceras and chimonanthuses, in all of which the choice is wide, although none of them give the rich floral colour of rhododendrons. Likewise hamamelises must be omitted, and another choice made from the same list.

Shade is of three kinds in the garden; one from big overhanging trees, another from buildings, and the third from small trees of one's own deliberate placing. This last category will obviously not concern us, for the inclusion of such a tree will have been done for the express purpose of providing an upper layer of greenery and flower, which will in turn be enjoyed by the specially chosen smaller things beneath it. Shade from a building is not very troublesome, in fact the majority of shrubs will thrive happily in it, although the quantity of flower produced in some kinds may be reduced. It benefits especially white-variegated shrubs and plants, but not golden-variegated forms of the same species, and allows shade-lovers to develop to their very best. But shade from overhanging trees, coupled with the inevitable suction of their roots, is often difficult. When once established, however, shrubs and plants, suitably chosen, will thrive well. If the shade is from greedy surface-rooting trees with a dense overhead canopy of leaves, like the beech, the ash, chestnuts and sycamores, despair may well reign. But if the oak with its deeply questing roots is the sole provider of shade, all is well; and scattered shade from old fruit trees, birches, larch and pines, and a host of garden trees, cherries and the like, is helpful in many ways, provided the branches are well aloft, and that shrubs and plants are not expected to thrive immediately around the boles of the denser trees.

A garden overhung, therefore, with light shade will provide almost ideal conditions for a very great number of shrubs and plants, among which rhododendrons of all kinds, mahonias, camellias, *Fatsia*, many daphnes, sarcococcas, ruscuses and skimmias, *Leucothöe*, ivies, *Iris foetidissima*, bergenias, ferns, cyclamens, primulas, pulmonarias, hepaticas, and many small bulbs may be expected to thrive.

Presuming that our border is to delight the eye, glass cloches and other structures will not be welcome, but where the principal *raison d'être* is to provide flowers for cutting, hoops of bent cane or hazel supporting a night-covering of sacking or straw mats will be found of the very greatest benefit in all but severe frost.

We will now consider the possibilities of a garden which has a warm and sheltered corner in it, bounded by buildings on its north and east

PLAN I

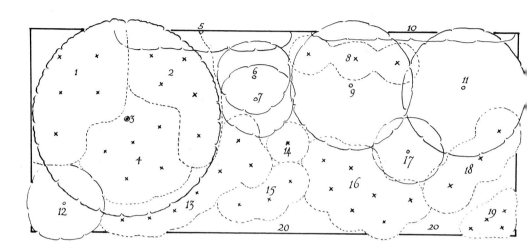

1. *Helleborus corsicus* (5)
2. *Helleborus orientalis* in variety (5)
3. *Hamamelis mollis* or variety (1)
4. *Helleborus niger* (5)
5. *Mahonia heterophylla* (*M. toluacensis*) (1) trained on wall
6. *Daphne mezereum* 'Bowles's White' (1)
7. *Polystichum munitum* (1)
8. *Helleborus kochii* and *H. atrorubens* (3)
9. *Viburnum farreri* (1), underplanted with *Viola odorata* and *V. alba*, with *Crocus* 'Vanguard'
10. *Hedera canariensis* 'Gloire de Marengo' (1) on wall
11. *Rhododendron mucronulatum* or *Camellia sasanqua* (1), underplanted with *Cyclamen hederifolium* and *Crocus tomasinianus*, *C. sieberi*, *C. laevigatus*, etc.
12. *Skimmia* × *foremanii* (1)
13. *Erica carnea* (*E. herbacea*) (7)
14. *Iris foetidissima* (1)
15. *Bergenia purpurascens* (3)
16. *Erica carnea* 'Springwood White' (7)
17. *Sarcococca hookeriana digyna* (1)
18. *Pulmonaria rubra* (3)
19. *Hepatica* × *media* 'Ballard's Variety' (3)
20. Small bulbs, with suitable small ground-cover

PLAN II

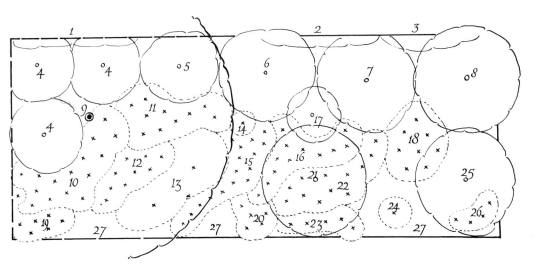

1. *Jasminum nudiflorum* (1) on wall
2. *Hedera colchica* (1) on wall
3. *Hedera helix* 'Angularis Aurea' (1) on wall
4. *Mahonia japonica* (3)
5. *Fatsia japonica* (1)
6. *Cornus alba* 'Elegantissima' (1), underplanted with bulbs
7. *Rhododendron* Nobleanum 'Venustum' or 'Chrismas Cheer' (1)
8. *Garrya elliptica* (1)
9. *Prunus subhirtella* 'Autumnalis', standard tree on 6 foot stem (1)
10. *Helleborus corsicus* (15)
11. *Helleborus kochii, H. atrorubens*, and *H. orientalis* forms (10)
12. *Iris foetidissima* (9)
13. *Hedera colchica* 'Dentata Variegata' (2)
14. *Polystichum munitum* (1)

15. *Erica carnea (E. herbacea)* (17)
16. *Erica × darleyensis* (12)
17. *Skimmia × foremanii* (1)
18. *Bergenia* 'Ballawley Hybrid' (7)
19. *Helleborus niger* and varieties (7)
20. *Erica carnea* 'December Red' (5)
21. *Hamamelis mollis* or variety (1) (underplanted with Nos 16, 22 and 23)
22. *Erica carnea* 'Springwood White' (12)
23. *Bergenia purpurascens* (5)
24. *Helleborus foetidus* (1)
25. *Chimonanthus praecox* or variety (1), underplanted with bulbs and hepaticas
26. *Saxifraga fortunei* (4)
27. Small bulbs, with suitable ground-cover

sides. Here all manner of delights will find a place. Tight against the
hottest wall the Algerian Iris will find its most congenial home, and
provide flowers almost without stopping, from September until
April; and in narrow borders with similar sun-warming, most of the
choicer small bulbs will especially thrive. Nerines, Kaffir lilies, sternbergias and zephyranthes, colchicums, *Helleborus lividus* and *Liriope*
will all enjoy the shelter and warmth, even in our warmer counties. It
will also be the best place possible for *Garrya*, *Mahonia lomariifolia* and
M. fremontii, *Erica lusitanica*, *Magnolia grandiflora*, *Daphne bholua* and
D. odora, *Edgworthia*, *Buddleia auriculata*, *Cytisus* 'Porlock', hebes,
grevilleas, *Chimonanthus* and azaras. On the walls the three clematises
and *Jasminum* × *mesneyi* will be likely to prosper. The daphnes and
Edgworthia mentioned above will need a cooler soil than the others,
and this can be provided by covering their area with slabs of stone;
where the soil is cool and shelter is present, *Camellia sasanqua* and its
varieties will, too, be happily accommodated, in lime-free soil, to give
fragrant blooms in October and November.

Cold, sticky, limy soils will usually suit *Daphne mezereum*,
hepaticas, *Cornus alba* and varieties, cotoneaster, viburnums, prunuses, bergenias, hellebores, snowdrops and *Eranthis*. Should a very
wet position be the only available site for a winter-colour planting,
C. alba varieties, and all willows and bamboos will be found to
provide an astonishing variety of colour. In short, there is no aspect or
soil in which there is a complete dearth of choice, short of the star-
vation of dense, overhanging trees. But who, having the glory of a
full-grown beech tree in the garden, that most delightful of our native
trees, with its ferny branches sweeping the ground, would wish to
dispense with its manifold beauties and grace in order to grow some
exotics?

17. Conclusion

Study is like the heaven's glorious sun
That will not be deep-searched with saucy looks;
Small have continual plodders ever won
Save base authority from others' books.

WILLIAM SHAKESPEARE
from *Love's Labour's Lost*

FOR BEGINNERS AND CONNOISSEURS

It cannot be denied that, were they given the protection of some vast glass structure during the winter, the majority of trees and shrubs and plants – particularly the latter – mentioned in this book would produce their flowers to greater perfection, unmolested by the fingers of Jack Frost. And so this last chapter shall be a revision of those preceding it, first outlining a few stalwarts that may be tried in almost every garden, then giving some suggestions for room decoration, followed by the cultivation of the more tender subjects in frames and houses.

We will continue with our plan of taking the largest first. If we want a tree or two, the Silver Birch in its common or its weeping or cut-leafed form, or one of the choicer species such as *Betula jacquemonti* with the Autumn Cherry (*Prunus subhirtella* 'Autumnalis') in its white or pink form, may suffice, with the possible addition of *Crataegus* × *lavallei* 'Carrierei' for the beauty of its long-lasting orange fruits.

The larger shrubs, up to some 12 feet or so, that may be counted upon to give pretty regular display are *Cornus mas*, and the Witch Hazels, of which the best, *Hamamelis mollis*, is the smallest in growth. With these we may group what is probably the best all-round holly, *Ilex aquifolium* 'J.C. van Tol', and the noble *Garrya* for sheltered gardens, with our old, inestimable, familiar friend the Laurustinus (*Viburnum tinus*) making a good third to these evergreens.

The following might be chosen for rather small growth, up to some 7 or 8 feet: *V. farreri* or *V.* × *bodnantense*, and *Camellia* × *williamsii* for flowers, *Cornus alba* 'Sibirica' for reddish bark, and the two superlative cotoneasters, *Cotoneaster conspicuus*, forming a dense arching hummock, and *C. serotinus*, of open habit, carrying their berries until May. With them I would choose my own prime favourite for shade, *Mahonia japonica*, first for foliage, scent and habit, and the first choice for any sunless corner.

For smaller shrubs we might have those two lovely skimmias, ×*foremanii* for berry, and 'Rubella' for the red-brown of its multitudes of tiny flower buds. On lime-free soils the pernettyas can be very lovely, together with *Rhododendron mucronulatum* or *R. dauricum*, and some *R.* Nobleanum forms. *Daphne mezereum* should be the choice on sticky, limy soils.

In the front we need some ground-cover, and for this there is nothing comparable to *Erica carnea* (*E. herbacea*) and its varieties; apart from the type species I would choose 'Springwood White' as a truly great garden plant, especially for slopes. Planted about 2 feet apart, they soon mingle and make an impenetrable carpet.

Among bulbs we could not miss out *Schizostylis coccinea* 'Viscountess Byng', whose stems give us such splendid flowers for the house in a shade of delicate pink that one would hardly expect in November, and two or three types of snowdrops must be included. I think I would choose the ordinary *Galanthus nivalis*, because it is cheap and one can therefore plant in quantity, and its double form, and the splendid 'S. Arnott'. By mixing snowdrops with Tommasini's *Crocus* several weeks of bloom may be obtained from the same place, and if some Lily of the valley can be grown with them, the area given will remain weed-free and work-free for the whole year. The Winter Aconite and the Christmas Rose are indispensable if they can be made at home; but they need, I think, a 'tacky' soil and coolness to make them thrive; this is also true of many snowdrops as well. Gardening as I do on sandy soil, my experience is that the Christmas Rose has hardly settled down yet after five years' trial, and aconites only increase by seed.

On the other hand, a more accommodating plant than the many forms of *Helleborus orientalis*, the Lenten Rose, could not be found. They appear to thrive anywhere, in any soil and in almost any situation, and can be most thoroughly recommended in their great diversity of colours.

For walls the Winter Jasmine and *Pyracantha angustifolia* and *P. atalantioides* (*gibbsii*) tie for first place, and I should not like to omit the great cream variegated ivy, *Hedera colchica* 'Dentata Variegata' for shady walls, while for sunny walls I would use instead *H. canariensis* 'Variegata'. And of course, at the foot of all sunny walls and the dry bases of hedgerows, lots of forms of the Algerian Iris should be planted, to provide exquisite flowers for picking. No corner is too hot or dry for them.

With this small selection of the numerous plants mentioned in this book much beauty could be obtained in even a small garden from the days of the latest Michaelmas daisy (*Aster tradescantii*) until the coming of the purple, white and gold of the spring crocuses. And except where stated they can be grown out of doors without protection in Surrey, and in the frequent mild spells which we experience in our winter will blossom forth regularly, while the leaves and coloured twigs, bless them, will be with us throughout all weathers, doing their indispensable part in furnishing the garden.

In a garden of half an acre it should be possible to provide flowers and other decorations for the house throughout the year. With a garden of an acre this becomes easy, even through the winter. It is easy to maintain a succession of Autumn Cherry in flower; I find that by cutting a good branch in November one obtains not only the first main crop which can sometimes be timed to flower just right for Christmas, but that if the same branch be kept long enough the second crop will appear, very white and winter-frail, a month later in a warm room. Meanwhile further branches can be cut to repeat the performance. I am seldom without Winter Jasmine in a vase; it opens successive crops from October until the spring, and is admirable for cutting with Christmas Roses and holly at Christmas. The rhododendrons like *Rhododendron mucronulatum* open well in water too, and I like to have these with a few pieces of *Mahonia japonica*, the contrast of colours is so excellent.

A word here about lasting qualities would be apposite, since the *Mahonia* only lasts a few days and then soon drops, and I have found no means of inducing buds to open; even hot water, so useful for short-lasting flowers, has not proved successful. Much the same may be said of the Fragrant Guelder, but I find all these troublesome flowers are greatly helped by being removed at night and put into the cool larder, where the dewy air greatly revives them. Mrs Constance Spry told me that the hot-water treatment had proved successful with the notoriously difficult Lenten Roses. Water as hot as one can bear it for one's hands should be put in the container, and this will often revive flagging stems and will also usually make them last much longer if used at first, after cutting. I always top up my vases in winter with warm water, especially if I am expecting flowers to open on cherry or Winter Sweet or *Hamamelis*. How deliciously these last two, or the Fragrant Guelder or *Mahonia*, will scent a room; even two or three small pieces will convey their sweetness around.

The spring-flowering trees can also very easily be forced into bloom in a warm room, and almost any early-flowering member of the *Prunus* tribe is suitable. The red buds of *Skimmia japonica* 'Rubella' are invaluable for winter arrangements.

But there is no need to rely upon the frail flowers only. Give them their legitimate company, the noble leaves – the great, broad-tinted blades of *Bergenia*, the striking grass-green blades of the Stinking Iris, and the great puckered foliage of *Viburnum rhytidophyllum*, all strongly contrasting with each other. An occasional piece of variegation will not come amiss, and a red twig or two from the Dogwood and a berried spray will light the whole.

In a large room under brilliant light a transparent glass container can be filled with the assorted colours of bare twigs of willow in orange and yellow, Dogwood in red and ochre, and the green of *Kerria* or *Leycesteria*, giving a clean, bright effect very suitable for February, when spring is just round the corner. And, of course, still more spring-like are the early types of Pussy Willow mentioned on page 30, and the catkins of hazel.

With all this easily grown variety, giving us ample variation in colour, form and line, the only difficulty is to know just how much of our small garden we can devote to these plants. But the comforting thought immediately comes that the bulk of the winter's invaluable leaves is from plants and shrubs whose flowers appear at other seasons.

There are cold spells which sometimes go on for weeks, and then the cut greenery indoors begins to look dusty and no fresh flowers are forthcoming outside. It is then that I wish I had a large, slightly heated, glass structure, where I would grow the early rhododendrons whose flowers are more frail than most, in large tubs, or even in the borders themselves. I would have *Jasminum polyanthum* and *Buddleia asiatica* to shed their fragrance around, and the many bulbs would flower untroubled by icy winds. Occasionally one comes across a greenhouse given over to such joys, but more often than not it is an unheated glasshouse and much can be done even then. But the flowers will suffer during frosty spells unless temporary heat can be used.

One of the most attractive ways of enjoying the tiny bulbs, the colchicums, snowdrops, crocuses and irises, the cyclamens and all the other small things mentioned, which so easily spoil out of doors, is to have a deep frame for them. An ordinary 'cold frame' is all that is needed, with brick sides built up to about 2 feet, covered with a sash frame or metal light. After ensuring that drainage is good, a light, gritty soil containing humus and bonemeal can be filled into the frame, leaving 9 inches or so air-space at the lower end. In this the bulbs will thrive and multiply, and can flower abundantly without being dashed to pieces by storms and pecked by birds.

The alpine house itself is not the ideal place for these winter-flowering bulbs, for, being unheated, a cold spell leaves them almost as badly cared for as they would be outside. They will not stand the cold so well in a pan or pot on staging as they will growing comfortably in a frame. The higher one can raise the frame the greater will be the enjoyment from the flowers, and the rich warm scent of *Crocus imperati* or *C. sieberi* in dark January is worth catering for in a careful and methodical way. Crocuses are particularly prone to damage by sudden storms, but they can stand a great deal of frost without being destroyed, while the snowdrop, having its flower the opposite way up, comes through most storms unscathed.

Other joys that come to mind are *Asphodelus acaulis*, *Tecophilaea cyanocrocus*, and the grey-and-blush *Ranunculus calandrinioides*, *Aster pappei*, *Lithospermum rosmarinifolium*, *Iberis semperflorens*, and *Raffenaldia primuloides*; these all deserve to have that little extra shelter that they need. And with them I would grow, of course, a bigger selection of the early saxifrages of the Kabschia and Engleria sections than the solitary very early species already mentioned, and the exquisite *Primula allionii*, a fragrant miniature with a long flowering season.

Having said my say, and gathered into these pages all the colour I can think of to warm our rooms and brighten our gardens during winter, I feel that a bewildering choice has been spread before those who are about to plant a few good things. I hope that the numerous less worthy plants that have crept into these pages will not obscure the more important and beautiful subjects. In any case, if the mere quantity of plants which I have attempted to display is such that it impresses future growers with their amazing variety and possibilities, the object of this book will have been achieved.

18. Planting Tables

In the following tables I have given a brief and concise picture of the height and width, period of beauty and colour of stems or other characters of practically all the trees, shrubs, bulbs and plants mentioned in this book. I hope that this handy form of reference may be of use to intending planters, but it should be borne in mind that, as I have stressed earlier in this book, I write from Surrey, and periods of flower and also ultimate growth may vary greatly over the counties. In particular the heights of the trees and shrubs should be 'taken with a pinch of salt'; for if all intending planters kept rigidly within the limits prescribed by their gardens far fewer trees and shrubs would be planted. They all grow much bigger than we realize, or than our appetite allows! Suffice it to say that it is always permissible to plant too closely provided one can harden one's heart and remove the overcrowding vigorous specimens later: a task few of us relish. But so much enjoyment can be obtained from the first ten years of a shrub's life that after ten years a shrub is often left to take care of itself; and so much uncertainty attends most of us in the second decade from the present that this is very understandable. In the smaller garden of today, therefore, the wise choice is the smaller-growing specimen, with temporary 'fillers' in between, to be rooted out later. But our smaller gardens are only very personal things and these counsels of perfection at times smack too much of a purist's advice.

It is in the greater, more permanent plantings – along our trunk roads and in our national parks and gardens, and the grounds of institutions – that circumspection is most needed; where the future will judge and decry planting which has been lavish and unattended.

In the same way the planting periods are also counsels of perfection, and may be varied according to the governing exigencies. It is possible to move almost anything at almost any time in one's own garden with complete success, but plants that have to be out of the ground for some days or weeks should be moved at a time most suitable to them. This I have endeavoured to indicate.

The words 'shade' and 'shelter' are given to show to which plants I would accord either type of protection here in the open in Surrey. Some plants thrive better in shade, or their foliage is at its largest size and best colour when not burned by the sun, or alternatively they may do equally well in either position, and thus they may be given shade, leaving full exposure to plants which derive greatest benefit from it. 'Shelter' means that I would give these plants the warmest positions available and cover the ground around them in the autumn with a deep mulch, and, where practicable and necessary, cover their parts above ground with evergreen branches or a wigwam of sacking for the winter. It is best not to put in new plants in this category until late spring, when danger of severe frost is past.

As explained in other chapters, many small bulbs require a deal of sunlight and need well-drained and sheltered positions; these words 'shade' and 'shelter' are therefore omitted from the bulbs lists on pages 198–200.

The particulars given are very brief; they are not meant to be more than a quick and easy reference, and more exact and greater details will be found not only in earlier chapters, but in specialist books on the various genera concerned, and in catalogues.

TREES, flowering	Height (approx)	Spread (approx)	Flowering period	Flower colour	Planting time
Alnus incana 'Aurea'	20 ft	10 ft	Feb–Mar	Orange	Oct–Mar
— *glutinosa*	70 ft	20 ft	,,	Yellow	,,
Arbutus × *hybrida*	15 ft	15 ft	Sept–Nov	Ivory	Mar–May
— *unedo*	,,	,,	,,	Ivory	,,
— — *rubra* ('Croomei')	10 ft	10 ft	,,	Pinkish	,,
Azara microphylla	15 ft	,,	Feb–Apr	Yellow	,,
Cornus mas	20 ft	20 ft	Jan–Mar	,,	Oct–Mar
Corylus colurna	70 ft	40 ft	Feb–Mar	,,	,,
Crataegus monogyna 'Biflora'	20 ft	15 ft	Intermittent	White	,,
Eucalyptus gunnii	100 ft	50 ft	Oct–Nov	Green	May
Parrotia persica	30 ft	60 ft	Jan–Mar	Reddish	Oct–Mar
Populus canescens	100 ft	50 ft	Feb–Mar	,,	,,
— *tremula*	40 ft	20 ft	,,	,,	,,
Prunus dulcis 'Praecox'	15 ft	15 ft	,,	Pink	,,
— *conradinae*	30 ft	30 ft	,,	,,	,,
— *davidiana*	20 ft	25 ft	Jan–Mar	,,	,,
— — *alba*	25 ft	12 ft	,,	White	,,
— *incisa* 'Praecox'	20–30 ft	10–20 ft	Feb–Mar	Blush	,,
— *kansuensis*	20 ft	20 ft	,,	,,	,,
— *mandschurica*	15 ft	10–20 ft	,,	,,	,,
— *mume* cultivars	,,	15 ft	Jan–Mar	Various	,,
— *serrulata*					
— — *semperflorens*	12 ft	12 ft	Nov–Apr	Blush	Oct–Mar
— *subhirtella* 'Autumnalis'	20 ft	30 ft	Oct–Mar	White	,,
— — 'Autumnalis Rosea'	,,	,,	Jan–Mar	Pink	,,

DECIDUOUS SHRUBS, flowering

	Height (approx)	Spread (approx)	Flowering period	Flower colour	Planting time
Abeliophyllum distichum	5–6 ft	5–6 ft	Feb–Mar	White	Oct–Mar
Chaenomeles speciosa 'Aurora'	5–8 ft	5–8 ft	Oct–Apr	Salmon	,,
Chimonanthus praecox	7–8 ft	6–7 ft	Jan–Mar	Greyish cream	,,
— — 'Grandiflorus'	,,	,,	,,	Dark yellow	,,
— — 'Luteus'	6–7 ft	5–6 ft	,,	Bright yellow	,,
Corylus avellana 'Contorta'	8–10 ft	8–10 ft	,,	Yellow catkins	,,
Daphne mezereum (shade)	3–4 ft	3–4 ft	Dec–Apr	Pink/White	,,
— — 'Grandiflora' (shade)	4–5 ft	,,	Oct–Dec	Old Rose	,,
Edgworthia papyrifera (shelter)	4–6 ft	4–6 ft	Feb–Apr	Creamy yellow	Apr–May
Forsythia giraldiana	6–8 ft	6–8 ft	Feb–Mar	Yellow	Oct–Mar
— *ovata*	4–5 ft	4–5 ft	,,	,,	,,
Hamamelis mollis	8–15 ft	8–10 ft	Jan–Feb	Yellow/Orange	,,
— *japonica*	7–10 ft	10–12 ft	Feb–Mar	Yellow	,,
— *vernalis*	6 ft	6 ft	,,	Creamy grey	,,
— *virginiana*	8 ft	8 ft	Sept–Nov	Lime yellow	,,
Lonicera fragrantissima	6–8 ft	6 ft	Nov–Mar	Cream	,,
— × *purpusii*	,,	,,	,,	,,	,,
— *setifera*	10 ft	10 ft	Feb–Mar	Pink	,,
— *standishii*	6–8 ft	6 ft	Nov–Mar	Cream	,,

	Height (approx)	Spread (approx)	Flowering period	Flower colour	Planting time
Nuttallia cerasiformis	6-8 ft	6-8 ft	Feb-Apr	Cream	Oct-Mar
Prinsepia utilis	10 ft	10 ft	Feb-Mar	Creamy	,,
Salix acutifolia	12 ft	,,	Jan-Mar	Yellow	,,
— aegyptiaca (medemii)	,,	12 ft	Jan-Feb	Yellow	,,
— daphnoides 'Aglaia'	15 ft	10 ft	Jan-Mar	,,	,,
— gracilistyla	6-10 ft	6 ft	Jan-Feb	,,	,,
— — 'Melanostachys'	4 ft	4 ft	Feb-Mar	Black	,,
— irrorata	10 ft	6 ft	Jan-Mar	Yellow	,,
Stachyurus chinensis	5-10 ft	5-8 ft	Feb-Apr	Cream	,,
— praecox	,,	,,	,,	,,	,,
Viburnum × *bodnantense* 'Dawn' and 'Deben'	11 ft	6-11 ft	Oct-Mar	Pink	,,
— × burkwoodii	7-8 ft	7-8 ft	Autumn-Spring	White	Autumn and Spring
— foetens	10 ft	10 ft	Oct-Apr	,,	Oct-Mar
— farreri	8-15 ft	8-15 ft	Oct-Mar	Blush	,,
— — 'Candidissimum'	,,	,,	,,	White	,,
— — 'Nanum'	3 ft	3 ft	,,	Blush	,,
— grandiflorum	10-15 ft	8-12 ft	,,	Pink	,,
— 'Park Farm Hybrid'	7-8 ft	7-8 ft	Autumn-Spring	White	Autumn and Spring

EVERGREEN SHRUBS, flowering

	Height (approx)	Spread (approx)	Flowering period	Flower colour	Planting time
Atherosperma moschatum	10-12 ft	8-10 ft	Feb-Mar	Cream	Oct-Mar
Buddleia auriculata (shelter)	6-9 ft	5-8 ft	Oct-Dec	Cream	Spring
Camellia × 'Cornish Snow' and 'Winton'	6-8 ft	5-6 ft	Feb-Mar	White/Pink	,,
— japonica and cultivars (shade)	10-15 ft	10-20 ft	Feb-Apr	Pink/White	Autumn and Spring
— 'November Pink'				Pink	,,
— reticulata and cultivars (shade and shelter)	,,	10-15 ft	Feb-Apr	Rosy red	,,
— saluenensis (shade)	6-8 ft	6-8 ft	,,	Pink	,,
— sasanqua and cultivars	,,	,,	Sept-Dec	Various	,,
— × williamsii 'Bow Bells' etc.	8-10 ft	8-10 ft	Feb-Apr	Pink	,,
Coronilla glauca (shelter)	4-6 ft	4-6 ft	Oct-June	Yellow	,,
— valentina ,,	,,	,,	,,	,,	,,
Cytisus 'Porlock' ,,	8-10 ft	6-8 ft	Intermittent	,,	,,
Daphne bholua ,,	7-8 ft	4-5 ft	Oct-Dec	Pink	,,
— blagayana	1 ft	Spreading	Jan-Apr	Cream	,,
— × hybrida (dauphinii)	3-4 ft	2 ft	Autumn-Spring	Lilac	,,
— jezoensis	9 ins	1 ft	Jan-Feb	Yellow	,,
— laureola (shade)	2-4 ft	2-3 ft	Dec-Apr	Green	,,
— odora (shelter)	3-4 ft	4-5 ft	Feb-Apr	Blush	,,
Elaeagnus × *ebbingei*	8-10 ft	8-10 ft	Oct-Dec	Creamy	,,
— macrophylla	10 ft	15 ft	,,	,,	,,

	Height (approx)	Spread (approx)	Flowering period	Flower colour	Planting time
Elaeagnus (cont.)					
— *pungens*	9 ft	10 ft	Oct–Nov	Cream	Autumn and Spring
Fatsia japonica (shade)	10–15 ft	8–10 ft	Oct–Dec	,,	Spring
Garrya elliptica and cultivars	6–12 ft	6–12 ft	Jan–Mar	Green	,,
Grevillea rosmarinifolia (shelter)	6–7 ft	6–7 ft	July–Nov	Pink	,,
Hebe 'Andersonii' (shelter)	4–6 ft	4–5 ft	July–Dec	Purple	,,
— 'Autumn Glory' (shelter)	1–3 ft	Spreading	Aug–Dec	,,	,,
— 'Bowles's Variety' (shelter)	3–4 ft	3–4 ft	,,	,,	,,
— 'Hielan' Lassie' (shelter)	3–5 ft	3–5 ft	,,	,,	,,
— 'Mrs Tennant'	,,	,,	,,	,,	,,
— *speciosa* and cultivars (shelter)	,,	3–4 ft	July–Dec	Various	,,
Mahonia acanthifolia (shelter)	8 ft	8 ft	Nov	Yellow	Autumn and Spring
— *bealei* (shade)	6–8 ft	4–6 ft	Oct–Apr	Lemon	,,
— × *media* cultivars	7–10 ft	7–8 ft	Nov–Dec	Yellow	,,
— *japonica* (shade)	6–8 ft	6–8 ft	Oct–Apr	Lemon	,,
— *lomariifolia* (shelter)	8–10 ft	4–6 ft	Oct–Dec	Yellow	Spring
Osmanthus heterophyllus	,,	8–10 ft	Oct–Nov	White	Autumn and Spring
Pieris japonica and cultivars	6–10 ft	6–10 ft	Feb–Mar	White/Pink	,,
Sarococca hookeriana digyna (shade)	4–5 ft	3–4 ft	Jan–Mar	Blush	,,
— *humilis* (shade)	1–2 ft	Spreading	,,	White	,,
— *ruscifolia* (shade)	2–4 ft	3–4 ft	,,	,,	,,
Sycopsis sinensis	21 ft	10 ft	Feb–Mar	Orange	,,
Viburnum tinus and cultivars	7–12 ft	10–15 ft	Oct–Apr	White	,,

HEATHERS, for flowers and foliage	Height (approx)	Distance apart for planting	Flowering period	Flower colour	Planting time
Calluna vulgaris, various	1–2 ft	18 ins–2 ft	Sept–Oct	Various (foliage)	Autumn and Spring
— — 'Hiemalis'	,,	1 ft	Oct–Nov	Lilac-pink	,,
Erica arborea alpina	6–8 ft	4 ft	Feb–May	White	,,
— *carnea* (herbacea) and cultivars	9–12 ins	1 ft	Dec–Mar	Pink/White	,,
— — 'Aurea'	,,	,,	Jan–Apr	Yellow (foliage)	,,
— *cinerea* 'Golden Drop'	6 ins	8 ins	Summer	Yellow (foliage)	,,
— — 'Golden Hue'	1 ft	10 ins	,,	,,	,,

	Height (approx)	Distance apart for planting	Flowering period	Flower colour	Planting time
Erica (cont.)					
— × *darleyensis*	18 ins	18 ins	Nov–Mar	Lilac pink	,,
— — 'Arthur Johnson'	2 ft	,,	,,	,,	,,
— — 'George Rendall'	1 ft	15 ins	,,	Pink	,,
— — 'Silberschmelze'	18 ins	18 ins	Dec–Mar	White	,,
— *erigena* (*hibernica*) cultivars	4 ft	18 ins	Feb–Apr	White/Pink	Autumn and Spring
— *lusitanica*	4–8 ft	4 ft	Dec–Apr	Pinky grey	,,

CLIMBING PLANTS, flowering	Height (approx)	Spread (approx)	Flowering period	Flower colour	Planting time
Clematis cirrhosa balearica	12–15 ft	Indefinite	Feb–Apr	Creamy green	Oct–Apr
— *napaulensis* (shelter)	30 ft	,,	Dec–Apr	Creamy yellow	Apr–May
Jasminum nudiflorum	12 ft	,,	Oct–Apr	Yellow	Oct–Apr
— × *mesnyi* (shelter)	15 ft	,,	Mar–Apr	,,	Apr–May
Lapageria rosea (shelter and shade)	,,	,,	July–Nov	White to crimson	,,

TREES AND SHRUBS with coloured bark	Height (approx)	Spread (approx)	Period of beauty	Bark colour	Planting time
Acer davidii	30–50 ft	30 ft	Winter	Red to green,	Oct–Mar
— *grosseri hersii*	20–30 ft	20 ft	,,	white	,,
— *laxiflorum*	40–50 ft	30 ft	,,	streaks	,,
— *palmatum* 'Sen-kaki'	20 ft	15 ft	,,	Coral red	,,
— *pennsylvanicum*	15–30 ft	20 ft	,,	Green, white streaks	,,
— — 'Erythrocladon'	20 ft	15 ft	,,	Scarlet, white streaks	,,
Arbutus menziesii	50 ft	20 ft	All the year	Snuff-brown	Mar–May
— *andrachnoides*	20 ft	15 ft	,,	Red-brown	,,
Berberis dictyophylla	6 ft	5–6 ft	Winter	Greyish	Oct–Mar
Betula albo-sinensis septentrionalis	70–90 ft	30–40 ft	All the year	Coppery	,,
— *ermanii*	60–80 ft	30–50 ft	,,	Buff	,,
— *grossa* (*ulmifolia*)	50–80 ft	20–40 ft	,,	Creamy	,,
— *nigra*	50–90 ft	,,	,,	Brown	,,
— *papyrifera*	60–100 ft	20–50 ft	,,	White	,,
— *pendula* (*verrucosa*)	50–60 ft	15–30 ft	,,	,,	,,
— — 'Dalecarlica'	,,	,,	,,	,,	,,
— — 'Fastigiata'	50 ft	15–20 ft	,,	,,	,,
— — 'Youngii'	30 ft	30 ft	,,	,,	,,
— *platyphylla szechuanica*	60–80 ft	30–40 ft	,,	,,	,,
— *utilis prattii*	60–70 ft	20–30 ft	,,	Coppery	,,

	Height (approx)	Spread (approx)	Period of beauty	Bark colour	Planting time
Cornus alba	8-10 ft	8-10 ft	Winter	Plum red	Oct-Mar
— — 'Elegantissima'	,,	,,	,,	,,	,,
— — 'Sibirica' ('Westonbirt')	6-8 ft	6-8 ft	,,	Bright red	,,
— *stolonifera* 'Flaviramea'	,,	,,	,,	Ochre green	,,
Kerria japonica	4-6 ft	3-5 ft	,,	Green	,,
Leycesteria formosa	5-8 ft	,,	,,	,,	,,
Philadelphus	3-12 ft	3-10 ft	,,	Grey and brown	,,
Pinus bungeana	15-20 ft	15-20 ft	All the year	Flaking, grey	Autumn and Spring
— *pinaster*	120 ft	40 ft	,,	Red-brown	,,
— *sylvestris*	70-120 ft	30-50 ft	,,	Reddish	,,
Platanus × *hispanica*	120 ft	80 ft	Winter	Flaking	Oct-Mar
— *orientalis*	100 ft	,,	,,	,,	,,
Prunus maackii	20-30 ft	10-20 ft	All the year	Brown	,,
— *serrula* (*tibetica*)	15-20 ft	10-15 ft	,,	Coppery	,,
Rubus biflorus	8-10 ft	8-10 ft	,,	White	,,
— *cockburnianus* (*giraldianus*)	,,	,,	,,	Grey-white	,,
— *lasiostylus*	6-8 ft	6-8 ft	,,	,,	,,
— *subornatus melanadenus*	6 ft ?	6 ft ?	,,	Mahogany	,,
— *tibetanus*	5-6 ft	Spreading	Winter	White	Feb-Mar
Salix alba argentea	30 ft	15 ft	,,	Reddish	Oct-Mar
— — *vitellina*	65 ft	30 ft	,,	Yellowish	,,
— — 'Britzensis'	,,	,,	,,	Red	,,
— *chrysocoma*	50 ft	50 ft	,,	Yellowish	,,
— *daphnoides* and varieties	15 ft	10 ft	,,	Bloom-covered	,,
— *fargesii*	6-10 ft	6-10 ft	,,	Red buds	,,
— *sepulchralis* (*salamonii*)	50 ft	30 ft	,,	Green-brown	,,
Sorbus aucuparia 'Beissneri'	40-60 ft	10-15 ft	,,	Coral red	,,
Stephanandra tanakae	6 ft	6 ft	,,	Red-brown	,,
Viburnum opulus 'Nanum'	2-3 ft	3-4 ft	,,	Ruddy	,,

FOLIAGE, Shrubs and Climbers	Height (approx)	Spread (approx)	Period of beauty	Foliage colour	Planting time
Arbutus unedo	30-40 ft	15-30 ft	All the year	Green	Autumn and Spring
Atriplex halimus	6 ft	6 ft	,,	Grey	,,
Aucuba japonica cultivars	6-8 ft	6-8 ft	,,	Variegated	Oct-Mar
Azalea (see Rhododendrons, pages 98-103)					

	Height (approx)	Spread (approx)	Period of beauty	Foliage colour	Planting time
Calluna (see page 186)					
Camellia japonica					Autumn and
varieties (shade)	10-30 ft	10-20 ft	All the year	Green	Spring
Cedrus atlantica 'Glauca'	120 ft	70 ft	,,	Grey-blue	,,
Chamaecyparis lawsoniana					
'Columnaris'	50 ft	4 ft	,,	Blue-grey	Oct-Mar
— — 'Ellwoodii'	20 ft	5 ft	,,	Grey-green	,,
— — 'Lanei'	50 ft	10-25 ft	,,	Yellowish	,,
— — 'Pembury Blue'	60 ft	10 ft	,,	Blue-grey	,,
— — 'Triompf van					
Boskoop'	80 ft	15 ft	,,	,,	,,
— *pisifera* 'Squarrosa'	60 ft	12 ft	,,	,,	,,
— — 'Boulevard'	10 ft ?	2-3 ft ?	,,	,,	,,
— *obtusa* 'Nana					
Gracilis'	20 ft	8 ft	,,	Rich green	,,
— — 'Sanderi'	4 ft	2 ft	Winter	Plum-purple	,,
Choisya ternata 'Sundance'	5 ft	8 ft	All the Year	Yellow	,,
Cordyline australis					
(tender)	40 ft	14 ft	All the year	Green	Apr-May
Cryptomeria japonica				Plum-	
'Elegans'	25 ft	25 ft	Winter	purple	,,
Cupressus glabra					Autumn and
(*arizonica*) 'Conica'	70 ft	12 ft	All the year	Grey	Spring
— 'Glauca'	,,	10 ft	,,	,,	,,
Cyathodes colensoi	9 ins	18 ins	Winter	Purplish-grey	,,
Cytisus scoparius					
(*Sarothamnus scoparius*)	6-10 ft	4-6 ft	,,	Green	,,
Danaë racemosa	2-4 ft	3-4 ft	All the year	,,	,,
Elaeagnus × *ebbingei*	8 ft	15 ft	,,	,,	,,
— *macrophylla*	10 ft	,,	,,	Grey-green	,,
— *pungens* 'Dicksonii'	8 ft	8 ft	,,	Yellow variegated	,,
— — 'Frederici'	6 ft	,,	,,	Cream variegated	,,
— — 'Maculata'	12 ft	,,	,,	Yellow variegated	,,
— — 'Variegata'	,,	,,	,,	Cream variegated	,,
— × *reflexa*	15 ft	10 ft	,,	Green	,,
Erica (see page 186)					
Eucalyptus gunnii	100 ft	30 ft	,,	Grey-green	Apr-May
Euonymus fortunei					Autumn and
'Coloratus'	3-4 ft	Spreading	Winter	Red reverses	Spring
— — 'Silver Queen'					
(on wall)	10-15 ft	6-10 ft	All the year	White-edged	,,
— — 'Variegatus'	12-18 ins	Indefinite	,,	Variegated	,,
Garrya elliptica	6-12 ft	6-12 ft	,,	Green	,,
Hebe, various	1-2 ft	2-3 ft	,,	Green, yellow, grey, purplish	,,

	Height (approx)	Spread (approx)	Period of beauty	Foliage colour	Planting time
Hedera canariensis 'Gloire de Marengo' (shade and shelter)	15–20 ft	Clinging or Prostrate	All the year	Variegated Variegated cream	Oct–Mar ,, ,,
— *colchica*	,,	,,	,,	Green	,,
— — 'Dentata Variegata'	,,	,,	,,	Variegated primrose	,,
— *helix* 'Arborescens' (Tree Ivy) (shade)	4–6 ft	4–6 ft	,,	Various	,,
— — Climbing cultivars	15–20 ft	Clinging or Prostrate	,,	,,	,,
Ilex × *altaclerensis* cultivars	30–60 ft	10–20 ft	,,	Various	Autumn and Spring
— *aquifolium* cultivars	,,	,,	,,	,,	,,
Juniperus horizontalis	6–12 ins	Spreading	Winter	Violet-blue	,,
Leucothoë fontanesiana (shade)	4–6 ft	4–6 ft	,,	Burnished	,,
Magnolia grandiflora	40–80 ft	12–30 ft	All the year	Green	,,
Mahonia aquifolium	2–4 ft	Spreading	,,	Burnished	Apr–May
— *fremontii* (shelter)	5–10 ft	4–6 ft	Winter	Violet-grey	,,
— 'Heterophylla' ('Toluacensis')	4–6 ft	,,	,,	Burnished	Autumn and Spring
— *japonica* (shade)	6–8 ft	6–8 ft	All the year	Green	,,
— *lomariifolia* (shelter)	5–8 ft	4–6 ft	,,	,,	Apr–May
— 'Moseri'	2–3 ft	2–3 ft	Winter	Reddish	Autumn and Spring
— *repens* (shade)	12–18 ins	Creeping	All the year	Green	,,
— 'Undulata'	8–9 ft	4–6 ft	,,	Burnished	,,
Phillyrea latifolia	10–15 ft	10–15 ft	,,	Green	,,
Phormium tenax and cultivars	6–8 ft	6–8 ft	,,	Various	Spring
— *cookianum* and cultivars	3–5 ft	3–5 ft	,,	Various	,,
Phyllostachys flexuosa	8–12 ft	8–12 ft	,,	Green	May–June
— *nigra*	8–12 ft	6–10 ft	,,	,,	,,
— — *henonis*	8–14 ft	,,	,,	,,	,,
— *ruscifolia*	3–4 ft	2–3 ft	,,	,,	,,
Picea pungens cultivars	40–100 ft	10–20 ft	,,	Grey-blue	Autumn and Spring
Pinus sylvestris 'Aurea' and 'Gold Coin'	10–30 ft	5–10 ft	Winter	Yellowish	,,
Prunus laurocerasus 'Magnoliifolia'	8–20 ft	8–15 ft	All the year	Green	,,
— — 'Otto Luyken'	8 ft ?	8 ft ?	,,	Dark green	,,
— — 'Zabeliana'	5–6 ft	12–15 ft	,,	Green	,,
Rhododendron ponticum 'Foliis Purpureis'	8 ft ?	8 ft ?	Winter	Plum-purple	,,
Rubus flagelliflorus	10 ft	Climbing	,,	Soft green	,,
— *irenaeus*	5 ft	Spreading	,,	,,	,,
Semiarundinaria fastuosa	20 ft	4–8 ft	All the year	Green	May–June

	Height (approx)	Spread (approx)	Period of beauty	Foliage colour	Planting time
Senecio 'Sunshine'	3 ft	6 ft	All the year	Grey	Autumn and Spring
Shibataea kumasasa, see *Phyllostachys ruscifolia*					
Sinarundinaria murieliae	6-10 ft	5-8 ft	,,	Green	May-June
Skimmia × *confusa* (*S. laureola*)	2-3 ft	2-3 ft	Winter	Green	Autumn and Spring
— *japonica* 'Rubella'	,,	,,	,,	Ruddy buds	,,
Thuja occidentalis 'Lutea'	60 ft	10-15 ft	All the year	Yellowish	,,
— — 'Rheingold'	5-10 ft	4-6 ft	Winter	Orange	,,
— *orientalis* 'Nana Aurea'	3-5 ft	1-3 ft	,,	Yellowish	,,
— — 'Meldensis'	4 ft	2 ft	,,	Plum-purple	,,
— *plicata* 'Atrovirens'	80 ft ?	25 ft ?	All the year	Rich green	,,
Trachycarpus fortunei	12-40 ft	6-8 ft	,,	Green	,,
Viburnum davidii	3-4 ft	4-6 ft	,,	,,	,,
— *rhytidophyllum*	10-15 ft	10-15 ft	,,	Green	,,

FOLIAGE (Herbaceous Plants)	Height (approx)	Period of beauty	Foliage colour	Planting time	Distance apart for planting
Arum italicum 'Pictum'	12 ins	Nov-Spring	Marbled	July-Aug	9 ins
Bergenia 'Abendglut'	9 ins	Winter	Plum	Autumn and Spring	1 ft
— 'Ballawley Hybrid'	12 ins	,,	Liver	,,	18 ins
— *purpurascens* and 'Sunningdale'	10 ins	,,	Plum	,,	1 ft
Blechnum chilense (shelter and shade)	2-3 ft	All the year	Green	,,	3 ft
Cyclamen hederifolium (shade)	6 ins	Winter	Marbled	July-Aug	9 ins
Dianthus 'White Ladies' and others	8 ins	All the year	Glaucous	Autumn and Spring	1 ft
Euphorbia myrsinites	Trailing	,,	,,	,,	,,
— *rigida* (*biglandulosa*)	18 ins	,,	,,	,,	,,
Helleborus corsicus	2 ft	,,	Pale green	,,	3 ft
— *foetidus*	,,	,,	Dark green	,,	2 ft
Iris foetidissima (shade)	,,	,,	Green	,,	1 ft
— — 'Variegata' (shade)	,,	,,	Variegated	,,	,,
Ophiopogon planiscapus nigrescens	6 ins	,,	Nearly black	,,	9 ins
Phormium tenax and cultivars	5-8 ft	,,	Various	Spring	3-5 ft
Polygonum affine and cultivars	12 ins	Winter	Brown	Autumn and Spring	18 ins
Polystichum munitum (shade)	2-3 ft	All the year	Green	,,	2 ft
Sisyrinchium striatum	18 ins	,,	Grey-green	,,	9 ins

BERRIES (Shrubs and Trees)	Height (approx)	Spread (approx)	Period of beauty	Colour of berries	Planting time
Callicarpa bodinieri (*giraldiana*)	6–10 ft	5–7 ft	Sept–Dec	Violet	Oct–Mar
— *dichotoma*	5–8 ft	4–6 ft	,,	,,	,,
Celastrus orbiculatus	30–40 ft	Twining	Oct–Dec	Orange	,,
— *scandens*	20 ft	,,	,,	,,	,,
Clematis tangutica obtusiuscula	10–12 ft	Climbing	Oct–Jan	Fluffy	,,
Cotoneaster conspicuus	4–7 ft	4–6 ft	Oct–May	Red	Autumn and Spring
— 'Cornubia' and 'St Monica'	12–18 ft	10–15 ft	Oct–Feb	,,	,,
— *frigidus*	20 ft	25 ft	,,	,,	,,
— *harrovianus*	4–7 ft	4–6 ft	Nov–Feb	,,	,,
— *horizontalis*	2–4 ft	Spreading	Oct–Mar	,,	,,
— 'Hybridus Pendulus'	1 ft	,,	Oct–Feb	,,	,,
— *lacteus*	8–12 ft	10–20 ft	Oct–Dec	,,	,,
— *microphyllus cochleatus*	1 ft	Spreading	,,	,,	,,
— *pannosus*	6–10 ft	5–8 ft	Nov–Feb	,,	,,
— *salicifolius*	12 ft	12 ft	Oct–Feb	,,	,,
— *serotinus*	8–10 ft	8–10 ft	Nov–Mar	,,	,,
— *simonsii*	6–8 ft	5–7 ft	Oct–Mar	,,	,,
— × *watereri* 'John Waterer'	12–18 ft	12–15 ft	Oct–Feb	,,	,,
Crataegus × *lavallei* 'Carrierei'	15–20 ft	10–15 ft	Nov–Feb	Orange	Oct–Mar
— × *grignonensis*	,,	,,	,,	Red	,,
Euonymus europaeus	8–15 ft	6–10 ft	Oct–Dec	Pink and orange	,,
— *myrianthus*	8–12 ft	,,	,,	Yellow and orange	,,
Hedera helix 'Arborescens'	5–6 ft	5–6 ft	Oct–Mar	Blackish	,,
Hydrangea macrophylla	6–10 ft	6–10 ft	Nov–Mar	Green and brown	Oct–Mar
— — Hortensia	4–8 ft	4–8 ft	,,	,,	,,
— *paniculata*	6–8 ft	4–6 ft	,,	Brown	,,
— — 'Grandiflora'	,,	,,	,,	,,	,,
— *serrata* 'Grayswood'	3–4 ft	2–3 ft	,,	Plum and brown	,,
Ilex × *altaclerensis* cultivars	30–60 ft	10–20 ft	Nov–Feb	Red	Autumn and Spring
— *aquifolium* 'Bacciflava' ('Fructu Luteo')	,,	10–15 ft	,,	Yellow	,,
— — 'Pyramidalis'	20–30 ft	,,	,,	Red/Yellow	,,
— — 'J.C. van Tol'	,,	,,	,,	Red	,,
— *verticillata*	6–8 ft	6–8 ft	,,	,,	,,
Ligustrum vulgare	8–10 ft	8–10 ft	Oct–Dec	Black	,,
— *compactum* (*yunnanense*)	10–20 ft	8–15 ft	,,	Maroon	,,
Malus 'Robusta'	20 ft	20 ft	Oct–Mar	Red	Oct–Mar
Pernettya mucronata	1–4 ft	Spreading	Sept–Nov	Various	Autumn and Spring

	Height (approx)	Spread (approx)	Period of beauty	Colour of berries	Planting time
Pernettya (cont.)					
— — 'Bell's Seedling'	1-4 ft	Spreading	Sept-Nov	Red	Autumn and Spring
— — 'Davis's Hybrids'	,,	,,	,,	Various	,,
Pyracantha angustifolia	10-12 ft	6-8 ft	Nov-Feb	Orange	,,
— *atalantioides*	20 ft	8-10 ft	Sept-Nov	Red	,,
— *crenato-serrata* (*yunnanensis*)	6-8 ft	,,	Nov-Feb	Coral red	,,
— 'Mohave'	8 ft	8 ft	Oct-Dec	Orange red	,,
— 'Teton'	,,	3 ft	,,	,,	,,
— 'Shawnee'	,,	8 ft	,,	Orange yellow	,,
— 'Watereri'	10 ft	10 ft	,,	Red	,,
— 'Waterer's Orange'	,,	,,	,,	Orange	,,
Ribes fasciculatum	4-5 ft	3-4 ft	Oct-Nov	Red	,,
Rosa 'Allen Chandler'	15 ft	Climber	Oct-Jan	,,	Oct-Mar
— *canina* 'Andersonii'	6 ft	8 ft	,,	Scarlet	,,
— 'Cantab'	8 ft	7 ft	Oct-Apr	Red	,,
— 'Cupid'	15 ft	Climber	Oct-Jan	Green and red	,,
— *damascena* 'St Nicholas'	3-4 ft	4 ft	,,	Dark red	,,
— *gallica officinalis*	4 ft	,,	,,	,,	,,
— 'Penelope'	7 ft	6 ft	Oct-Feb	Subtle	,,
— *rubiginosa* (*eglanteria*)	6 ft	8 ft	Oct-Jan	Scarlet	,,
— 'Scarlet Fire'	6-8 ft	8-10 ft	Oct-Jan	Red	,,
— 'Wilhelm'	6 ft	5 ft	Oct-Feb	Green-red	,,
— 'Will Scarlet'	,,	,,	,,	,,	,,
Ruscus aculeatus (shade)	1-3 ft	1-3 ft	Oct-Dec	Red	,,
Skimmia × *foremanii* (shade)	3-5 ft	3-5 ft	Oct-Mar	,,	Autumn and Spring
— 'Nymans' (shade)	6-7 ft	5-6 ft	,,	,,	,,
— *japonica* (shade)	3-5 ft	3-5 ft	,,	,,	,,
— *reevesiana* (shade) (lime-free soil)	2-3 ft	2-3 ft	,,	,,	,,
Sorbus aucuparia 'Fructu Luteo'	20-40 ft	15-30 ft	,,	Yellow	Oct-Mar
— *commixta* 'Serotina'	,,	,,	Nov-Jan	Red	,,
— *esserteauiana*	,,	20-30 ft	Oct-Jan	Red/Yellow	,,
— *hupehensis*	20-30 ft	10-20 ft	Oct-Nov	White/Pink	,,
Stranvaesia davidiana	10-30 ft	10-15 ft	Oct-Dec	Red	Autumn and Spring
— — *undulata*	8-10 ft	,,	,,	,,	,,
Symphoricarpos × *chenaultii*	3-5 ft	3-5 ft	Sept-Dec	White	Oct-Mar
— 'Constance Spry'	4-6 ft	4-6 ft	,,	,,	,,
— New hybrids	2-4 ft	2-4 ft	Nov-Jan	Pink/White	,,
— *orbiculatus*	4-6 ft	4-6 ft	Sept-Dec	Lilac-crimson	,,
— *albus laevigatus* (*rivularis*)	,,	,,	,,	White	,,
Viscum album (parasitic)	2-3 ft	2-3 ft	Nov-Mar	Pearly	Affix seeds in March

BERRIES (herbaceous plants)	Height (approx)	Period of beauty	Colour of berries	Planting time	Distance apart for planting
Iris foetidissima (shade)	18 ins	Nov–Dec	Red	Autumn and Spring	1 ft
— — 'Citrina' (shade)	,,	,,	,,	,,	,,
Physalis franchetii	1–2 ft	Sept–Nov	,,	,,	,,

RHODODENDRONS

The following table seeks to present the manifold characters of the genus. It will be realized that many rhododendrons of value in winter for bark or leaf colour may not flower during the period under review, but their flower colour and season have been included for ease of reference. Planting may be carried out from autumn until the spring with hardy species and varieties; late spring for those which are tender.

The rating in the extreme right column denotes degree of hardiness according to the *Rhododendron Handbook* 1980 (Royal Horticultural Society).

H4 = Hardy anywhere in the British Isles and may be planted in full exposure if desired.

H3 = Hardy anywhere in the British Isles but requires some shade to obtain best results.

H2 = Hardy in south and west but requires shelter even in warm gardens inland.

The same letters in italics indicate a similar rating, added from the author's judgement.

RHODODENDRONS

	Height (approx)	Width (approx)	Flower colour	Flowering period	Foliage	Group rating
'Alix'	15–20 ft	10 ft	Red	Feb–Apr	Dark green	*H3*
arboreum	30–40 ft	30 ft	White/crimson	Jan–Apr	Dark green, medium	H2
auriculatum	15–20 ft	20–30 ft	White	Aug	Long, green	H3
auritum	6–8 ft	5–6 ft	Pale yellow	Apr–May	Narrow, greyish beneath	H2
barbatum	15–30 ft	15–20 ft	Scarlet	Feb–Mar	Dark green, medium	H3
basilicum	30 ft	30 ft	Pale yellow	April	Immense, felted beneath	H3
'Bo-Peep'	7–8 ft	7–8 ft	Creamy yellow	Feb–Mar	Bronze-green, small	H2
'Bric-a-Brac'	5 ft	6–7 ft	White	,,	Dark green	H2
bureavii	6 ft	10 ft	Reddish	April	Glossy and felted	H3
callimorphum	4–9 ft	8–10 ft	Rosy pink	Apr–May	Grey-green, rounded	H3
calophytum	30–40 ft	30–40 ft	White/pinkish	Feb–Apr	Grey-green, long	H3
caloxanthum	3–5 ft	3–5 ft	Yellow	April	Grey-green, round	H2
campanulatum 'Knap Hill'	6–12 ft	12–18 ft	Lilac-blue	,,	Rusty felt beneath	H4
campylocarpum	8–12 ft	4–8 ft	Yellow	Apr–May	Grey-green, round	H3
'Carex'	12–15 ft	12–15 ft	Blush-white	Feb–Apr	Greyish, medium	H2

	Height (approx)	Width (approx)	Flower colour	Flowering period	Foliage	Group rating
charitopes	3-5 ft	3-5 ft	Pink/white	Apr-May	Felted beneath, small	H3
'Choremia'	5 ft ?	5 ft ?	Red	Feb-Mar	Dark green, felted beneath	H3
'Christmas Cheer'	5-6 ft	8-10 ft	Blush pink	Jan-Apr	Green, medium	H3
ciliatum	6 ft	6 ft	White	Mar-Apr	Dark green, small	H2
Cilpinense	3-6 ft	3-6 ft	White	Feb-Mar	,,	H2
cinnabarinum and varieties	8-12 ft	15-20 ft	Reddish	May-June	Grey-green, round	H3
concatenans	5-8 ft	7-10 ft	Yellow	Apr-May	Grey, medium	H3
'Cornubia'	20-30 ft	10-15 ft	Red	Feb-Apr	Grey-green, round	H2
'Crossbill'	7-8 ft	4-5 ft	Yellow	,,	Green, small	H2
dauricum	8 ft	6 ft	Magenta pink	Jan-Mar	Bronze-green, small	H4
degronianum	7-8 ft	10-12 ft	Pink	May	Rolled, green	H4
dichroanthum apodectum	2-4 ft	7-8 ft	Orange/crimson	June	Small	H4
eclecteum	7-12 ft	7-12 ft	Pink/white	Jan-Mar	Fresh green, broad	H2
falconeri	40-50 ft	40-50 ft	Creamy yellow	Apr-May	Immense, felted beneath	H2
fictolacteum and *rex*	15-45 ft	15-45 ft	White/rosy	April	,,	H3
fortunei	15-20 ft	15-20 ft	Pink/lilac	May	Purple stalks	H3
fulvum	20 ft	20 ft	White/pink	Feb-Apr	Rusty, felted beneath	H3
geraldii	8-12 ft	15-20 ft	White/lilac	Feb-Mar	Grey-green, long	*H3*
'Golden Oriole'	5-6 ft	3-4 ft	Yellow	Feb	Small, dark	H2
griffithianum	14-20 ft	14-20 ft	Blush/white	May	Light green	H2
hippophaeoides ('Haba Shan', 'Sunningdale')	3-5 ft	3-5 ft	Lilac-blue	Apr	Greyish, tiny	H4
hodgsonii	12-20 ft	15-25 ft	Purplish	,,	Immense, felted beneath	H3
hyperythrum	5-8 ft	5-8 ft	White	June	Rolled, green	H4
impeditum	6-18 ins	8 in-5 ft	Purplish blue	Apr-May	Violet-grey, tiny	H4
intricatum	3 ft	3 ft	Cool lilac	Feb-May	Grey-green, tiny	H4
'Jacksonii'	6 ft	8-10 ft	Rosy red	Mar-Apr	Dull green, medium	H4
kiusianum ('Kirishima and Kurume Azaleas)	18 in-5 ft	18 in-6 ft	Various	Apr-May	Bright green, tiny	H4-H2
lepidostylum	2 ft	5 ft	Pale yellow	May-June	Grey-green, small	H3
leucaspis	3 ft	6 ft	White	Feb-Mar	Dark green, small	H2
lutescens	6-8 ft	6-8 ft	Yellow	Feb-Apr	Bronze green, small	H2
macabeanum	45 ft	45 ft	Yellowish	March	Immense, felted beneath	H3
makinoi	3-7 ft	5-6 ft	Pink	June	Rolled, green	H3
mallotum	10-20 ft	10 ft	Red	April	Dark green, felted	H3
moupinense	4 ft	4 ft	White/pink	Feb	Dark green, small	H3

	Height (approx)	Width (approx)	Flower colour	Flowering period	Foliage	Group rating
mucronulatum	8 ft	8 ft	Magenta-pink	Dec–Mar	Bronze-green, small	H3
multiflorum	4–6 ft	4–6 ft	Blush-pink	Feb–Apr	Green, medium	H3
'Ninette'	8–10 ft	8–10 ft	Pale rose	June	Yellow stalks	H3
× *nobleanum* 'Album'	6 ft	6–8 ft	White	Dec–Mar	Dull green, medium	H3
— 'Coccineum'	,,	,,	Rosy red	,,	,,	H3
— 'Venustum'	8 ft	8–10 ft	Pink	Nov–Apr	,,	H3
'Olive'	6–8 ft	4–5 ft	Mauve	Feb	Small, dark green	H4
orbiculare	10 ft	10 ft	Pink	Apr	Grey-green, round	H4
parvifolium	3 ft	3 ft	Dark magenta	Jan–Mar	Dark green, tiny	H4
ponticum 'Foliis Purpureis'	15 ft	15 ft	Mauve	May–June	Coppery purple	H4
Praecox	4–6 ft	4–6 ft	Lilac-pink	Feb–Apr	Dark green, small	H3
praevernum	6–12 ft	12–15 ft	White/lilac	Feb–Mar	Dark green, long	H3
proteoides	1–3 ft	3 ft	Yellow	Apr	Dark green, fawn beneath	H3
'Red Admiral'	15–20 ft	10 ft	Red	Feb–Apr	Mid-green	H2
rirei	18 ft	18 ft	Soft purple	Feb–Mar	Grey-green, long	H3
'Rosa Mundi'	5–6 ft	5–6 ft	Blush-pink	Jan–Apr	Dull green	H4
roxieanum	4–9 ft	4–9 ft	White/pink	Apr–May	Narrow, felted	H3
saluenense	2 ft	3 ft	Purple/crimson	,,	Purplish, tiny	H4
scabrifolium	4–6 ft	4–6 ft	White/pink	Feb	Bronze-green, small	H2
Shilsonii	12–20 ft	12–20 ft	Red	Feb–Apr	Blue-green	H2
'Silkcap'	3 ft ?	3 ft ?	Blush	Feb–Mar	Small, dark	H3
sinogrande	20–30 ft	20–30 ft	Creamy	Apr	Immense, felted beneath	H2
smithii	10–15 ft	10–15 ft	Scarlet	Feb–Mar	Dark green, medium	H3
soulei	6–12 ft	6–12 ft	White/pink	May–June	Grey-green, round	H3
spiciferum	6 ft	6 ft	Pink	Feb–Apr	Bronze-green, small	H2
stewartianum	3–7 ft	3–7 ft	Pink/white yellow	,,	Dark green	H3
strigillosum	12–20 ft	12–20 ft	Scarlet	Feb–Mar	Dark green, medium	H2
sutchuenense	10–20 ft	10–20 ft	White/lilac	,,	Grey-green, long	H3
'Tessa'	7–8 ft	7–8 ft	Lilac-rose	Feb–Apr	Dark green, small	H4
thomsonii	10–20 ft	10 ft	Crimson	,,	Grey-green, round	H3
'Titness Park'	10 ft ?	10 ft ?	Deep pink	,,	Large, long	H3
vernicosum	25 ft	25 ft	Pink	May–June	Shining	H3
wardii	15–20 ft	10–15 ft	Yellow	,,	Grey-green, round	H3
williamsianum	3–5 ft	3–5 ft	Pink	April	Soft green, round	H3
yakushimanum	5 ft	7–8 ft	Blush	May	Small; white felt, turning brown	H3

HERBACEOUS PLANTS, **flowering**		Height (approx)	Flowering period	Colour	Planting time	Distance apart for planting
Adonis volgensis		6–12 ins	Feb–Apr	Yellow	September	1 ft
Aster tradescantii (of gardens)		2–4 ft	Oct–Nov	White	Spring	2 ft
Bergenia × *schmidtii*		12–18 ins	Feb–Apr	Pink	Autumn and Spring	1 ft
— *ligulata* (shelter)		6–12 ins	Feb–Mar	Blush	Spring	,,
Chrysanthemum, Korean		3–4 ft	Oct–Dec	Various	,,	18 ins
Helleborus atrorubens (shade)		9–18 ins	Dec–Apr	Purplish	Autumn and Spring	2 ft
— *corsicus*	(shade)	1–3 ft	Jan–Apr	Green	,,	,,
— *cyclophyllus*	,,	9–18 ins	Feb–Mar	,,	,,	1 ft
— *foetidus*	,,	,,	,,	Green	,,	,,
— *kochii*	,,	9–12 ins	Jan–Mar	Primrose	,,	,,
— *lividus*	,,	1–2 ft	Jan–Apr	Green	,,	18 ins
— *niger*	,,	9–12 ins	Dec–Mar	White	,,	,,
— × *nigericors*	,,	1–2 ft	Jan–Apr	Greenish white	,,	,,
— *olympicus*	,,	9–18 ins	Feb–Apr	White	,,	2 ft
— *orientalis*	,,	12–18 ins	,,	Various	,,	,,
— *purpurascens*	,,	9–18 ins	,,	Purplish	,,	1 ft
— *torquatus* (of gardens)	,,	8–10 ins	,,	,,	,,	,,
— *viridis*	,,	9–18 ins	,,	Green	,,	,,
Hepatica × *media* 'Ballard's Variety' (shade)		4–9 ins	,,	Powder blue	Apr and Sept	9 ins
— *nobilis* (shade)		3–8 ins	,,	Various	September	,,
— *transsilvanica* (angulosa) (shade)		,,	,,	,,	Apr and Sept	,,
Ionopsidium acaule (shelter)		2 ins	Winter	Pale lilac	September	Sow thinly
Liriope muscari (shelter)		8–12 ins	Oct–Dec	Violet	Spring	1 ft
Petasites fragrans		9–18 ins	Jan–Mar	Grey	,,	See text
— *japonicus*		1–3 ft	Feb–Apr	White	,,	3 ft
Polygala chamaebuxus		3–6 ins	Autumn and Spring	White and yellow	Autumn and Spring	10 ins
— — *grandiflora*		,,	,,	Magenta and yellow	,,	,,
Primula acaulis sibthorpii		3–5 ins	,,	Pink	Spring	9 ins
— *boothii*	(shade)	,,	Feb–Apr	,,	,,	,,
— *bracteosa*	,,	,,	,,	Lilac	,,	6 ins
— *edgworthii*	,,	,,	,,	,,	,,	9 ins
— — 'Alba'	,,	,,	,,	White	,,	,,
— *gracilipes*	,,	,,	,,	Pink	,,	,,
— *megaseifolia*	,,	6 ins	,,	Magenta	,,	,,
Pulmonaria rubra		6–12 ins	Jan–Mar	Coral	Autumn and Spring	18 ins
— *saccharata*		,,	Feb–Apr	Pink	,,	,,
Pulsatilla vulgaris 'Budapest'		9–15 ins	Feb–Mar	Powder blue	Spring	1 ft
Ranunculus ficaria forms		3–6 ins	Feb–Apr	Various	Any time	6 ins
Saxifraga fortunei (shade)		9–15 ins	Oct–Nov	White	Spring	1 ft
— *kellereri*		3–4 ins	Jan–Mar	Pink	Sept and Spring	6 ins

	Height (approx)	Flowering period	Colour	Planting time	Distance apart for planting
Viola florairiensis	4–6 ins	Feb–Dec	Various	Autumn and Spring	4 ins
— *odorata* and *V. alba*	3–5 ins	Feb–Nov	,,	,,	6 ins
— Winter Pansies	4–6 ins	Autmn and Spring	,,	,,	,,

BULBOUS PLANTS,

flowering   Depth of planting: except where mentioned specifically otherwise, bulbs should be planted to a depth twice the bulb's own height.

	Height (approx)	Flowering period	Colour	Planting time	Distance apart for planting
Arisarum vulgare	6 ins	Feb–Apr	Brown/white	Autumn	6 ins
Colchicum bifolium (*szovitzii*)	2–3 ins	Nov–Mar	White or pink	June–Aug	4 ins
— *decaisnei*	2–4 ins	Oct–Nov	Pink and white	,,	,,
— *doerfleri*	,,	Jan–Feb	Rosy lilac	,,	,,
— *hungaricum*	,,	,,	White to pink	,,	,,
— *kesselringii*	,,	Feb	,,	,,	,,
— *luteum*	,,	Feb–Mar	Yellow	,,	,,
— *ritchii*	,,	Jan	Pink or white	,,	,,
Cyclamen coum and *vernum*	3–5 ins	Nov–Feb	White to purple	August	6 ins
— *libanoticum*	4–6 ins	Feb–Apr	White to pink	,,	,,
Eranthis	2–6 ins	Jan–Feb	Yellow/white	Feb–Mar	4 ins
Hyacinthus azureus	4–8 ins	Feb–Apr	Blue	Sept–Nov	3 ins
Ipheion uniflorum	6–8 ins	Feb–May	,,	Summer	5 ins
Merendera sobolifera	2–4 ins	Feb–Mar	Lilac-pink	June–Aug	3 ins
Muscari schliemanii	4–8 ins	,,	Blish	,,	,,
Narcissus 'Ard Righ'	12–18 ins	,,	Yellow	Sept	8 ins
— *asturiensis*	2–3 ins	Feb–Apr	,,	,,	3 ins
— 'Bartley'	1½–2 ft	,,	,,	,,	6 ins
— *bulbocodium*	4–8 ins	,,	,,	,,	3 ins
— — *riffanus*	,,	,,	Pale yellow	,,	,,
— — *romieuxii*	,,	,,	,,	,,	,,
— 'Cedric Morris'	6–8 ins	Dec–Jan	Yellow	,,	6 ins
— *clusii*	4–8 ins	Feb–Apr	White	,,	3 ins
— *dubius*	6–8 ins	,,	Yellow	,,	4 ins
— 'February Gold' and 'Jana'	9–12 ins	,,	,,	,,	6 ins
— 'Forerunner'	12–18 ins	,,	,,	,,	,,
— *hedraeanthus*	2–3 ins	,,	,,	,,	3 ins
— *lobularis*	6–9 ins	,,	,,	,,	4 ins
— *obvallaris*	10–15 ins	,,	,,	,,	6 ins
— 'Rijnveld's Early Sensation'	12–18 ins	Jan–Mar	,,	,,	8 ins
— *watieri*	4–6 ins	Feb–Apr	White	,,	3 ins
Nerine bowdenii	12–18 ins	Sept–Nov	Pink	August	,,
— — 'Aurora'	1–2 ft	,,	Salmon	,,	8 ins
— — 'Fenwick's variety'	1–2½ ft	,,	Pink	,,	,,

	Height (approx)	Flowering period	Colour	Planting time	Distance apart for planting
Schizostylis coccinea and cultivars	1-2 ft	Sept-Nov	Red/pink	Spring	6 ins
Scilla bifolia and *praecox*	4-8 ins	Feb-Apr	Blue	Sept-Nov	3 ins
— *tubergeniana*	6 ins	Feb-Mar	Pale blue	Sept-Oct	5 ins
Sternbergia cretica	3-4 ins	Sept-Dec	Yellow	August	3 ins
— *macrantha*	4-6 ins	Sept-Nov	,,	,,	,,
— *maroccana*	5-7 ins	Sept-Dec	,,	,,	,,
— *sicula*	4-6 ins	Sept-Nov	,,	,,	,,
Zephyranthes candida	8-10 ins	,,	White	Spring	,,

CROCUSES

Crocus					
alatavicus	3-4 ins	Feb	White	July-Sept	3 ins
ancyrensis	2-3 ins	Jan-Feb	Orange-yellow	,,	,,
aureus	3-5 ins	Feb-Mar	Yellow	Sept-Nov	,,
balansae	2-4 ins	,,	Orange	July-Sept	,,
banaticus (likes shade)	6 ins	Nov	Purple	July	6 ins
biflorus	3-4 ins	Feb-Mar	White to blue	July-Sept	3 ins
cancellatus	3-6 ins	Sept-Dec	White to purple	July-Aug	,,
chrysanthus	3-4 ins	Feb-Mar	Various	July-Sept	,,
crewei	,,	Feb	White	,,	,,
dalmaticus	,,	Feb-Mar	Mauve	,,	,,
fleischeri	4-5 ins	Feb	White	,,	,,
heuffelianus	4 ins	Jan-Feb	Purple	,,	,,
imperati	3-4 ins	,,	White to lilac	,,	,,
korolkowii	3-6 ins	Feb-Mar	Yellow	Aug-Oct	,,
laevigatus	,,	Oct-Mar	Lilac	July-Aug	,,
longiflorus	4-6 ins	Oct-Nov	,,	,,	,,
nevadensis	3-4 ins	Jan	White to lilac	July-Sept	,,
ochroleucus	3-6 ins	Oct-Dec	Creamy	July-Aug	,,
olivieri	2-4 ins	Feb-Mar	Orange	July-Sept	,,
sieberi	3-4 ins	Jan-Mar	Lilac	July-Sept	,,
susianus	2-4 ins	Feb	Orange	,,	,,
tomasinianus	3-5 ins	Feb-Mar	Various	,,	,,
tournefortii	2-5 ins	Oct-Nov	Lilac	July-Aug	,,
'Vanguard'	4-6 ins	Feb-Mar	Grey-lilac	July-Sept	,,
versicolor	2-4 ins	,,	White, etc.	,,	,,
vitellinus	2-5 ins	Nov-Mar	Orange	,,	,,

IRISES

Iris					
bakeriana	6-9 ins	Feb-Mar	Bluish	July-Sept	4 ins
caucasica	9-12 ins	,,	Yellow	,,	8 ins
danfordiae	4-6 ins	Jan-Feb	,,	,,	4 ins

	Height (approx)	Flowering period	Colour	Planting time	Distance apart for planting
Iris (cont.)					
histrio	4–6 ins	Dec–Feb	Lilac-blue	July–Sept	4 ins
— *aintabensis*	,,	Feb–Mar	China blue	,,	,,
histrioides	,,	Jan–Feb	Spode blue	,,	,,
'Katharine Hodgkin'	5 ins	,,	Greenish grey	September	6 ins
persica	4–8 ins	Feb	Grey-blue	July–Sept	4 ins
planifolia (alata)	6–9 ins	Nov–Jan	Blue-purple	,,	6 ins
reticulata	,,	Feb–Mar	Purple/blue	Aug–Oct	4 ins
rosenbachiana	6–8 ins	Jan–Mar	Purple, etc.	July–Sept	6 ins
— *baldschuanica*	4–6 ins	,,	Pale yellow	,,	,,
sindjarensis (aucheri)	4–8 ins	Feb–Mar	,,	,,	,,
'Sindpers'	,,	,,	,,	,,	,,
unguicularis (stylosa)	6–12 ins	Sept–Apr	White to purple	Spring or Autumn	1 ft
vartanii	4–6 ins	Dec–Jan	Lilac	July–Sept	4 ins

SNOWDROPS and SNOWFLAKES
(will thrive in shade)

	Height (approx)	Flowering period	Colour	Planting time	Distance apart for planting
Galanthus allenii	6–8 ins	Feb–Mar	White	After flowering	5 ins
— *byzantinus*	,,	Nov–Jan	,,	,,	,,
— *caucasicus*	,,	Feb–Mar	,,	,,	,,
— *cilicicus*	5–6 ins	Nov–Mar	,,	,,	4 ins
— *corcyrensis*	4–6 ins	Nov	,,	,,	,,
— *elwesii*	6–9 ins	Jan–Feb	,,	,,	5 ins
— *graecus*	4–6 ins	Dec–Feb	,,	,,	4 ins
— *ikariae latifolius*	5–7 ins	Feb–Mar	,,	,,	,,
— 'Merlin'	6–8 ins	,,	,,	,,	5 ins
— *nivalis* and cultivars	5–8 ins	Jan–Mar	,,	,,	4 ins
— — 'Straffan'	6–8 ins	Feb–Mar	,,	,,	,,
— *plicatus*	,,	Jan–Mar	,,	,,	5 ins
— *rizehensis*	5–7 ins	Feb–Mar	,,	,,	,,
— 'S. Arnott' and other large flowered	7–10 ins	Jan–Mar	,,	,,	6 ins
Leucojum vernum	4–6 ins	,,	,,	,,	,,
— — *carpathicum*	,,	,,	,,	,,	5 ins
— — *wagneri*	6–10 ins	,,	,,	,,	6 ins

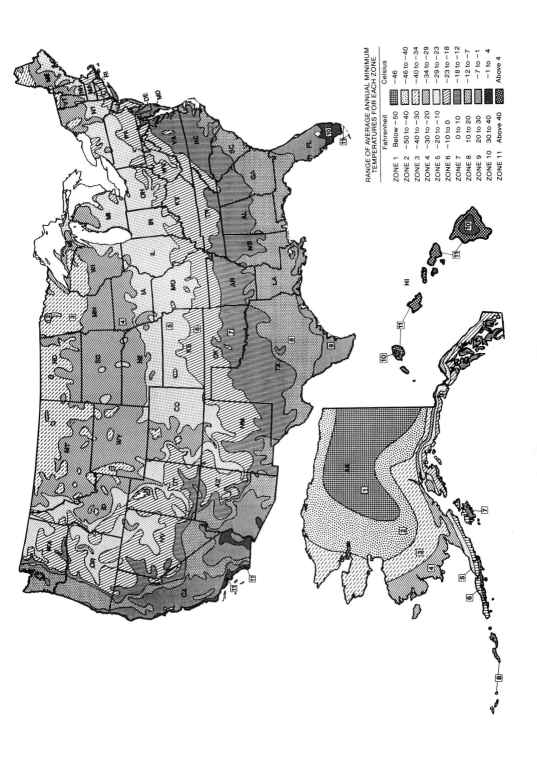

RANGE OF AVERAGE ANNUAL MINIMUM
TEMPERATURES FOR EACH ZONE

	Fahrenheit	Celsius
ZONE 1	Below −50	−46
ZONE 2	−50 to −40	−46 to −40
ZONE 3	−40 to −30	−40 to −34
ZONE 4	−30 to −20	−34 to −29
ZONE 5	−20 to −10	−29 to −23
ZONE 6	−10 to 0	−23 to −18
ZONE 7	0 to 10	−18 to −12
ZONE 8	10 to 20	−12 to −7
ZONE 9	20 to 30	−7 to −1
ZONE 10	30 to 40	−1 to 4
ZONE 11	Above 40	Above 4

Bibliography

List of metric equivalents

(approximate figures)

Bean, W. J. 8th Edition, *Trees and Shrubs Hardy in the British Isles*. John Murray, London, 1970–80.

Bowles, E. A. *A handbook of Crocus and Colchicum*. Martin Hopkinson, London, 1924.

Bowles, E. A. *A Handbook of Narcissus*. Martin Hopkinson Ltd, London, 1934.

Brickell, C. D., and Mathew, B. *Daphne*. Alpine Garden Society, Woking, 1976.

Hillier & Sons. *Manual of Trees and Shrubs*, 3rd edition. Winchester, 1973.

Lynch, R. Irwin. *The Book of the Iris*. John Lane, London, 1904.

Mathew, Brian. *Dwarf Bulbs*. B.T. Batsford, London, 1973.

Rehder, Alfred. *Manual of Cultivated Trees and Shrubs*, 2nd edition, New York, 1940.

Rose, Peter Q. *Ivies*. Blandford Press, Poole, Dorset, 1980.

Royal Horticultural Society. *The Dictionary of Gardening*. Oxford University Press, 1951; Supplement, 1969.

Royal Horticultural Society. *The Rhododendron Handbook*. London, 1980.

Royal Horticultural Society. The International Rhododendron Register. London, 1958.

Saunders, Doris E. *Cyclamen*. Alpine Garden Society Bulletin, revised 1973.

Thomas, G. S. *Perennial Garden Plants*. J. M. Dent & Sons Ltd., London. Third edition 1990.

1	in		2.50	cm	
1½	ins		4.00	cm	
2	ins		5.00	cm	
2½	ins		6.00	cm	
3	ins		7.50	cm	
6	ins		15.00	cm	
10	ins		25.50	cm	
12	ins	(1 ft)	30.00	cm	
18	ins		45.00	cm	
2	ft		60.00	cm	
3	ft		100.00	cm	(1 metre)
4	ft		1.20	m	
5	ft		1.50	m	
10	ft		3.00	m	
15	ft		4.50	m	
20	ft		6.00	m	
30	ft		9.00	m	
40	ft		12.00	m	
50	ft		15.00	m	
100	ft		30.00	m	

Index of Latin Names of Plants

The hardiness zones in the United States are indicated by the numbers in bold type. See map on p201.

Zones beside each entry indicate the geographical survival range of each plant
Numbers in *italics* refer to line drawings; numbers in **bold** refer to colour photographs